Transforming Faith

Transforming Faith

Individual and Community in H. Richard Niebuhr

JOSHUA DANIEL

☙PICKWICK *Publications* • Eugene, Oregon

TRANSFORMING FAITH
Individual and Community in H. Richard Niebuhr

Copyright © 2015 Joshua Daniel. All rights reserved. Except for brief quotations in critical publications or reviews, no part of this book may be reproduced in any manner without prior written permission from the publisher. Write: Permissions, Wipf and Stock Publishers, 199 W. 8th Ave., Suite 3, Eugene, OR 97401.

Pickwick Publications
An Imprint of Wipf and Stock Publishers
199 W. 8th Ave., Suite 3
Eugene, OR 97401

www.wipfandstock.com

ISBN 13: 978-1-4982-0448-4

Cataloging-in-Publication data:

Daniel, Joshua

    Transforming faith : individual and community in H. Richard Niebuhr / Joshua Daniel.

    x + 216 p. ; 23 cm. —Includes bibliographical references and index.

    ISBN 13: 978-1-4982-0448-4

    1. Niebuhr, H. Richard (Helmut Richard), 1894–1962. 2. Christianity and culture. I. Title.

BR115.C8 D37 2015

Manufactured in the U.S.A.   09/04/2015

For Megg,
Agnes, and Isaiah

Contents

Acknowledgments | ix

1 Introduction: Recovering the Individual, Chastening Community | 1

2 Loyalty Atoning through Interpretation: Individual and Community in Josiah Royce's Philosophy of Christianity | 23

3 Democratization through Novelty: Individual and Community in George Herbert Mead's Social Psychology | 56

4 Radical Faith and Responsible Transformation: Locating Individual Creativity in H. Richard Niebuhr's Theological Ethics | 93

5 The Transformation of Faith, to Transform Faith: Locating Radical Creativity through Christ | 148

6 Conclusion | 201

Bibliography | 207
Index | 213

Acknowledgments

I would like to thank those who read earlier versions of this work and provided me constructive criticism: Kristine Culp, Hans Joas, Kathryn Tanner, and in particular William Schweiker, whose severe humanity has taught me the shape of responsibility. I would also like to thank those friends and colleagues who have wittingly and unwittingly contributed to the final form of this work: Mandy Burton, Kristel Clayville, Rick Elgendy, Michelle Harrington, David Newheiser, Myriam Renaud, Mike Sohn, Elizabeth Sweeny Block, and Michael Turner.

I am grateful to all of those at Wipf and Stock and Pickwick who have played a role in ushering my work into published form.

Finally, I would like to acknowledge my family, who are all responsible for shaping me into the sort of person who is able to write a book in the first place. Thank you.

— 1 —

Introduction
Recovering the Individual, Chastening Community

AFTER A NUMBER OF conversations concerning this book—a motivating factor of which is to restore the individual to a significant place within Christian moral reflection—I have found that many react to the word individual with the same discomfort and antipathy that often greet words like modernity and liberalism. Isn't excessive individualism the problem to which the restoration of a tradition-rich morality, such as can be discerned in historical Christianity, is the solution? And isn't such individualism the deliverance of modernity and the symptom of a lingering liberalism that has run its course but refuses to die? These interlocutors have been well meaning and supportive, and so rather than advise me to abandon the project in which I had invested so much time and energy, they exhorted me to add a qualifier every time I utter "individual." To discuss the "individual" as adjectivally unencumbered has been depicted as a sort of academic faux pas: "Haven't you received the telegram that the Enlightenment is over?"[1] Better to say complex or situated or multidimensional individual. Continually surprising is that there seems to be a conceptual short-circuit from individual to individualism, triggered by the common-sense-status of a narrative in which modernity and liberalism are responsible for unmooring us from the personal bonds that compose families and local communities, and for insisting that intellectual truth, moral validity, and political legitimacy can only

---

1. This is not hyperbole; someone actually asked me this question.

be secured by appeals to universal, impersonal norms. According to this narrative, the individual is a self-enclosed, autonomous entity whose intellectual aspirations, moral motivations, and political obligations necessarily remain self-referential. Descartes's search for certainty and Kant's account of morality both entail the dismissal of tradition, as well as a focus on the resources of the individual's own capacities, while Hobbes's political vision is simply the best of all possible avenues for atomistic individuals to achieve self-preservation. On the one hand, the individual is understood to be a theoretical construct; in fact, humans are dependent and encumbered, such that the intellectual and moral ideals of Descartes and Kant are necessarily inhuman. On the other hand, insofar as the individual is what the social constructs of modernity and liberalism intend to support and promote, we are all being formed according to its image. Ultimately, the unencumbered individual and its stunted, vacuous mode of life are hardly worth restoring, especially as a moral resource.

Thankfully, other interlocutors have responded to my project less suspiciously, even positively. The main reason for this difference is that these interlocutors agree with me on the character of the individual. Our shared assumption is that the individual, and particularly the human individual, is constitutively situated, complex, and multidimensional. Without such qualities there is no individual properly speaking, just an example or an item. A human is constituted as an individual by her distinction from other humans; yet a distinction is not a separation. The human individual is distinct in and through, not despite or outside of, her various communal ties. Individuality is achieved by the manner in which we occupy our communal memberships. In this case, there is no fundamental contrast between the individual and the communal member or participant. Instead, the significant contrast is between manners of membership. All members occupy a posture within the community; individuals take on a posture towards the community.

One way to picture the contrast between more and less individualized members is through that between reflective and non-reflective members. Reflective members occupy a critical distance from their community's norms, which enables them to articulate a reasoned account of those norms that can serve as a critique or endorsement of those norms. Non-reflective members, on the other hand, follow communal norms mechanically, critically neither motivated nor honed enough to judge them. Individuality refers to a reflective manner of communal membership, whereby one stands within and outside the community at the same time, orienting one's life within the community according to what is discerned from one's external stance.

There are two advantages of picturing the contrast between individual and non-individual this way. First, it suggests that individuality is an achievement. Socialization into any community or communal endeavor almost always requires a period of trusting acceptance. In order to enter the community of chess players, I have to accept my chess instructor's account of the moves that the individual pieces are allowed to make, and it is reasonable to accept his account of the best moves to make in common situations. However, if new members are going to carry their community forward over time, into novel circumstances that community elders are unlikely to have faced, then communal fidelity requires getting some critical purchase on community norms, in order to make them responsive to new situations. A chess player who achieves individuality will be able to account for why certain moves are better than others in common situations, which both entails an ability to critically reflect on the competence of his instructor, and provides resources for succeeding in new situations. Picturing the contrast between individual and non-individual as that between reflective and non-reflective membership also prevents a premature moralizing of the conceptual distinction between individual and community. Individual/community is equivalent to neither good/bad nor bad/good. We can affirm that individuality and community are goods of human life while recognizing that particular individuals and communities lack goodness. Something similar can be said about critical reflection. It too is a good of human life, and achieving it ideally enables us to recognize bad aspects of communal life. However, this recognition does not necessarily lead us to engage in internal critique of our communities, especially when we are perceived to be in competitive, hostile relations with other communities. It is hasty to characterize zealous patriots in a time of war as un-reflective nationalists, for they are just as likely to be reflective nationalists, able to rationally justify the bad aspects of their own national life—"Sure, it may be technically illegal to hold a certain population in prison without bringing charges against them, but [insert justification here]." These two points—that individuality can be understood as the final achievement of communal formation, and that the critical distance that characterizes such an individual is not unambiguously good—will be essential for my argument throughout. For immediate purposes, I mean to show that the individual is necessarily encumbered, and that its mode of life is neither stunted nor vacuous.

Or rather, if the individual's mode of life is stunted and vacuous, then the culprit is just as likely to be community as individuality. This is a third point, equally crucial for my argument. I will articulate it with the help of sociologist Randall Collins, whose work stands in a theoretical tradition that can be traced back to George Herbert Mead, a social theorist to whom my argument is heavily indebted. Collins remarks, "We are historical products of a period that has developed an increasingly widespread and increasingly penetrating cult of individuality; thus we are constrained to think of ourselves as autonomous, inward, individuals."[2] Those suspicious of the individual would agree. The individual is the result rather than the author of social and historical factors. The cunning of these (modern, liberal) factors is to have erased their tracks, beguiling us into thinking that the individual is self-evident or a priori, something to take for granted such that community becomes the contentious task of assembling members rather than a given good of human life. To valorize the individual is to be complicit in the project of jettisoning historical particularities, and can have no place in a form of ethics that is anchored in the historical life of a particular person, himself anchored in the historical life of a particular community. In short, to appeal to individuality is to cease doing distinctly Christian ethics.

I have just said that this view presumes a misleading depiction of the individual. Just as significant, it presumes a misleading depiction of the community, whereby the point of socialization, of induction into a particular community, is to ensure a certain sameness of experience among its members. If the individual is understood as a self-enclosed, autonomous monad, and if the existence of such entities is the problem of modern moral life, then the easy solution lies in community, in binding us together to undertake common tasks. What makes this solution even easier is that an uncontroversial reading of the history of Christian ethics yields community as a predominant good to be pursued.

Significantly, Collins resists this move. He admits, "We are deeply socially constituted beings, from the moments as babies when we begin to make noises and gestures in rhythm with our parents, through the adult networks that induct us into cults of experience that we elaborate in our inner lives. Symbols make up the very structure of our consciousness. Symbols are the lenses through which we see." And yet, he appreciates, "We do see something through [these symbols]. That experience is a reality, concrete, particular, individual; sometimes of the highest value to ourselves. That the pathway to those experiences is deeply social does not take anything away from them."[3] Socialization into a set of normative symbols is a pre-requisite for our capacities, not only for experiencing anything at all, but also for irreducibly individual experiences, the sort of things "that cannot be com-

---

2. Collins, *Interaction Ritual Chains*, 372–73.
3. Ibid., 373–74; emphasis mine.

municated to others, that are often best savored alone." Regarding such experiences, Collins asserts, "being with someone else at these moments is often a distraction, and attempting to relate the experience in the clichés of conversation tends more to destroy the experience than to expand it."[4] The suggestion is not only that there are individual experiences, which are funded yet ultimately unable to be captured by communal norms, but also that the attempt to submit these experiences to communal circulation can violate them. The demand that one articulate such individual experiences so that they are easily communicable to one's fellows within a particular community can be a form of tyranny, especially if such articulation eradicates the individual qualities of these experiences. In these cases, it is community that stunts our life and renders it vacuous.

While Collins's point seems to be more about the relationship between experience and language than that between individual and community, it does help address the latter tension. On one hand there is a concern about whether or not language can adequately capture experience, and on a related hand there is a concern about whether or not a community can adequately recognize or appreciate the individuality of its members. To be sure, we cannot neatly align individual with experience and community with language, but Collins's comments imply a triadic structure of human experience that will animate the argument of this dissertation. At the first pole is the individual self, socially constituted and thereby encumbered, but irreducible to communal membership. At the second pole are the individual self's social companions, those others through whom the community represents itself and socially constitutes us. At the third pole is what we experience, or more simply, reality. The point of this triadic structure is to disarticulate reality from social inheritance. The individual self has two kinds of relations, irreducible to each other though connected: to reality and to its self-constituting community. The individual's relations to her social companions enable her to negotiate relations with others, through patterns of response and imitation that culminate in the acquisition of language and conceptual inheritance by which she is able to cooperate with others as they transact with reality. Thus, the individual's relations to social companions include relations to reality, since the point of most social relations is to deal better with an impinging world. In this sense, we can talk about social experience as a function of what a particular community's language and conceptual inheritance enable its members to experience individually.

Meanwhile, according to this triadic structure, the individual has a relation to reality irreducible to her socially mediated relation to reality. If the

---

4. Ibid., 373.

community is responsible for initiating the individual self into organized relations with reality, there will come a time when an individual's experience of reality grates against, or does not quite match, social experience. My wife and I agree that blue and purple are two distinct colors, and we do not worry that our daughter will fail to discern their difference in our collective, pedagogical hands. Still, sometimes we see a shade on a work of art or piece of clothing that provokes disagreement, one of us discerning blue, the other purple. If our social inheritance has the final word on reality, if our only true relation to reality is socially mediated, then one of us is right and the other wrong. Our shared community would simply pass judgment and settle our controversy. On the other hand, if we each do have an irreducibly individual relation to reality, which is to say, if our socialization conditions but does not determine our experience of reality, and if our shared community recognizes this, then our conflicting discernments would be allowed to stand together. Collins might say that compelling one of us to see the color the other sees, or compelling both of us to see some compromise color, say blue-purple, would strip the personal significance from our own experience of that color.

The stakes become higher once we move to moral and religious contexts. Earlier I cautioned against being pejorative about patriots: we should not assume they are unreflective. We should also not be pejorative about patriotism. According to the triadic structure of human experience, service to one's own nation can be understood as devotion to some moral cause that one's nation is understood to represent and exemplify. The patriot serves his own nation because he perceives it as the best available agent for promoting the moral cause to which he is devoted. Again, it is possible that the individual's experience of that moral cause will grate against social experience of it, and so disagreements can arise regarding, e.g., what America stands for. Prosperity or freedom? What sort of prosperity, and what sort of freedom? Freedom rendered by prosperity, or freedom understood more severely, as a moral cause indifferent to the prosperity of its agents and promoters? How those in power answer these questions, and the institutional policies they recommend and promote, can have a serious, concrete impact on social life and experience. Even disagreements among citizens not in power effect social life. If my neighbor and I radically disagree about America's purpose, can I trust her? And if I decide I cannot trust her, how healthy can my domestic life be? More is at stake at this level of human life than the personal significance of individual experience.

Moreover, a particular danger arises here: the collapse of the moral cause that America serves, with American life itself, that is, the collapse of the third and second pole of the triadic structure. In this case, American life itself becomes equated with freedom, prosperity, or whatever its moral cause is understood to be. The danger here concerns international life. If other nations believe that America is not serving some moral cause that exceeds it, but rather promoting its own interests and rhetorically dressing it up as a moral mission, America's international reputation will become increasingly eroded. This danger also concerns individual life. If individual citizens devoted to the moral cause that America claims to serve, do not believe that America is living up to the cause, they should be motivated to critique American life in light of their individual devotion to that cause. If American life has collapsed its moral cause into itself, this critique will be taken simultaneously as treason and immorality, as the betrayal of America itself and of freedom, prosperity, etc., rather than as concern for the moral character of America. In fact, such critique must be taken so in this case. The collapse of moral cause into social life effectively invalidates the possibility of an individual experience of that moral cause that might contest social experience of it.

Consider religious life, in a broadly Christian context. Individual Christians come together and form communities of like-enough-minded Christians to worship a God they understand to have created, to presently sustain, and to ultimately redeem, the universe. Such worship involves agreed-upon language and behavior that somehow refers to God, though God is simultaneously understood to be essentially un-capturable by such communal norms. As with patriots and patriotism, so with religious believers and belief: no need to be pejorative. Religious believers may submit themselves to communal norms, but the point of such submission is an individual devotion, to a God whose power operates beyond those norms but which is best expressed through those norms. Yet again, there is the possibility that individual experience of God will grate against the social experience of God institutionalized in communal norms, and disagreements may arise regarding the appropriateness of religious language and behavior. If one experiences God as primarily caring, is it appropriate to refer to God as "Father," or can we allow God to be invoked as "Mother"? If one experiences God as impersonal power bearing down on all of reality, is it even appropriate to use personal language at all in God-talk? Similarly, if one experiences God as primarily empowering, is it appropriate to kneel and bow, or should we worship with our heads held high and our eyes fixed on heaven? If the latter, shouldn't the religious demeanor expressed in the rest of our interpersonal lives be one of confidence rather than acquiescence, especially if we are women? Again, more is at stake here than the personal significance of our experience. These sorts of disagreements fracture religious communities and often alienate individuals from such communities.

Meanwhile, the danger of collapsing reality and social inheritance here is nothing less than the danger of idolatry. If communal norms of religious language and behavior are understood as sufficient for relating to God, then being an obedient member of a particular religious community becomes equated to being in relation with God. This danger concerns the life and mission of the church. If those to whom God is witnessed by the religious believe that the church is not serving the God who exceeds it, but rather witnessing to themselves in elevated language, then the purpose of the church's mission will become radically undermined. Again, this danger also concerns individual religious life. If individual believers do not discern that their religious community is witnessing to the God it claims to worship, then they will be motivated to submit its communal norms to critique, in light of their individual experiences of God. If the religious community has collapsed God into its norms, this critique will likely, and in fact must, be taken simultaneously as betrayal of the community and of God, rather than as critical concern for the religious community's relation to God. Again, the collapse of God into social religious life effectively invalidates the possibility of an individual experience of God that might contest social experience of God. Stated religiously, such a collapse means that a religious community will discern idolatry in the criticism from its own individual members, as well as in that from other communities, but not in its own activity.

This is the spiritual problem that motivates my book: the tendency of religious communities to idolatrize themselves. As my example of American life and its moral cause should attest, I believe there are secular versions of this problem, whenever some community that claims to serve some reality beyond itself effectively collapses its mode of service with all legitimate service to that reality. Thus, I expect that my argument would have resonance outside of religious communities. Still, the motivating problem of this project and my own attempt to address it, are thoroughly theological. With the rise of secularizing social processes and the apparent decreasing influence of religious institutions in public life, a persistent worry of recent Christian thought has been the accommodation of Christian communities to prevailing social forces and norms, which is understood to radically undermine the churches' existence and mission. Arguably, this worry was initiated by the work of Karl Barth, who discerned a connection between the crest of nineteenth-century liberal theology, which attempted to make Christian claims answerable to prevailing intellectual and moral standards, and the rise of German nationalism.[5] Barth responded with his *Church Dogmatics*, an understanding of theology as a dogmatic inquiry that serves the church,

---

5. Barth, "Evangelical Theology," 14.

rather than as a general intellectual inquiry that serves the public. Broadly speaking, its theme is the priority of Christ as the norm of theological inquiry and human existence, which functions to cut off accommodation at the root: God's "Yes" to human life only arrives after God's "No" to all human attempts to live righteously before God. John Howard Yoder, who studied under Barth, spun this christological priority in a sociological direction, using the term "Constantinianism" to refer to the state of Christian communities who have accommodated their mission to align with the purposes of the powers that be, whether that be the Roman Empire or the United States of America.[6] Barth and Yoder have given impetus to a trajectory in recent Christian thought, often called post-liberalism, two of whose most renowned articulators I will discuss briefly below, which aims to stave off accommodation by calibrating the task of Christian thought and ethics as the recovery and explication of the distinctively Christian mode of life and reflection. Consider the flourishing of trinitarian theology in the twentieth century and into the twenty-first.[7] Whether or not all of the thinkers who contribute to this trend understand themselves to be post-liberal, it helps differentiate Christianity both from the other monotheisms and from surrounding social and cultural practices. Such trends are signs of the power of the worry over accommodation.

The worry over accommodation does instantiate a worry over a form of idolatry. If the Christian community's mission simply aligns with prevailing social practices and norms, then those practices and norms have been effectively elevated to a divine status. The worry is that, for example, *ultimate concern* is less a way to construe God than a divinization of some human phenomenon, or that the liberation of human life from forces of oppression is less a way to construe discipleship than the replacement of Jesus' teachings with a secular political agenda. The worry that motivates this book is a response to these sorts of worries. The attempt to overcome accommodation by focusing on Christian distinctiveness easily leads to a focus on forms of thought and life rather than on God. With the addition of an appreciation of humans as socially constituted, the focus on Christian distinctiveness becomes a focus on the Christian community, such that formation and membership in that community is understood to provide the only significant access to God. Meanwhile, if the prevailing social practices and norms from which we are supposed to differentiate Christianity, are understood to instantiate a form of invidious individualism, then the turn

---

6. See, paradigmatically, Yoder, *The Politics of Jesus*.

7. Among many others, LaCugna, *God for Us*; Moltmann, *The Trinity and the Kingdom*; Gunton, *The Promise of Trinitarian Theology*.

to community is further bolstered. Ultimately, membership in Christian community becomes the distinct alternative to the individualistic mode of life somehow (demonically?) held together by liberal society. This solution to accommodation bequeaths its own spiritual problem, namely, a tendency for the Christian community to idolatrize itself.

The problem is two-fold. First, this turn to community performs a turn away from God. Obviously the Christian tradition includes a number of reasons for understanding the church to serve a decisive, irreplaceable function in God's economy. Still, a turn to the Christian community that is focused on distinctiveness can easily become more concerned with how its practices and norms compare to those of other communities, than with how its practices and norms contribute to life before God; or worse, that distinctiveness will be understood to ensure worshipfulness. Ironically, we need a renewed Barthian turn, toward God and away from humanity.[8] Second and unsurprisingly, the turn to Christian community as the fundamental antidote to liberal individualism performs a turn away from legitimate individuality. In particular, this turn to community occludes recognition, much less appreciation, of individual relations to God. The Christian tradition includes a number of ways to articulate a plural divine relation to the world: two cities, two kingdoms, two governments, law and gospel, reason and revelation, etc. I would argue that we can understand God to relate to each human individual in a direct, unique, and particular way, without neglecting or denying that God relates to humans on a social level as well, whether generally, through the ordering of human life in communities from families up to global orders, or more specifically, through the church whose head is the divine son and whose purpose is more divinely distinctive than those of other communities.[9] Scripture supports this: the patriarchs, Moses, and the prophets are paradigmatic instances of God relating to individuals directly. These can be distinguished from instances in the wisdom literature where God is characterized as ordering creation on a more general level, providing the basic structures of human sociality. Moreover, the point of God's individual relations are social. God covenants with the patriarchs and Moses to create God's people; God calls the prophets to call that people back to that covenant.

The prophetic example illustrates well the dynamic I articulate in this dissertation. Prophecy presumes a social relationship between God and

---

8. See Biggar, *Behaving in Public*, where he argues for integrity rather than distinctiveness as the proper Christian aspiration, and begins to articulate a "Barthian Thomism."

9. I have no intention of aligning the individual/social distinction of God's relation to the world, with any of the other distinctions mentioned in the prior sentence.

humans. God has made a covenant with a particular people, and those people are carrying out their end of it through social actions, e.g., sacrifices. However, these social actions are missing the point of the covenant, and so warping divine-human relations as well as human social relations: instead of doing justice, loving kindness, and walking humbly with their God, God's people are engaging in oppression and attempting to cover it over with luxurious sacrifices (e.g., Micah). In response, God calls an individual prophet to reorient them to the point of their original covenant. This provides a good model for articulating God's direct relation to individual humans. Just as prophecy presumes a socially mediated relation between God and the Israelites, since God's covenant is with Israel, so the socially mediated relations between God and Christians as borne out in church life. Individual Christians come to learn who God is through the reading of Christian scriptures, participation in the liturgy, and the various other activities connected to the life of particular church. Since human life before God is meant to be social, it is essential that we create and order a form of social life dedicated to living before God. At the same time, church life teaches us about the ineradicable character of human sin, both individual (e.g., Cain murdering Abel) and social (e.g., Israel neglecting the oppressed, but sacrificing to God). Moreover, we have learned that the church is not any more immune from such sin than any other community, even if only the church is able to articulate it. Individual Christians and the church itself have sinned and continue to sin. The prophetic example implies that one way that God works to get the church to recognize its own social sin is to directly relate to individuals in such a way that they are enabled to discern the sinful aspects of their religious communal life and then speak and act in a way so as to critique these aspects while remaining faithful to the divine purpose that is meant to animate that communal life. The prophet works against her own religious community, for the sake of the divine purpose, and thus, for the sake of her community, and ultimately all other communities.

The task of this book is to articulate how this might work, and the task is timely given the rise of post-liberalism within Christian discourse. The concern over Christian distinctiveness plays right into the hands of the Christian community's susceptibility to idolatrize itself, and in the process shapes that community to create strategies for immunizing itself against prophetic critiques that arise from within it, especially if these critiques align with non-Christian critiques of the community. One way to address this susceptibility is to recover a conception of individuality that recognizes the significance of the self's social constitution without claiming that being socially constituted is the point of an individual self's existence. That is, the recognition that we are socially constituted through and through often stops short of wondering what the point of that constitution is. This means that to recover such a conception of individuality requires re-conceiving the task of social constitution, or what I will call moral formation throughout. I argue that the point of moral formation is individuality. Moral communities should aspire to develop their members' individuality, rather than simply solidify their membership, because it is through the individuality of their members that such communities themselves develop: individuals are the agencies through which communities are spurred to broaden and deepen the scope of their moral concern. This holds for Christian communities too. Each individual occupies a direct relation to God, ultimately irreducible to those social relations with others responsible for traditional, communal accounts of God; from this relation, each individual can develop the church. The point of moral formation, in Christian communities, is to promote such theo-centric individuality.

H. Richard Niebuhr, the guiding theological light of my project, argues that the "Barthian correction" to "Schleiermacherian" trends in theology, the renewed focus on the objectivity of God over against a focus on the subjective aspects of religious life, though essential, became an overcorrection; faith became understood as right belief in correct theological formulations, rather than as right existence before a personal, active God.[10] Similarly, the post-liberal turn to community is essential, but insufficient and potentially excessive: essential in the sense that it emphasizes the social constitution of the self and so suggests that moral formation is a fundamental task for Christian thought to consider; insufficient in the sense that it neglects the socially irreducible individuality of community members as an essential concern of moral formation; excessive to the degree that it denies that individuals have direct, socially irreducible relations to God from which the communal life of the church can be resisted and critiqued. Just as Niebuhr grants Barth's point about the sovereignty of God over all human endeavors as the presupposition of all theological work, I grant the post-liberal emphasis on the significance of community for shaping our experience and thought. And just as Niebuhr contends that Barth's point occludes recognition of the significance of our felt experience of God, I contend that the post-liberal emphasis fails to entertain the possibility of individual experience of God that grates against socially constituted experience of God. Moreover, this failure exacerbates the tendency of communities, especially churches, to idolatrize themselves.

Before turning to my chapter outline, I take stock of the post-liberal trend in recent Christian thought, as evidenced in the works of George

---

10. Niebuhr, "Reformation: Continuing Imperative," 142.

Lindbeck and Stanley Hauerwas. Both thinkers affirm the primacy of community but fail to conceptualize adequately the individuality of community members. Moreover, they fail to articulate and address the dangers of too exclusively focusing on community, namely, the dangers of a form of conservative authoritarianism that brooks no disagreement or criticism.

THE POST-LIBERAL ECLIPSE OF THE INDIVIDUAL

If the personalities and dynamics of modernity are responsible for articulating the individual as an entity constitutively unencumbered by social relations, then those of post-modernity—or those that respond to paradigmatic achievements of modernity, whether or not they themselves or anyone else has actually left modernity—are responsible for the articulation of historical communities as the matrices from and into which we are destined to live. The recognition of various social and cultural groups confronts us with the possibility that there are multiple ways of thinking and behaving in the world, and that making sense of them requires being formed into the communities that exemplify them. This provokes philosophical questions about the nature and status of truth and reality, as well as ethical issues regarding how we deal with differences that morally affront us. One option is to deny "Truth" and "Reality" and affirm human conceptual schemes, language-games, social inheritances, etc., as the only game in town, so that moral differences are something to be coped with, rather than something to be solved. This option licenses, among other possibilities, a refusal to put one's community's norms and criteria to the test, since any possible available standard would simply be that of another community. The post-liberal trend in recent Christian thought tends towards this option.

Two contemporary Christian thinkers are sharply critical of appeals to individuality and experience in their attempts to recover what they take to be the specifically Christian mode of moral life and religious reflection. While they do not directly or compellingly contest the major theological figure of this book, H. Richard Niebuhr, my own argument, which builds off of Niebuhr's work, is motivated by dissatisfactions with their positions.[11] While I will not be engaging them directly in the dissertation, I briefly discuss them for the sake of critically contextualizing my own argument.

11. For a discussion of Hauerwas and Niebuhr, which sees the former as more rather than less indebted to the latter, see Werpehowski, *American Protestant Ethics and Legacy of H. Richard Niebuhr*, chapters 5–6. In general, Werpehowski understands Niebuhr to have held together what subsequent Protestant ethics fractured into conflicting positions. For a discussion of Lindbeck (among others) and Niebuhr, see Cook, *The Open Circle*.

Stanley Hauerwas, the immensely influential Christian ethicist reputed to be responsible for the return and prominence of themes like narrative, virtue, and church, blames the combination of particular notions of "freedom" and "foundation" for the loss of the distinctively Christian character of Christian ethical reflection. For Hauerwas, this loss is fatal for Christians, because performatve witness "is at the heart of the Christian life": Christian convictions "cannot be learned except as they are attested to and exemplified by others."[12] This is why "the first social ethical task of the church is to be the church," to manifest those features that constitute it as the church.[13] Unfortunately, modern ethics is characterized by an emphasis on individual freedom as the essence of the moral life and a corollary search for a universal foundation for the moral life, which is disconnected from the histories of particular communities and so able to be chosen by unencumbered individuals. The result is mutually exacerbating self-deception and violence. The modern ideal of individual freedom, whereby the moral life is a matter of freely pursuing our desires in a way that does not impinge on others' free pursuits, is deceptive because it implies that it is possible to act and live in a way that does not impinge on others' freedom. The fact that we are biologically, socially, and culturally constituted gives the lie to this: to have a child and raise her in a particular historical community is necessarily to impinge on the child's freedom. Meanwhile, founding morality on some universal, inherent characteristic of the human—the signal example being rationality—can fund moral coercion: "If others refuse to accept my account of 'rationality,' it seems within my bounds to force them to be true to their 'true' selves."[14] The Christian life provides an antidote to this moral chaos, precisely by witnessing to a particular truth that depends on a witness that must be peaceful.[15]

Such an antidote entails re-anchoring morality in particularity, in the material content of an historical community rather than in the formal features of human beings. According to Hauerwas, the character of Christian ethics follows from the fact that "Christian convictions take the form of a story, or perhaps better, a set of stories that constitutes a tradition, which in turn creates and forms a community."[16] Christian ethics is the function of a particular community (the church) formed by a particular narrative

---

12. Hauerwas, *The Peaceable Kingdom*, 14–15.

13. Ibid., 99. Elsewhere, Hauerwas asserts that the issue of the church-world relation is more primary than that of the grace-nature relation (ibid., 60).

14. Ibid., 6–12

15. Ibid., 15

16. Ibid., 24

(God's life with Israel, Jesus, and the church). Enacting such ethics requires the training of our desires through the development of disciplined skills, or virtues, that enable us to tell the narrative and become members of the community. Christian morality turns out to be grounded in the acquisition of the particular virtues that life in a particular community requires, rather than in universal principles that can be rationally understood.[17] It is essential to understand that Hauerwas is not asserting that Christian ethics is distinctively Christian because it focuses on virtue, narrative, and community, though such focus is a feature that distinguishes it from certain forms of ethics (e.g., Kantian). Instead, the distinctiveness of Christian ethics is a matter of the content of the convictions that animate the Christian narrative responsible for the character of the church and its members.[18] Christian ethics shares an attention to virtues with ancient Hellenistic and Roman eudaimonistic ethics, but the particular narrative that constitutes the church determines the character of the virtues by which Christians are members of the church; Christian courage and patience are distinct from their ancient counterparts because of their distinctive narrative context.[19] The most distinctive aspect of the Christian narrative is Jesus, whose teaching and life embody "the announcement of the reality" of God's kingdom, which is "the possibility of living a life of forgiveness and peace with one's enemies."[20] While Jesus proclaimed the presence of God's kingdom and not himself, that presence can be grasped only by discerning how Jesus exemplified the truth and peace of the kingdom.[21] Becoming Christian, which is to say becoming truthful and peaceful, is a matter of mastering the specific content that constitutes the tradition that identifies a particular historical community as Christian.

Like Hauerwas, George Lindbeck, the titular founder of post-liberal theology, is concerned about the loss of Christian particularity, now in the discourse of doctrine rather than ethics. A major contributing factor in this loss that Lindbeck identifies is "experiential-expressivism," a theory of religion in which doctrines are understood as "noninformative and nondiscursive symbols of inner feelings, attitudes, or existential orientations."[22]

17. Ibid., 18. Hauerwas appreciates rules, so long as they are understood to orient moral behavior within particular communities rather than to be impersonal moral justifications.

18. Ibid., 69.

19. Hauerwas and Pinches, *Christians Among the Virtues*.

20. Hauerwas, *The Peaceable Kingdom*, 85.

21. Ibid., 74.

22. Lindbeck, *The Nature of Doctrine*, 16. Lindbeck mentions another theory, "cognitive-propositionalism," in which doctrines are understood as true propositions about objective realities; while he judges it to be inadequate, it does not threaten Christian particularity as much.

Religion as a distinct human phenomenon regards a universal experience—of the Ultimate, of the Holy, of the mysterium fascinans et tremendum, etc.—that is shared, though likely not thematized, by every individual; particular, historical religions are so many "expressions or objectifications" of this experience, whose validity is a function of their "reference to the experience."[23] This theory is a child of Western modernity, the product of an "experiential tradition" traceable to Kant, who cleared the intellectual ground for "the romantic, idealistic, phenomenological-existentialist streams of thought that have dominated the humanistic side of Western culture," ingraining in our very souls "habits of thought" that push us to understand religion as primarily rooted in pre-reflective experience, from which—and only from which—religion's public forms flower. Meanwhile, certain "psychosocial pressures" enable and promote experiential-expressivism: "the individualism, rapid change, and religious pluralism of modern societies" compel us "to meet God first in the depths of [our] souls and then, perhaps, if [we] find something personally congenial, to become part of a tradition or join a church."[24] For Lindbeck, these intellectual and cultural dynamics have created a crisis for Christianity: "There seems to be less and less communal sense of what is or is not Christian." The *sensus fidelium* that is meant to constitute Christian communities, that is, what Christians "discover they believe in times of crisis and are willing to die for," has become lost, and this threatens the viability of Christian churches.[25] Thus, the loss of Christian particularity effected by Western modernity, simultaneously symbolized and fed by the experiential-expressivist theory of religion, must be met with the recovery of the Christian *sensus fidelium*, aided and abetted by an alternative approach to religion.

This recovery is essentially tied to that of the classical biblical hermeneutics practiced by premodern Christians. Lindbeck identifies four formal characteristics of such hermeneutics: first, the Bible was interpreted canonically, as a unified work; second, such canonical interpretation was guided by something akin to rules of grammar "embedded in the speech and practices" of the interpreting community; third, the Bible was interpreted primarily as a narrative; fourth, the Bible was interpreted through figuration, both intra- and extra-textually. Together, these characteristics render the Bible "a cross-referencing, interglossing semiotic system" able "to assimilate by redescription all the worlds and world views which human beings construct."[26] By revitalizing this hermeneutics, churches will rediscover the Bible as a

---

23. Ibid., 31.
24. Ibid., 20–22; alterations mine.
25. Lindbeck, "Scripture, Consensus and Community," 202.
26. Lindbeck, "The Gospel's Uniqueness," 234–35.

text that projects an 'imaginatively and practically habitable world,'[27] which will provide an interpretive framework within which Christians understand reality and order their lives.[28] Connected to this recovery is Lindbeck's cultural-linguistic theory of religion. According to this theory, religions are understood as cultural or linguistic frameworks, competency in which requires the sort of learning and practice that feeds learning a language and how to participate in socially meaningful activities. Unlike the experiential-expressivist theory, in which a religion's public forms derive from some universal human experience, for the cultural-linguistic alternative such public forms become primary, playing the leading role over experience by shaping it according to its framework.[29] Meanwhile, rather than understand doctrines as symbols that articulate experience, this alternative understands doctrines to be rules for speaking and acting that constitute the form of life accessible through the Bible's projected world. Importantly, this does not mean that doctrines are formulations to be repeated word-for-word unthinkingly. Rather, doctrines are paradigms to be followed, structures that enable a certain variety in speech and action; doctrines are authoritative grammar, not necessarily changeless vocabulary.[30] Still, Lindbeck is clear about the shape of the solution to the crisis of the loss of *sensus fidelium* and a related approach to mission: "Instead of redescribing the faith in new concepts, [Christian should seek] to teach the language and practices of the religion to potential adherents" and to each other. In short, the recovery of the *sensus fidelium* requires a recovery of a catechetical method of formation.[31] As with Hauerwas, for Lindbeck becoming Christian is a matter of mastering the specific content, now in the form of grammar, that constitutes the tradition whose interpretive framework can only be embodied in particular, historical churches.

For both thinkers, a return to historical, communal particularity is the best way to combat the enervating combination of individualism and universalism bequeathed by modernity, according to which the individual is an unattached entity left to freely pursue its own desires and whose only morally constitutive relation can be to some universal entity accessible through private experience. Hauerwas, Lindbeck, and their many followers seek to restore the social aspect of human life, those historically particular communities in which individuals are formed and from which universals

---

27. Lindbeck, "Scripture, Consensus and Community," 218.
28. Lindbeck, *The Nature of Doctrine*, 117.
29. Ibid., 32–41.
30. Ibid., chapter 4.
31. Ibid., 132.

are articulated. Such restoration, given its own historical circumstances as a dissatisfied response to a certain view of liberalism and modernity, must emphasis socialization as the most significant mode of moral formation. Granting the significance of socialization to human moral development, questions still remain regarding the moral status of the individual within communities and checks against conservative authoritarianism with a communitarian position. A crucial aspect of this book is to show what is theologically at stake in taking these questions seriously.

THE ARGUMENT AND OUTLINE

The argument of my dissertation is that socialization, though an essential task of moral formation, is insufficient, because the proper aim of moral formation is individual development. The point of the argument is not only to address tendencies towards conservative authoritarianism discernible in recent enthusiasm for the task of socialization, but also to recover individuality as a crucial agent of communal development. Moral communities tend to contract the scope of their moral care and concern until self-defense becomes their posture towards other communities, a tendency that an emphasis on socialization abets. However, individuals within them can transcend their socialization and so resist such contraction, and insofar as they gain a following, their moral communities can expand and become vulnerable to transformation, both within and without. This account of individuality and communal development is funded by a Christian theological account whereby individuals are understood to have a direct relation to God that is irreducible to their social relations with each other, even and especially their social relations with other Christians within the church. This direct relation to God enables individuals to transcend their socialization in various communities and so creatively enact communal transformations. As it terms out, the theological diagnosis is that it is a warped direct relation to God that motivates the contraction of one's moral communities and so the emphasis on socialization. For these multiple reasons, individual development must be recovered as the aim of moral formation.

My argument consists of a conceptual reconstruction of Niebuhr's theological ethics through the accounts of individual and community found in Josiah Royce and George Herbert Mead. Niebuhr is an appropriate figure for this project because he offers a triadic construal of faith that appreciates the importance of tradition and socialization for the moral life conducted before and for God, while protecting a significant place for individuality within that life. Niebuhr recognizes that we have valid socially mediated relations with God, but insists that we each, as individuals, occupy a direct relation to God irreducible to those relations, from which we can critically reflect upon and transform those relations. This makes sense in light of his combination of Barth's Christian particularism and Troeltsch's social historicism with an evangelical piety animated by Blaise Pascal, Soren Kierkegaard and Jonathan Edwards. However, I articulate the complementary tension between individuality and community in Niebuhr's work against his more immediate American social-philosophical background, specifically Royce and Mead. Their work focuses acutely on the question of the relationship between individual and community, and so is the best background against which to interpret Niebuhr for my purposes.

My argument unfolds in the four following chapters. Chapters 2 through 4 provide my argument for a theological account of individuality and individual creativity based on an interpretation of Niebuhr's account of faith as read through the intellectual background of Royce and Mead. In chapters 2 and 3, I argue that Royce and Mead, respectively, betray a robust appreciation of socialization while understanding human moral development to culminate in the development of individual creativity. Royce offers a reparative model of individual creativity in his philosophical interpretation of Christianity. He regards socialization into a community with its own history and destiny, as the saving of individuals from vicious social dynamics that cause us to shuttle back and forth between the extremes of individualism and collectivism. Membership in a community provides us a way to be self-expressive that contributes to, rather than hinders, a life shared with others. However, the community is vulnerable to acts of treason that literally tear it apart, and can only be repaired by individuals who respond creatively to such acts as opportunities for making the community stronger and better than it was, in light of the ideal of the Beloved Community, the universal community of minded beings. Mead, on the other hand, offers a disruptive model of individual creativity. His account of human moral development turns on the distinction he makes within the self between the "me" and the "I." The "me" refers to the self as socially constituted, as having internalized a community's social inheritance. The "I" refers to the self as able to creatively respond to, rather than merely participate in, this inheritance. Mead refers to those individuals with strong "I's" as social geniuses: they tap into latent or neglected elements of their social inheritance in order to broaden and deepen communal relations. Such individual creativity is disruptive because it conflicts with forms of community life comfortable in their current state and exclusions. Social geniuses and their followers open their communities up to transformation, paradigmatically when their communities sees no reason to change. Thus for both thinkers, communal development occurs through individual creativity, but each has a different model of that creativity.

Niebuhr was influenced by the work of both Royce and Mead. In his account of faith as the combination of trust and loyalty, the notion of loyalty derives from Royce. In his account of responsibility as rooted in responsive, anticipatory relations, the characterization of these relations derives from Mead. In chapter 4, I argue that Niebuhr's use of Royce is contextualized within a conceptual structure that is more indebted to Mead than Niebuhr himself attests, and that it is this structure that enables us to articulate a theological account of disruptive individual creativity. The method I employ in this argument is conceptual reconstruction, that is, an interpretation of Niebuhr's thought through the lens of concepts available to though not exploited by him, primarily Mead's I/me distinction. Niebuhr's references to Royce and Mead are few and under-discussed, but rather than determine precisely what Niebuhr understood himself to be using from each thinker, I aim to show how he could have used Mead, in order to articulate the argument in chapter 4. An exegetical upshot of my reconstruction is that it explains why Niebuhr used Royce's philosophy of loyalty, but not his interpretation of Christianity. I argue that Niebuhr's triadic account of faith can be read as an articulation of the self's I/me relation before God: while the "me" still refers to the self as socially constituted, the "I" now refers to the self as related directly to God in a way that is irreducible to her social relations. In Niebuhr's own terms, the "me" refers to the self's social faith, while the "I" refers to the self's radical faith, which works in and through social faith. The life of faith exemplified and enabled by Jesus Christ is the life of radical faith that takes the form of trust in God as good, and loyalty to God's cause, the universal community of being. This form of radical faith transforms our various social faiths, and so underwrites a form of radical individual creativity that must disrupt our finite social lives in order to press them into divine service. Radical creativity is disruptive because the radical faith that funds it is itself the transformation of a radical distrust in and disloyalty to God that results in the idolatrizing of social faith and the funding of a form of social creativity that simply defends the community against internal and external criticism. Radical faith, our irreducibly individual relation to God, transforms our social faiths, our socially mediated relations to each other and our common pursuits; radical faith then funds radical creativity, action in direct response to God, which transforms our social creativity so it is self-transformative rather than self-defensive. Ultimately, a Mead-oriented reading of Niebuhr enables me to articulate a theological account of individuality and individual creativity.

In the fifth and final chapter, I tie up one loose end and illustrate my argument with some examples. The loose end that needs tying is an account of the individual self's direct, socially irreducible relation to God. Here,

I characterize this relation as one of existential resonance, by extending some suggestions from Niebuhr's later work. Existential resonance is my construction for what Niebuhr appeals to when he appeals to feeling and emotion, a construction with which I hope to improve on these latter terms. With this account of the self's direct relation of God, I then discuss two forms of the radical creativity that would follow from a radically trustful form of that relation, symbolic and virtuous creativity. Radically creative symbolic novelty refers to the multiplication of symbols for God that follows from recognizing the unique existential resonance that each individual member of the Christian community undergoes in relation to God. Importantly, such novelty does not entail an abandonment of traditional symbols, but rather a transformative renewal of such symbols in interaction with new symbols. I illustrate this dynamic by arguing that a new symbol like "God the mother" can both critique the traditional symbol "God the father" in its more patriarchal modes and renew it by drawing out its personal resonances with the new symbol. Meanwhile, radically creative virtuous novelty refers to the transformation of moral virtues from self-defensive service to their host moral communities, to self-transformative service to God's cause, the universal community of being. Such transformation comes in two stages: first, the transformation of radical faith from distrust to trust; second, the subsequent transformation of moral virtues as expressive of radical trust, rather than radical distrust. While symbolic novelty prevents the collapse of symbol and reality, virtuous novelty prevents the collapse of virtue and deed: because moral virtues are vulnerable to transformation, specific actions traditionally associated with them cannot ensure their presence. I end the chapter by showing how God can be understood to morally form us through Jesus Christ, who exemplifies and enables symbolic and virtuous creativity. Such creativity is ineradicably individual, but oriented in a social rather than solipsistic direction.

CONTRIBUTIONS

I intend my book to make two sorts of scholarly contribution. First, I hope to enrich Niebuhr scholarship through my in-depth analysis of the influence of his American intellectual heritage. While I have found isolated discussions of his conceptual interactions with Royce and Mead, none are adequately thorough, and none have attempted to discern how he negotiates the influence of two thinkers different enough from each other to warrant such an attempt. One ramification of this analysis is an enrichment of our portrait of Niebuhr. While it is common to note that Niebuhr was ahead of the curve in appreciating the social construction of the human, it is not often discerned that one stream feeding this appreciation—the American intellectual scene—also contributed to his appreciation of the irreducibility of our individuality. In this way, I hope to suggest that Niebuhr's evangelical piety is not some lingering primitive remnant that ought to have been abandoned once he robustly accepted social theory, but rather can be conceptually renewed and deepened as a significant aspect of such theory. Finally, I hope that my own extensions of Niebuhr's work in the final chapter reflect that his work remains immediately fecund for contemporary theological ethics. While his influence is indisputable in American Protestant ethics, he deserves as large a place within the field as his brother is currently enjoying.

Second, in my final chapter I hope to enrich the field of theological ethics. My rhetorical strategy of discussing symbolization and virtue together is to disrupt somewhat settled distinctions within the field. Those for whom virtue is a major category, like Hauerwas, tend not to use the category of symbol, probably because of its associations to thinkers associated with liberal modernity. Meanwhile, those for whom symbol remains a relevant category often do not use the category of virtue, perhaps because of its associations to their post-liberal critics. In other words, stances within the field of theological ethics may overdetermine topics of inquiry, and I hope to show that this is unnecessary. I also hope to contribute to an understanding of each topic. My notion of God's accommodation to human symbolic activity is meant to contest the notion that such activity is necessarily anthropocentric, in the sense of being human work independent of divine agency. Appreciating human mediation of the divine does not entail denying the priority of divine activity, but rather taking that priority seriously. On the other hand, my account of virtues as hermeneutical responsive dispositions is meant to suggest that virtuous activity does not have to be conceived along Aristotelian-Thomistic lines. The point is to contextualize virtue within a vision indebted to responsibility, just as Niebuhr encourages us to think about man-the-maker along the lines of the man-the-answerer: virtues dispose us to respond to God and the world responsibly. Simply put, to appreciate human symbolic activity is not to have drunk the Kool-Aid of modern, autonomous individualism, just as to appreciate virtue is not to have drunk the Kool-Aid of a communitarianism that wishes to re-institute the Middle Ages. This leads to the overarching contribution I intend to make: individuality is a legitimate and significant phenomenon for theological inquiry and a moral agency for communal development that demands theological-ethical attention.

— 2 —

Loyalty Atoning through Interpretation
Individual and Community in Josiah Royce's Philosophy of Christianity

As STATED IN THE introduction, the point of the first chapters is to draw out from H. Richard Niebuhr's major works a theo-ethical vision of human life before God in which the individual self occupies a position irreducible to her position in her religious community (or any human community), and from which she is enabled to critique and reconstruct that (or any other) community. According to such a vision, the aim of moral formation within the religious community cannot be socialization, installment or absorption into the community as a functioning member. Rather, moral formation must aim at the individual development of community members, not only out of respect for their irreducibly individual relationships to God, but also because the progress of communal life before God depends on such relationships. This is not to say that socialization is not a necessary part of moral education; it is essential, but ultimately under-determining. We can draw such a vision of human life from Niebuhr if we read him against the background of two American thinkers that he engaged, Josiah Royce and George Herbert Mead, who both provide accounts of human moral development that appreciate the necessity of socialization while ultimately carving out a space for individual creativity. The point of the next two chapters, then, is to show how Royce and Mead characterize the dynamic relationship between individual and community in their accounts of human development, through a close reading of their major works that Niebuhr references or quotes. This chapter will accomplish its task by focusing on

Royce's *The Problem of Christianity*, as well as the earlier work that paved its way, *The Philosophy of Loyalty*. My argument in this chapter is that Royce's philosophical account of Christianity articulates atonement as an interpretive process that requires irreducibly individual and creative acts, ultimately oriented toward the betterment and moral improvement of community. For moral formation, this means that socialization must be completed in individual development.

As stated, my intention is less to trace intellectual-historical connections from the earlier thinkers to Niebuhr, than to articulate constructively a vision that can be drawn from Niebuhr in light of Royce and Mead. In chapter 4 I will suggest reasons as to why Niebuhr takes up Royce's account of loyalty, but not his interpretation of Christianity, and these turn on, I will argue, Niebuhr's more fundamental utilization of Mead for his theo-ethical vision, as well as on instabilities in Royce's position. Of course, this critical suggestion requires understanding Royce's interpretation of Christianity, and this chapter is meant to contribute precisely to such an understanding. At the same time, my intention is less to compare Royce and Mead directly, than to show how they interact within Niebuhr's work. The question for me less regards which thinker more adequately accounts for the dynamic between individual and community, than which account Niebuhr deems more adequate, as seen through how and to what extent he takes up each in his own work. That said, Royce's work had, and continues to have, a reputation that would contest this chapter's argument that Royce promoted individual creativity and social transformation. Before turning to the core of this chapter, an exegesis of Royce's *The Problem of Christianity*, a brief discussion of this reputation will provide some context for the exegesis.

ROYCE AS SOCIAL CONSERVATIVE?

In an article that compares Royce and Mead on the relation between the human self and social processes, ultimately endorsing the latter, scholar of American thought David L. Miller implies a stark contrast: Royce's philosophy is a form of conservative idealism that can only demand conformity to existing institutions, while Mead's thought provides the sort of progressive pragmatism that accounts for human selves' ability to direct and change social processes. The crucial difference is that "Royce founded his system on the belief that man is born into a moral order, an order that is there apart from man's thinking or doing and antedates the appearance of man." According to Miller, this moral order is necessarily a fixed, closed society, in response to whose demands humans can only be loyal or rebellious, because Royce is simply providing idealistic metaphysical backing for taken-for-granted Christian beliefs: "If the individual is to be saved he must enter into a pre-established institution, the Church Universal."[1] To assume such an institution means, "one is not asked to construct a system of moral rights and obligations."[2] Mead offers a stark contrast: he presumes no moral order independent of human construction, and so can account for individual humans' capacity to create, direct, and change the social processes that constitute a moral order, enabling us to see that there are more subtle ways to respond to the moral order than simply loyalty or rebellion. Miller grounds this social-anthropological difference between the two in their hermeneutic differences. On Miller's account, Royce understands meaning to consist in cognition, while Mead understands it to consist in response. Royce's hermeneutics is thus merely syntactical, concerned only with the relation between signs, while Mead's hermeneutics is pragmatic in the linguistic sense of being concerned with the relation between signs and the environment in which they are used.[3] In other words, Royce is a formalist and Mead is a proto-use-theorist concerning language and meaning. Thus, Miller can suggest that Royce discerns meaning to subsist in a realm disconnected from human life, such that knowing, besides behavior, becomes a matter of conformity to an external order, while Mead discerns meaning to arise in the midst of human life, such that knowing requires constructive activity. In short, there is simply no room for individual creativity in Royce's thought on Miller's account.

Miller's article is a response to an interpretation of Royce as moving away from Hegelian idealism and toward Peircean pragmatism in his later work, including and especially *The Problem of Christianity*.[4] For Miller, this move, when truly undertaken, is toward naturalism, and insofar as Royce remains an idealist who articulates some notion of an "absolute," this apparent move is only a shift in vocabulary. Miller implies a rather blunt connection: if naturalism, then room for individual creativity within human society; if any sort of supernaturalism, then only room for conformity or rejection to pre-existing moral orders. Since Miller, Royce scholars have argued that changes in his thought are much more than terminological. John E. Smith in particular argues for the deep impact of Charles Peirce on Royce, and Frank Oppenheim, extending Smith's work, also discerns connections

---

1. Miller, "Josiah Royce and George H. Mead," 73–77.
2. Ibid., 85.
3. Ibid., 68–69.
4. In particular, Fuss, *The Moral Philosophy of Josiah Royce*.

between Royce and the other classical pragmatists.⁵ One is hard-pressed to find any support for Miller's characterization of Royce in this scholarship, because it is generally recognized that Royce's thought moves throughout his career towards an account of the "absolute" that grounds and promotes, rather than obscures, individuality and particularity. For Royce, individual lives do ultimately fit into a larger, absolute life, but this fit requires individual expression and creativity more than mere conformity. In short, accept the influence of pragmatism on Royce, and the significance of the individual becomes clear.

More recently, Dwayne Tunstall has argued that Royce was as, if not more, deeply influenced by his early debate with personalist philosopher George Holmes Howison. At stake in this debate is whether or not individuality, particularly in the sense of moral autonomy, could be preserved with a monistic conception of the 'absolute'; Royce thought it was possible, Howison did not. For Tunstall, the entire trajectory of Royce's work can be read as the working out of a response to Howison's criticism, ultimately issuing in an articulation of idealism as "an ethical and panentheistic personalism," according to which "we are seen as participants in the divine life, but insofar as we live out the divine's eternal purpose in our own unique way."⁶ *Pace* Miller, this reading depends on disconnecting the possibility of individual creativity from a thorough-going naturalism, and so depends on the possibility of a supernatural theism that can ground and promote individuality. Tunstall argues that the panentheism implicit in Royce's metaphysics of community provides this sort of theism. In this regard, it is relevant to mention that Royce understood his work *The Problem of Christianity* to be a response to William James's *The Varieties of Religious Experience*. While James focuses on individual religious experience, Royce focuses on "a form of social religious experience." Moreover, whereas James supposes churchly religious experience to be merely conventional, "lacking in depth and in sincerity," Royce declares this a mistake, insisting, "All experience must be *at least* individual experience; but unless it is *also* social experience, and unless the whole religious community which is in question unites to share it, this experience is but as sounding brass, and as a tinkling cymbal . . . This is the essence of Christianity."⁷ In short, according to recent scholars and the thinker himself, Royce offers a thoroughly communal *and* religious vision

---

5. Smith, *Royce's Social Infinite*; Smith, *America's Philosophical Vision*, chapters 7–10; Oppenheim, *Reverence for the Relations of Life*.

6. Tunstall, *Yes, But Not Quite*, 6, x.

7. Royce, *Problem*, 40–41.

which grounds and promotes individual creativity. This chapter intends to articulate this vision.

In light of this recent consensus, my exegesis is not idiosyncratic, and so does not attempt to carve a significant space for itself within Royce scholarship regarding the nature of the development of his thought, the character of his theism, the character of his philosophical method, the relation between the different aspects of his thought (e.g., logic, epistemology, metaphysics), and so on. Rather, for the purposes of this book, I intend to interpret one significant work, and others as they are relevant to this task, through the lens of one particular dynamic of human life. Smith asserts, "Royce's whole philosophy could be interpreted as the story of the cooperation and tension between individual and community."[8] This chapter should demonstrate that this is certainly true of *The Problem of Christianity*. While my interpretation is not idiosyncratic, the order of my exposition differs from the usual model, and in doing so reveals a problem that other scholars have failed to notice. While most accounts begin with Royce's ideas of community and interpretation as the norm that orders their ensuing discussion, I follow the trajectory of the story of moral development Royce has to tell, which means my account arrives at community and interpretation. My argument proceeds in three sections, each discussing one of the leading ideas that Royce identifies as essential to Christianity, though not in the order of his identification. The first section discusses his second idea, the Lost Individual, while the second section discusses his first idea, the Beloved Community; the third section discusses the third idea, Atonement. There is a reason for interpreting the work in this order. The idea of the Lost Individual describes the problematic human situation to which the idea of the Beloved Community describes the solution. However, this Community makes possible another, deeper and more significant problematic human situation, treason, to which the idea of Atonement describes the solution. This stutter exposes a problem in Royce's account of community. Ultimately, the argument of *The Problem of Christianity* turns on the possibility of interpretation as a human capacity for individual creativity.

THE PROBLEM OF EDUCATION IN THE PROBLEM OF CHRISTIANITY

Royce distinguishes "two principal and contrasting characteristics" of Christianity. First, Christianity can be understood as what was taught and lived out by Jesus Christ: it is an "art of living" composed of "the teaching,

---

8. Smith, *The Spirit of American Philosophy*, 91.

the personal example, and the spirit of the Master." Second, and more expansively, Christianity includes the interpretation of Jesus Christ and his religion "in the light of some doctrine concerning his mission, and also concerning God, [humanity], [humanity's] salvation," a doctrine which goes beyond what Christ himself taught. This interpretive aspect of Christianity is illustrated both by the significance of the suffering, death and resurrection of Christ to the Christian tradition, which the disciples could only relate to his teachings through their own interpretation, and by the parabolic expression of those teachings themselves, which required interpretation by the disciples' further, latter insight in order to be fully understood.[9] In an earlier article, Royce claims: "What is vital in Christianity must be, if anything the Christian interpretation of human life, and the life lived in the light of this interpretation," an interpretation of which Christ's teachings are a "partial presentation."[10] Royce's point is that Christ's teachings and activities were *intended* by him to be supplemented and fulfilled by the latter interpretations of his disciples for the sake of human life. Thus, Royce's own interpretation of those teaching and activities can be understood as a form of hermeneutic discipleship.

Indeed, Royce is clear that his delineation of Christianity's three essential ideas—the Beloved Community, the Lost Individual, and the Atonement—constitute his interpretation of Paul's interpretations of Jesus Christ's original teachings and activities. Importantly, interpretation has more than methodological significance. It is not only the mechanism by which communities understand themselves, but also the mechanism by which they are reconstituted when threatened with dissolution. This should become clear by the end of the chapter. Now I turn to Royce's notion of the Lost Individual.

The problem that Christianity articulates is the problem of education manifesting as malforming socialization, which Christianity purports to solve. This problem is identified in Royce's second essential idea of Christianity, the Lost Individual, or otherwise stated, the Moral Burden of the Individual: "The individual human being is by nature subject to some overwhelming moral burden from which, if unaided, he cannot escape. Both because of what has technically been called original sin, and because of the sins that he himself has committed, the individual is doomed to a spiritual ruin from which only a divine intervention can save him."[11] While this may

---

9. Royce, *Problem*, 65–69; cf., Royce, "What Is Vital in Christianity?," 140–43.

10. Royce, "What Is Vital in Christianity?," 130, 143.

11. Royce, *Problem*, 100. Smith asserts that Royce's account of sin separates him from American liberal theology (*Royce's Social Infinite*, 141), but Royce's view on the interpretation of Christianity as mediating an historical tradition with contemporary wisdom complicates any strict separation.

seem an individualistic notion of sin, Royce insists that social processes render the individual's moral burden. It is education in the sense of malforming socialization that renders lost individuals in need of salvation through the Beloved Community.

To delineate this idea, Royce turns neither to the Genesis narrative, nor to a doctrine or theory of original sin, but rather "to [humanity] as we empirically know [it]," taking the position of an "observant naturalist" of human conduct.[12] Taking this position is a matter of gleaning from human experience, instead of starting with philosophical abstractions or merely reiterating the historical sources. On this experiential view, conduct is understood to result "from the training which our hereditary predispositions, our instinctive tendencies, get, when the environment has played upon them in a suitable way, and for a sufficient time."[13] With this training, "our instincts become interwoven into complex habits, and thus are transformed into our voluntary activities," so that our conduct becomes "more and more definite," whether "for good or for ill."[14] Royce discerns two kinds of training. The first kind is purely *ecological*, establishing "in us a given form of conduct," without awareness of what that form is or means. Human beings share this ecological training with, and so our conduct remains bound to that of, all living beings. The second kind is specifically *social* training, providing an awareness of our form of conduct, a "grade or sort of consciousness" that accompanies our conduct. Social training provides the practical self-knowledge or moral self-consciousness—"our knowledge about what we do, and about why we do it"—that separates us from other living beings. Thus, social training requires a specifically social environment.[15] While ecological training into conduct only requires interaction with an environment hospitable enough to sustain us, social training into consciousness of conduct requires interaction with fellows and with a social will within such an environment.

Social training is responsible for both moral self-consciousness and consciousness of the social will, that is, of the demands of the social environment. In fact, they increase in direct proportion to each other, because the social will develops as a response to the fall-out of the development of moral self-consciousness. Moral self-consciousness regards our "power to form ideals, and . . . to develop any sort of conscience."[16] According to Royce's moral anthropology as set out in an earlier, pivotal work, our moral self is

12. Royce, *Problem*, 104–5.
13. Ibid., 107.
14. Ibid., 105.
15. Ibid., 106–7.
16. Ibid., 109–10.

constituted by living according to an ideal life-plan, and our conscience is that ideal understood as our moral personality, as the present command to live according to it.[17] Social training contributes to this by providing social contrasts: "Contrasts, rivalries, difficult efforts to imitate some fascinating fellow-being, contests with my foes, emulation, social ambition, the desire to attract attention, the desire to find my place in my social order, my interest in what my fellows say and do, and especially in what they say and do with reference to me" all cultivate self-consciousness. In other words, there is an inevitable tension in our social life due to the social contrasts that result, not from natural depravity or the "graver vices," but from our natural differences and mutual misunderstandings. The sharper these contrasts are, the more conscious we become of our own selves, of our conduct and ideals, *precisely in opposition to those of others*: "moral self-consciousness is bred in me through social situations that involve . . . some form of social conflict,—conflict such as engenders mutual criticism."[18] Paradoxically, the moral self, which strives for unity and coherence, is born from and into social chaos. This is a rather dire account of primary moral development. As we will see in later chapters, both Mead and Niebuhr understand some level of cooperation to be more fundamental to moral self-consciousness than conflict. However, this social chaos does not yet comprehend Royce's idea of the 'moral burden of the individual.'

As social training renders moral self-consciousness, it also renders consciousness of the social will. Because of the inevitability of social tension and chaos, a social force that Royce calls the *social will* arises, developing codes and laws to make social life hospitable. The result is a more conscious, deliberate phase of social training, constituted by the transmission of a "customary morality" and the application of "social discipline." Ironically, in this effort to mitigate the destructive tendencies of the social contrasts between selves and others, the social will introduces "still new and more complex kinds of tension,—new social contrasts" between itself and each moral self it attempts to socialize. Because moral self-consciousness is a product of contrasting the self with others, the moral self rendered by social training is compelled to oppose itself to the social will as well. Royce explains that "precisely in proportion as society becomes more skilled in the external forms of culture, it trains its servants by a process that breeds spiritual enemies." The moral self will obey the social will in conduct, but "will naturally revolt inwardly." Cultivation, the social training of people through cultural forms of moral discipline not to destroy each other, breeds individualism in the sense

17. Royce, "Loyalty," 921–32.
18. Royce, *Problem*, 110–11.

of "spiritual self-assertion." Individuals are cultivated to emphasize "every sort and grade of more skillful opposition to the very social will that trains it."[19] In this phase, the paradox thickens: not only is the moral self born from and into social chaos, but the very attempt to deal with such chaos trains the moral self to become a skillful social rebel. *This* is the moral burden of the lost individual: while moral self-consciousness and consciousness of others and the social will increase in direct proportion, the valuation of the self increases in inverse proportion to the valuation of society and others.

The problem here is not the person's self-valuation as such, but the tendency of that valuation to be contrasted to the valuation of others and society. In other words, the problem is *individualism*, "the tendency to prefer what the individual [person] demands to what the collective will requires," but not *individuality*.[20] Royce asserts that social training breeds self-assertion, but a subtler way to describe this is that social training renders all forms of self-expression and self-development oppositional. Under social training, individuation is not accomplished simply by differentiation, but appears to require distance and isolation from others and society. The social will reacts to this individual self-valuation at the expense of others, with social training and moral cultivation, but also with its own form of self-valuation opposed to that of individuals, what Royce calls *collectivism*. Under collectivism, the social will is compelled to express itself in a form that suppresses individuality. This, in turn, compels individuals into individualism, as the cycle continues. Just as self-consciousness and consciousness of the social will increase in direct proportion, so individualism and collectivism intensify each other.[21] Ultimately, the problem is the constitution of false forms both of human individuality and human community, forms that feed off each other to destroy each other. As will be elaborated below, the solution to this unceasing conflict will require truer forms of human individuality and community, what recent Royce scholar Jacqeulyn Kegley calls "genuine individuals and genuine communities" that feed off each other to support each other.[22]

In light of the discussion in chapter 1, it is interesting to note that Royce understands the structure of individualism as a "highly potent social tendency" of self-assertion against others and the social will to be transhistorical, though it requires some level of civilization: "Savages appear to know little about individualism."[23] My point is that Royce does not under-

19. Ibid., 112–14.
20. Ibid., 127.
21. Ibid., 116.
22. Kegley, *Genuine Individuals and Genuine Communities*.
23. Royce, *Problem*, 113–14.

stand individualism to be the product of modernity, that period of time following the Middle Age; individualism is what Paul diagnoses in Romans 7. Thus, the solution to the problem of socialized individualism is similarly trans-historical, even if articulated paradigmatically by historically located individuals and communities. Stated otherwise, the Beloved Community, Royce's first essential idea of Christianity, is irreducible to even if constituted by particular historical communities. To this idea I now turn.

LOYALTY AND COMMUNITY: THE PROBLEMATIC SOLUTION

Royce articulates the solution to the problem of socialized individualism in his idea of the Beloved Community. Visible, historically particular churches create—and the appropriate understanding of creation here will be articulated below—the Beloved Community as a salvific community, by providing escape from society's moral (mal)formation of individualistic selves and its own collectivist response. Such salvation still requires some form of grace, but significantly, this form is interpretive.

According to Royce's interpretation of Paul, "salvation comes through loyalty," specifically loyalty to the Beloved Community, which is incarnated in our loyalties to the other communities of which we are members.[24] However, while loyalty and community alleviate the moral burden of the lost individual, providing a dynamic between individuality and community that is mutually generative rather than destructive, they also bring their own moral burdens. In the description of the moral burden of the individual quoted above, Royce makes a distinction between original sin and voluntary sin.[25] Social training and the chaos that ensues is Royce's account of original sin: it is something we inevitably suffer, something that causes irresistible reactions, *not* something we voluntarily do, *not* a sin "in the stricter sense."[26] Loyalty and community remain problematic because, while they save us from the original sin of social training, they create the conditions for voluntary sin in the sense of treason against the community to which we have devoted our loyalty. Having in the first section given an account of Royce's second essential Christian idea, the point of this section is to provide an account of loyalty and the beginnings of an account of the first Christian idea, the Beloved Community, as setting up the problem of treason, to which Atonement, the third Christian idea, provides the solution, thus completing

---

24. Ibid., 119.
25. Ibid., 100.
26. Ibid., 144.

the account of the Beloved Community. This requires a detour through an earlier work, *The Philosophy of Loyalty*, whose ideas Royce reconstructs in *Problem*.[27]

Loyalty

The Problem of Christianity is not the first work in which Royce discusses loyalty, though it is here that he introduces the significance of community. In *The Philosophy of Loyalty*, loyalty functions as the solution to a particular moral paradox: "I, and only I, whenever I come to my own, can morally justify to myself my own plan of life . . . Yet I, left to myself, can never find a plan of life."[28] Stated differently, moral autonomy is a good that needs an end.[29] Social training appears here as an inadequate solution, foreshadowing the more developed later account: it provides us with plans of life, and yet it provides too many and various plans which are so imperfectly ordered, that we are thrown back on ourselves in opposition to the social order, leading to a "seemingly endless play of inner and outer."[30] The adequate solution is loyalty, which Royce defines as "*The willing and practical and thoroughgoing devotion of a person to a cause.*"[31] A *cause* should be understood here as an ideal demanding realization, providing an outer, objective plan of life, an end, while devotion to it is the good that provides the inner, subjective autonomous justification of that plan, such that self-sacrifice for and obedience to our cause is transformed from social conformity to self-expression.[32] Importantly, Royce is *not* arguing that personal devotion to a cause of itself morally justifies that cause. Rather, it is personal devotion in the sense of our will's voluntary approval and assent to a cause that justifies loyalty as

---

27. I am attempting to disentangle these two works, in order to get some clarity on what changes between them. Other accounts, in my judgment, too tightly entangle these two works, along with others, to give a singular account of Royce's thought (see Kegley, *Genuine Individuals and Genuine Communities*, chapter 4; Smith, *The Spirit of American Philosophy*, chapter 3), and others treat the former as mere background to the latter (see Smith, *Royce's Social Infinite*, 34–63; Oppenheim, *Royce's Mature Ethics*, 73–78; Oppenheim, *Royce's Mature Philosophy of Religion*, 25–28). Because Niebuhr takes up Royce's notion of loyalty, but not his later Christian construal of it, my project demands disentangling the two works, while leaving the former its integrity.

28. Royce, "Loyalty," 867.

29. Ibid., 891.

30. Ibid., 867–68.

31. Ibid., 861.

32. Ibid., 871.

a good *in place of* social conformity or external authority. Because of this, loyalty is always good, even if a particular cause to which we are loyal is not.

The objectivity or "super-individuality" of a cause consists in more than providing a life-plan that is external to individuals. By providing the same life-plan to various individuals, a cause is able "to join many persons into the unity of a single life."[33] Loyalty, while not authoritarian or conformist, remains social by uniting many and various individuals through their personal devotions to the same cause. This is another aspect of loyalty's goodness: it unites us in a manner superior to social conformity, by uniting us through, rather than abrogating, the autonomy and particularity of our personal devotions. This social good of loyalty is essential to the moral adjudication of causes. Royce asserts, "a cause is good, not only for me, but for [human]kind, in so far as it is essentially a *loyalty to loyalty*, that is, is an aid and a furtherance of loyalty in my fellows." Good causes encourage and inspire loyalty in others, while evil causes destroy such loyalty.[34] The cause of loyalty to loyalty, which Royce also calls the cause of universal loyalty, is not a cause among others. Hence, individuals cannot be devoted to it in addition to being devoted to friendships, families, nations, etc. Instead, the cause of universal loyalty is served through our devotion to other causes, so that causes are understood to be good insofar as they promote devotion to universal loyalty.[35] Moreover, if the cause of universal loyalty entails devotion to all loyalty everywhere, then it ultimately unites all loyal human life into a single life.[36] Again, this universal union of humankind occurs through the autonomy and particularity of our devotions to particular causes, not by overriding or abrogating them. Simply put, loyalty renders forms of social life, particular *and* universal, that require our individual autonomous self-expression and self-development.

Two more aspects of his philosophy of loyalty deserve attention. First, individuals need to be trained for loyalty: social training is to be resisted by "loyalty training." Royce mentions three factors of this training: first, "the influence of personal leaders"; second, "higher forms of training for loyalty involve a momentous process which I shall call the Idealizing of the Cause"; and third, "loyalty is especially perfected through great strains, labors, and sacrifices in the service of the cause."[37] I take the second factor to be the most controversial; the first and third simply note that loyalty requires an

33. Ibid., 897.
34. Ibid., 901.
35. Ibid., 908–9.
36. Ibid., 904.
37. Ibid., 961–62.

exemplar to incarnate our cause, in order to train us how to incarnate that cause through service to it. In the second factor, Royce is arguing that a cause can become idealized only once it becomes a lost cause, a cause that has historically failed. As examples, he notes Irish and Polish loyalty to their "idealized, although no longer politically existent nationality" (we could note the current situation of Palestinians), Judaism and Christianity, and the cause of universal loyalty itself. Because a lost cause cannot be realized "by any possible present deed," it can become idealized and so "demand that its followers should plan and work for the far-off future, for whole ages and aeons of time." Thus, loyalty to lost causes is inevitably accompanied by grief and imagination, but in specific forms: grief understood as a spur to the active recovery of what is lost, rather than as passive lamentation; and imagination as a vision of such future recovery that directs present deeds, rather than as consoling fantasy.[38] The implication for moral formation is bold: besides exemplars and our own labors, training for loyalty advances through historical failure *and* our loyally appropriate response to that failure through imaginative grief.

Second, loyalty "has its own metaphysic," that is, our experience of loyalty pushes us to hold that certain realities obtain, if we are to continue to be loyal.[39] While this brief account cannot do justice, it must be mentioned for the sake of accounting for Royce's final definition of loyalty. It was noted above that the cause of universal loyalty unites all of human life. The nature of this unity is implied when Royce states, "The loyal serve a *real whole of life*, an *experiential value* too rich for any expression in merely momentary terms."[40] This real whole of life is "the real whole conspectus of experience" that includes all temporal happenings, and Royce calls this the 'eternal.'[41] The cause of such a whole, such an experience, must historically fail, since it is impossible for it to be fully realized in any historical moment, and so it can only bear loyalty if idealized into a lost cause. Thus, Royce's final definition of loyalty: "*Loyalty is the will to manifest, so far as is possible, the Eternal, that is, the conscious and superhuman unity of life, in the form of the acts of an individual Self.*"[42] Metaphysically, loyalty demands the existence of an absolute unity of human and divine life, understood experientially. Morally, loyalty is our personal, autonomous expression of this unity *through* our

---

38. Ibid., 964–69.

39. Royce, "Loyalty," 993. Royce notes that the real world is defined by our ideal needs, which I take to mean that the real world is defined according to what needs to be the case if the pursuit of ideals through loyalty to causes is to make sense.

40. Ibid., 986; emphasis mine.

41. Ibid., 992.

42. Ibid., 996.

lives as individual selves, which are composed of our particular devotions to particular causes, enacted through particular deeds.

This metaphysic expresses the "latent union of morality and religion": at its peak, the moral life of loyalty involves belief in the reality of the "Eternal" as a cause. When Royce states, "Loyalty means a transformation of our nature," he means that loyalty to the eternal cause transforms our natural loyalties.[43] In other words, those loyalties—e.g., to friendships, families, nations—that admit of historical success are transformed by becoming vehicles for universal loyalty. Natural loyalties are not meant simply to last, or only to satisfy their devotees, but rather to become modes of serving the eternal cause. Insofar as our patriotism excludes concern or care for other nations, it is morally inferior to a patriotism that is concerned and cares for the global community. Of course, what such concern and care concretely entails in particular situations is an open question, but behind this is a metaphysical point. For Royce, it is *not* the case that the "Eternal" "is *first* eternally complete, but *then* asks us, in an indifferent way, to copy its perfections." Rather, loyalty requires us to perform unique deeds, unique not in the sense of genius, but in the sense of autonomous and voluntary. Such deeds express the universal, *not* simply as exemplary imitations, but as actual contributions to the "Eternal" itself: "If my deed were not done, the world-life would miss my deed," for this world-life is and needs "all our lives in one."[44] This seems to support Tunstall's argument that Royce is panentheist.[45] Whatever the precise character of Royce's theism, my point is that loyalty requires our irreducibly individual, autonomous self-expression and self-development.

Community

Perhaps because of the nature of this earlier work as an exposition of the reality and moral value of loyalty, Royce does not discuss the constitutive problem of loyalty: its creation of the opportunity for voluntary sin as treason. This discussion appears in *The Problem of Christianity*, which can be understood as Royce's interpretation of his own philosophy of loyalty in light of Christianity.[46] Here, he replaces the notion of *cause* with that

---

43. Ibid., 1008–9.

44. Ibid., 1012.

45. Tunstall, *Yes, But Not Quite*, 47–50. Tunstall's argument comprehends more than Royce, "Loyalty."

46. See Smith, *Royce's Social Infinite*, 66–77, for a beginning account of community that parallels mine.

of *community*, and the cause of universal loyalty with the first essential Christian idea, the Beloved Community: "There is a certain universal and divine spiritual community. Membership in that community is necessary to the salvation of [humankind]." This community is the "fitting realm wherein alone the Kingdom of Heaven which the Master preached can find its expression, and wherein alone the Christian virtues can be effectively practiced."[47] The Beloved Community is *not* to be confused with the visible church, or with any historical community, but rather is the ideal of the Universal Community to be expressed and realized through historical communities like visible churches, just as the cause of universal loyalty is served through our particular loyalties. The Beloved Community thus serves as the moral standard for visible, historical churches. When Royce explains that the church that realizes that standard "is still a sort of ideal challenge to the faithful, rather than an already finished institution," he is implying that the standard expressed by the Beloved Community is a lost cause.[48] As we will see, the structure of the loyal life will remain intact in Royce's account of community, despite the conceptual shift.

The shift from *cause* to *community* is occasioned by an anthropological claim: there are two different grades or levels of human being. On the one hand are *individuals*, whose words and deeds express or manifest particular minded lives, distinct from those of all other individuals. On the other hand are *communities*, whose particular minded lives are expressed or manifested in communal realities like languages, customs, and religions. There are individual minds tied to the organic lives of particular bodies, and social minds with "a sort of organic life of their own" and a different psychology. Royce, following psychologist Willhelm Wundt, is deliberately vague about the precise nature of the minded life of communities, calling it a "fair 'working hypothesis'" for further investigation. His point is to insist that communities are *more* than collections of individuals: individual minds can*not* produce languages, customs, or religions unless they are united in community, i.e., unless they are participating in a particular social mind.[49] There is an essential distinction to be made here between community and society. Society is that social environment in which social training occurs. Here, individuals are merely collected since, as was shown above, society on this understanding divides individuals both from each other and from itself, rendering a pernicious dynamic of mutually enforcing individualism and collectivism. Community is an *ideal* environment, in which individuals

---

47. Royce, *Problem*, 72.
48. Ibid., 77.
49. Ibid., 238–39.

are united but remain distinct, becoming members through participation in its social mind. This is not to suggest that communities are not embedded in, dependent on or creative of particular forms of ecological and social environments: the Beloved Community requires the visible church for its realization, which in turn requires certain ecological dynamics in order to exist. The point is that communities live by exceeding such ecological and social environments.[50] Society is united by a social will, which conflicts with the individuals collected within it. Community is united by a social mind, which can unite individuals across particular societies.

The question is how individuals participate in a particular social mind, how they occupy the ideal environment that is a community. Royce identifies three conditions for community. The first is "the power of an individual self to extend his life, in ideal fashion, so as to regard it as including past and future events which lie far away in time, and which he does not now personally remember."[51] Recall that, for Royce, the moral self is constituted by an ideal life-plan. Here, he is emphasizing time as an essential factor in the formation of moral selfhood: "my idea of myself is an interpretation of my past,—linked also with an interpretation of my hopes and intentions as to my future."[52] The moral self is constituted by memory and hope, in the sense that the present self constitutes itself by interpreting its past self to its (interpreted) future self.[53] To ideally extend one's self in time is to claim as one's own, as constituting one's very self, past and future deeds and events of distant others, as well as physical things (e.g., a samurai's sword) and spiritual objects (e.g., grace) that no longer or have yet to or only ideally exist.[54] Simply put, participation in a social mind requires the capacity to participate in histories and destinies that exceed our biographies by ideally identifying with them.

The second condition for community is "the fact that there are in the social world a number of distinct selves capable of social communication, and, in general, engaged in communication." This condition makes it clear that communities require a social environment to exist. For Royce, the significance of this condition lies in its emphasis on the distinctness of individual selves: the unity of the community does not entail "any reduction or melting of these various selves into a single merely present self, or into a mass of passing experience." In other words, the ideal does not necessitate

50. Ibid., 262.
51. Ibid., 253.
52. Ibid., 245.
53. Ibid., 287.
54. Ibid., 254.

the mystical, if this is understood to involve loss of self. Instead, community members should keep their individuality in order to contribute their "own edifying gift to the common life."[55] This is consistent with the earlier claim that loyalty requires the autonomous self-expression of its devotees, and makes it all the more clear that the individual self's ideal identification with a community's past and future is *not* a matter of conformity.

Finally, the third condition for community is "the fact that the ideally extended past and future selves of the members include at least some events which are, for all these selves, identical."[56] Community is created when distinct selves claim the same ancestral past and are oriented to the same future goal, just as distinct loyal selves are united by their devotion to the same cause. Important insights are hidden here. It is not the *strictly empirically* experienced past that constitutes communal memory, but the *ideal* past experienced as presently significant. In other words, a particular group's experienced suffering will not make them a community *unless* that suffering is interpreted as part of an ideal history of suffering that extends beyond the experience of that group's members, yet is claimed by them. On the other side, it is not a *realizable* goal that constitutes communal hope, but an *ideal* goal that directs present action. A realizable goal would spell the end of community *unless* that goal is understood as progress toward an ideal goal. Stated otherwise, community is created when distinct selves *idealize* their personal memories and hopes so that they become part of the community's ideal history and goal.

These three conditions account for the possibility of community, but not for the actual and continuing conscious common life of community. Besides an ideal past and future, community requires common deeds and a common love. Such deeds are essentially cooperative, performed with fellow-members. This cooperative activity requires a social environment, which poses a paradoxical problem. Recall that the social environment is where social training reigns, resulting in the destructive dynamic between collectivism and individualism, between imposed socialization and reactive rebellion. The form this dynamic—the original sin of civilization—takes regarding cooperation is that civilized society "breeds cooperation at the expense of a loss of interest in the community." This is exacerbated by social complexity, which renders cooperation dependent on vaster networks, and so puts more and more distance between those who must cooperate with each other. The result is that the cooperation imposed by society must appear to the individual "as a mere process of nature, and not as his own

55. Ibid., 255–56.
56. Ibid., 256.

work,—as a mechanism and not as an ideal extension of himself."[57] Thus, the vicissitudes of the modern social environment, within which cooperation *must* be performed, make cooperation appear merely ecological rather than potentially ideal.

The solution to this problem is common love, by which the community renders its cooperative deeds ideally present. Royce notes three stages in the self's ideal extension: first, it reaches to a common past and future; second, to those fellow selves who share that common past and future; third, to the present life and deeds of these fellow selves. Participation in the social mind of the community ultimately requires memory of its ideal past and hope for its ideal future that are "enlivened" by love for its ideal present deeds. Love is our ideal extension into the present, for it entails "*acting as if we could survey*, in some single unity of insight" the wealth and variety that constitute the cooperative activities in which we participate, but which, under conditions of social complexity, we cannot cognitively grasp.[58] *Love* here is Royce's interpretation of Pauline charity, Christian love taking on the form of loyalty. Recall that, for Royce, Pauline Christianity is an interpretive extension of Jesus' teachings. In this case, Paul's experience of and in the Christian community allowed him to transform Jesus' doctrine of love—which had two objects, God and neighbor—into a doctrine that includes love for the community as a third object. According to Royce, this inclusion made neighbor-love a less mysterious and abstract, and more concrete, enterprise. For Paul neighbor-love must be mediated through community-love: charity means that we love our neighbors as fellow community members, which entails loving the community first.[59] At the same time, charity is an interpretation: "The ideal extension of the self gets a full and concrete meaning only by being actively expressed in the new deeds of each individual life."[60] Charity turns our present, individual deeds into interpretations of that common activity *as* cooperative, *as* constitutive of the community.

Now we can see why the first essential idea of Christianity is of the specifically *Beloved* Community. When interpreted through Paul, devotion to a cause becomes loyal love for a community. Importantly, the idea of the Beloved Community is the "specifically Christian form" of the idea of the universal community. The latter, more general, idea is grounded in the social nature of humankind manifested in communities, and comes to be

57. Ibid., 260–65.
58. Ibid., 265–67.
59. Ibid., 89–98.
60. Ibid., 268.

valued by all who learn loyalty.⁶¹ The Beloved Community connotes "the idea of a spiritual life in which universal love for all individuals shall be completely blended, practically harmonized, with an absolute loyalty for a real and universal community."⁶² Part of Royce's point in insisting that the idea of the Beloved Community *is* the idea of the universal community is to deny that it could be identified with any visible Christian church. In *The Philosophy of Loyalty*, loyalty to a particular cause became universal loyalty because of the inner dynamic of the goodness of loyalty itself. Here, love for one's particular church is to be constituted by and expressive of love for all humankind. Royce formulates the following imperative for Christians: "So live together that the Church may be worthy of Christ who loves it." This might sound as though he is asserting that Christ loves only those who gather to confess and worship him. In fact, Christ's love for the church manifests an infinite concern for both levels of human being: for all humans as individuals *and* for humankind as a communal unit.⁶³ For a Christian community to be worthy of Christ requires that its members' love for it manifest Christ's love for humankind. Loving the neighbor as a fellow-member of the Beloved Community does *not* mean loving her only insofar as she confesses and worships Christ, but only insofar as she is a member of the universal human community. Thus, a Christian community that excludes care and concern for this universal community is less worthy of Christ than one that includes them. The members of a worthy Christian community must see its cooperative activity as connected to the cooperative activity of the universal human community. At the same time, the only way to show care and concern for, and to cooperate with the activity of, the universal human community, is through care and concern for, and cooperative connection with, other particular human communities. Hence, the Beloved Community is incarnated in the visible Christian church only insofar as that church spreads the Beloved Community abroad.

Again, the concrete particulars of such care, concern and cooperative connection cannot be defined in advance. This underscores Royce's constant insistence: love for the community, whether our particular church or humanity itself, means being "joined in a life in which we shall be both preserved as individuals, and yet united to that which we love."⁶⁴ Royce explains, "Unless each man knows how distinct he is from the whole community and from every member of it, he cannot render to the community

61. Ibid., 101.
62. Ibid., 98.
63. Royce, *Problem*, 95–97.
64. Ibid., 270.

what love demands,—namely, the devoted work."⁶⁵ Our participation in our community's cooperative activity must be uniquely individual—not in the sense that our individual work must be novel or different from everyone else's, but that it must be autonomous and voluntary. As with loyalty, love for community requires personal self-expression and self-development. This entails that our community's cooperative activity cannot be some determinate task. If the Christian community is called to the ideal challenge of manifesting the Beloved Community, and *not* to the reproduction of some fixed institution, than our unique, individual deeds as members will in fact be creative of the Beloved Community as a present reality.

It should be noted that the above account of the conditions of the possibility for and life of the community is entirely anthropological, but not exhaustively so, as the appeal to Christ might have hinted. Recall that in Royce's description of the moral burden of the individual, humans can only be saved through some form of divine intervention. This is not inconsistent with salvation coming through loyalty, but rather indicative of loyalty being a matter of divine intervention. Royce notes that the Beloved Community "must be an union of the members who first love it," but also that "the unity of love must pervade it, before the individual member can find it lovable." Whence the love? If love originates from the individual members, there is no accounting for how it can be oriented toward the community, given the conditions of social training and civilization. If love originates from the community leader, there is no accounting for the origin of the leader's love for the community without positing a community with members who love it. According to Royce, the only way out of this circle is to posit "some miracle of grace" in the form of a leader who can create the community that she loves and bids others to love. Such a leader must appear to be both an individual member *and* "the spirit—the very life" of the community, such that "his origin will be inexplicable in terms of the processes which he himself originates."⁶⁶ While we can give an account of community and love for it as anthropological phenomena, we cannot account for their supernatural origins. This inexplicable origin can only be discussed with reference to the idea of *grace*, that "power that gives to the Christian convert the new loyalty" to the new—beloved—community.⁶⁷

Christianity conceives of this power as the work of Christ. Paul can describe the Beloved Community as the Body of Christ because Christ himself—after his death, resurrection and ascension—"*is now identical with the*

---

65. Ibid., 268.
66. Ibid., 129–31.
67. Ibid., 125.

spirit of this community."⁶⁸ Royce notes a parallel between the doctrine of the two natures of the Christ and his notion of the two levels of humankind.⁶⁹ Insofar as Christ appeared as a member of the Beloved Community, he must be understood to be a human individual; insofar as he appeared as the spirit or life of the Beloved Community, he must be understood to be, somehow, the human community itself. Recall that Christ's love, and so Christian love, is *of* all particular individuals and *of* humankind as a singular community. Significantly, this union of the two levels of humankind is not exclusive to the incarnation of Christ; it is trans-historical. Royce explains, "Such union of the two levels has its place in our daily lives wherever the loyalty of an individual leader shows to other men the way that leads them to the realm of the spirit," i.e., their community.⁷⁰ There are unanswered questions here about the relation between divine grace and human work. Suffice it to say for now that, though Royce opens up the work of grace, understood as the very initiation of loyal love to community, to the strictly human realm, his claim is *not* that human leaders can accomplish of themselves what Christ did. Rather, the claim seems to be that human leaders can now accomplish what Christ did in and for their communities *because* Christ has already done it in and for humankind. If the work of Christ is grace, then *because* of that grace we can accomplish a similar work.

The Problem of Loyalty and Community

It should be clear how loyalty and community solve the problem posed by social training, how the idea of the Beloved Community contains the solution to the problem expressed in the idea of the Moral Burden of the Individual. While our interactions in the social environment render us antagonistic to each other *and* society, provoking society to impose its will on us and so initiating a destructive dynamic between individualism and collectivism, loyalty to and love for community provide an avenue to express and develop our individual, particular selves in a way that builds up community, uniting us with others internally through our orientation toward the community. Instead of atomized individuals and undifferentiated masses, loyal love to community renders "genuine individuals and genuine communities." Before turning to the concept, suppressed so far, that serves as the glue of Royce's exposition of Christianity and community—*interpretation*—we must turn to Royce's account of the voluntary sin rendered

68. Ibid., 131.
69. Ibid., 138.
70. Ibid., 140.

possible by loyalty and community. This order is important, because the argument will be that it is precisely insofar as communities are communities of interpretation that they are able to confront sin in the stricter sense. Meanwhile, the work of Christ and the loyal love it enables will only be *fully* understood once we see how it overcomes such sin.

Loyal love for community makes possible the voluntary sin of *treason*. Royce notes two conditions that constitute a traitor. First, the traitor must be a member of a community to which he is loyal and to whose cause he is actively devoted. That person, still caught in the dynamic of individualism and collectivism and having yet to find a community to which to be loyal, cannot be a traitor. Only the person who has been saved from the original sin of social training can voluntarily sin.[71] I do not think that Royce commentators have appreciated how odd this account is, given the extent to which it separates original and voluntary sin: voluntary sin does not proceed from a state of original sin, but rather from a state of being saved from original sin.[72] The second condition of treason is that the traitor must perform a voluntary act in which he betrays his own cause. Voluntary here means not simply non-coerced, but also expressive of the inner self: treason is "an affair of the heart."[73] Royce does not explain what *motivates* treason, *why* a person who has been saved by loyalty to community would then betray that community, but the lack of explanation makes a point. Royce calls treason a person's "morally 'impossible' choice," and the impossible is precisely what eludes explanation.[74] Treason may be a possibility concomitant with loyalty, but there is *no reason* why a loyal person would commit it. This entails that treason can*not* simply be understood as a residue of self-assertion left from our social training, for Royce does give an account of what motivates that.

If treason is ultimately a mystery, it does have objective consequences for the self and the community. By committing treason, we consign ourselves to the "*hell of the irrevocable.*" Treason is *irrevocable* because no matter how saintly we become afterward, we will *always* have committed it, it will *always* be part of our past selves. Treason is *hellish*, "moral suicide," because to betray our cause is to betray the life-plan that constitutes us as moral selves. If loyalty to a cause unites one's individual and communal, inner and outer, natures by providing a way of self-expression that contributes to the building up of community with others, then disloyalty literally

---

71. Ibid., 168.

72. Smith is simply wrong when he asserts that voluntary sin proceeds from the chasm between individual and community created by social training. See Smith, *Royce's Social Infinite*, 159.

73. Royce, *Problem*, 168

74. Ibid., 154.

tears the self apart.[75] Again, this is not simply a reversion to the condition of social training: the dynamic of individualism and collectivism prevents the genesis of the unity of the self, but it does not disrupt an existing unity. This is clear when it is recognized that treason also destroys the community.[76] To commit treason is to betray the cooperative activity through which the life of the community subsists and the love that unites the members to each other and the community. This too is irrevocable: Royce notes that, while love for the traitor may be restored, it will always be love scarred by the fact that it is for that member who was once a traitor.[77] The task made necessary by treason is a new work of grace, one that will re-create the sundered community.

INTERPRETATION AND ATONEMENT

Community saves us from the social chaos that follows from social training, but it provides the conditions for treason, the voluntary sin that threatens community itself. I have noted that Royce's account of original and voluntary sins leaves them oddly disconnected from each other: what saves us from original sin, enables voluntary sin. Moreover, Royce does not seem to appreciate the complexity of his own account of community. On the one hand, treason is conceivable only within the ideal environment of some community, not the social environment. On the other hand, community can only be fully realized once treason is overcome within it. Thus, there seems to be two stages of community, the pre-treason stage in which communal bonds are strong enough to overcome social chaos and so be susceptible to treason, and the post-treason stage in which the community has recreated itself after some act of treason. This section completes the account of community I began last section; last section I accounted for pre-treason community, and in this section I account for post-treason community. As we will see, the interpretive relations that bind community together in the first place, are the same sort of relations through which the process of atonement heals a community broken by treason. Despite the communal character of atonement, it requires the irreducibly individual acts of particular community members. This section proceeds in two parts, first offering an account of Royce's notion of interpretation, and then offering an account of his notion of atonement as a process of interpretation.

75. Ibid., 162.
76. Ibid., 174–75.
77. Ibid., 177–78.

Interpretation as Cognitive Process

Following Charles Sanders Peirce, Royce identifies interpretation as a third type of cognitive process distinct from perception and conception.[78] While perception is the immediate apprehension of some singular datum or thing, and conception is the abstraction from data and things of some universal character, type or quality, interpretation is the cognitive grasp of mental or spiritual objects. Interpretation is our *only* mode of access to the processes that go on in other minds through the signs that manifest them. Royce likens interpretations to exchange values: to communicate with others is like "crossing the boundary of a new country," and standing "in the presence of a largely strange world of perceptions and conceptions" which we must come to understand in the terms of our own perceptions and conceptions. Interpretation effects this exchange or translation, allowing us to understand other minds and act accordingly, just as exchanging currency and translating speech allow us to travel within a foreign country and interact with its inhabitants appropriately.[79] Royce's imagery is suggestive. When communication between individuals in general is interpreted on the model of foreign travel, communication between foreigners in particular becomes paradigmatic of, rather than especially problematic for, communication itself. In other words, communication between foreigners becomes more the inevitable deliverance of the interpretive process and less a hindrance to it.

Interpretation is a process that relates three terms in a determinate order. The first term is the person of the interpreter. The second term is the object of interpretation. This object is always personal: when we interpret another person, we are interpreting some particular product of that person's mind, such as a gesture, speech, text, etc. In short, the object of interpretation must be construed as a *sign* of something personally significant. The third term is the person to whom the interpretation is addressed. Thus, interpretation is the process of one mind interpreting another mind to yet another mind. It is now clearer how the moral self can be understood as an interpretation, for it is constituted by the present self interpreting the past self, via some *sign* of this past self, to the future self.[80] Interpretation

---

78. On the influence of Peirce on Royce's notions interpretation and community see Smith, *Royce's Social Infinite*, 21–31, 69–74, and Smith, *America's Philosophical Vision*, chapter 10. Tunstall (*Yes, But Note Quite*) contests a strong influence of Peirce on Royce's metaphysics of community, but Royce's use of Peirce to articulate interpretation is undeniable.

79. Royce, *Problem*, 277–83.

80. Ibid., 286–87.

is essentially interpersonal—Royce calls it a "conversation"[81]—for it connects persons who are foreign to each other, whether simply because our minds are necessarily separate from each other (and in this sense we are all somewhat foreign to each other), or also because we are separated by time, geography, language, culture, etc.

To call interpretation a *process* is to foreground its temporal dimension. Kegley argues that each term in the interpretive process is connected to a specific dimension of time: the interpreter is in the present, interpreting a sign of something past to a future addressee.[82] This suggests the interminability of interpretation. Royce notes that the process of interpretation issues in *an* interpretation, a *product* that may seem to consummate the process. However, this interpretation is itself a sign, manifesting the mind of the interpreter who is struggling to understand her own object of interpretation. This sign can then be taken up into another process of interpretation, which in turn will issue in its own interpretation-sign that can be taken up into yet another interpretive process, such that "the social process involved is endless." While perception and conception are self-limiting processes, stopping once objects are sensed or categorized, interpretation appears to be a self-perpetuating process, ultimately beyond the control of any individual interpreter.[83] The ramifications of this for moral formation are incredible. If moral education is neither purely perceptual, nor purely cognitive, but rather interpretive, then it is an endless temporal process. Any community that aspired to practice such moral formation would open itself to endless novelty. Royce does not go all the way in this direction, given his understanding of atonement, but the point is suggestive and promoted by Mead and, I will argue, Niebuhr.

Royce is less interested in interpretation as a process that continuously exceeds the grasp of our intention and agency, than as a community building process that binds us to others. The interpretive process is ultimately perpetuated by what Royce calls the "Will to Interpret," a social (and ultimately divine) dynamic in which three tasks circulate between three intentions. The interpretive process creates community between the three persons involved insofar as the interpreter's will to interpret is met by and fulfilled in the interpreted's will to be interpreted[84] and the addressee's will to receive the interpretation. The aim of interpretation for each of these

81. Ibid., 289.
82. Kegley, *Genuine Individuals and Genuine Communities*, 43.
83. Royce, *Problem*, 289–90.
84. Kegley notes, "The will to interpret also involves a willingness to have one's ideas tested and compared against the ideas of others; to risk . . . error and change" (*Genuine Individual and Genuine Communities*, 45).

wills is "complete mutual understanding," which can only be realized in time as the spiritual unity of a 'community of interpretation.'[85] Royce is not describing a different kind of community than those already described: all communities that meet the conditions described above are communities of interpretation, and triads of persons have already been delineated for certain examples of interpretation. The point here is to show how the unity of community can be attained while preserving individuality. Each person in the interpretive process has her own task, differentiated from that of the others, which must be *individually willed*; e.g., if our addressee does not will to receive our interpretation, there will be no community. At the same time, the tasks will shift between persons. The interpreter must will *to* interpret, but once she has offered her interpretation, she must will *to be* interpreted herself and will *to receive* further interpretations, if the community is to continue.[86] Such individual willing and performance of tasks within the interpretive process is not a matter of genius, but it is creative of meaning and community.

The preservation of purposive individuality is defended in Royce's metaphysics of community, what he calls the *doctrine of signs*, just as personal, autonomous self-expression and self-development is defended in his metaphysics of loyalty. Again, while this brief account cannot do justice to his metaphysics of community, it is appropriate to include it. According to Royce's metaphysical thesis, "The universe consists of real Signs and of their interpretations," or stated more directly, "the universe is a community of interpretation."[87] In other words, the universe is *not* ultimately composed of universals and particulars, and so can*not* ultimately be known through perception and conception. Rather, the universe expresses mindedness through signs, and so can only be known by minds through interpretation.[88] This is not to deny that there are real things in the universe to be perceived and conceived,[89] but rather to insist that such things are ultimately expressive of mind, such that their significance is only accessible through interpretation. In line with this understanding of reality, Royce asserts that the divine should be conceived "in the form of the Community of Interpretation, and above all in the form of the Interpreter, who interprets all to all"; he also refers to "God the Interpreter." To participate in the interpretive process is

---

85. Royce, *Problem*, 314–19.

86. Ibid., 315.

87. Ibid., 345, 340.

88. Hence, Royce is an idealist, even if he is also a voluntarist (Smith), pragmatist (Oppenheim), or personalist (Tunstall).

89. Oppenheim, *Royce's Mature Philosophy of Religion*, 162.

both to be inspired by and to participate in the "Will to Interpret," divinely construed.[90] While these quotes certainly raise more questions than they answer,[91] parallels with the metaphysics of loyalty are evident. The notion of "community of interpretation" replaces that of the "Eternal" here, but both notions are inclusive and non-effacing of personal individuality and both refer to a dynamic process rather than a fixed, complete substance or institution. Just as the eternal is composed of individual experiences and deeds, so the community of interpretation requires the personal willing of individual tasks; just as the eternal is not a perfect object to which one conforms, so the community of interpretation is an illimitable process in which one must personally participate. Royce's metaphysics of community thus *grounds* personal, autonomous self-expression and self-development.

Atonement as Interpretive Process

The question remains in what sense interpretation can instantiate an atoning process, and so we must turn to Royce's notion of atonement. Recall that treason is any irrevocable deed that forever scars the community *and* the life of the (heretofore) loyal member who commits it. Because of the irrevocability of past deeds and events, atonement cannot consist in the undoing of treason. Rather, through atonement the traitor must become "tragically,—sternly,—yet really, reconciled, not only to himself, but to his deed of treason, and to its meaning in his moral world," and just as importantly, to the community and the meaning of that treason in its moral world. Royce distinguishes this notion from two historical Christian theories. Against satisfaction theories of atonement, Royce insists that reconciliation must occur between the traitor and his community, and within the traitor himself, but not with some angry God. Against moral theories, Royce insists that reconciliation must occur through concrete deeds that effect a more objective transformation than the influencing of subjective states: atonement is "*not* something about Christ's work, which merely arouses in sinful man love and repentance," but rather that work itself, changing the moral world of the traitor and his community.[92] For those familiar with Gustaf

90. Royce, *Problem*, 318–19. At this point it seems appropriate to register my agreement with Tunstall that there are panentheist tendencies in this particular work of Royce's.

91. In particular, there are hints of both Trinitarianism and panentheism. In this regard, there are striking parallels with the work of Lutheran theologian Robert W. Jenson. See Jenson, *Systematic Theology*. At the same time, it is unclear what place the doctrine of creation might hold in Royce's metaphysics.

92. Royce, *Problem*, 169–75, 185.

Aulen's typology of atonement theories, it is clear that Royce, by contesting satisfaction and moral theories, is clearing the way to articulate a version of the "Christus Victor" theory, according to which the atonement consists in Christ's triumph over evil.[93] In early forms of "Christus Victor," the atonement is Christ's victory of the devil, and in more contemporary forms, victory over social structures and forces that perpetuate evil.[94] For Royce, atonement is the triumph over *treason*, that is, the triumph over some willed evil act, rather than triumph over personified or social evil, and it includes both objective and subjective dimensions.

While treason is a destructive deed that rends the moral world of the traitor and his community, atonement is constructive, a "triumph of the creative will" that creates a new world. Royce explains that atonement "can only be accomplished by the community, or on behalf of the community, through some steadfastly loyal servant who acts, so to speak, as the incarnation of the very spirit of the community itself." This loyal servant performs a "creative work," the very possibility of which was opened by a particular act of treason. Genuine atonement occurs when the world transformed by this creative work turns out *"better than it would have been had all else remained the same, but had that deed of treason not been done at all."* Such atonement "transforms the meaning of that very past which it cannot undo" by effecting the "transfiguration of the very loss into a gain that, without this very loss, could never have been won."[95] Royce illustrates this with the biblical story of Joseph and his brothers. The brothers' treason against the family in their treachery towards Joseph ultimately leads to Joseph's high position in Pharaoh's court, from which, as the incarnation of the spirit of the family, he is able to reunite it and save it from famine, ultimately materially bettering and morally improving its condition.[96]

My contention here is that it is only insofar as the community is one of interpretation whose members manifest the will to interpret, be interpreted and receive interpretation, that it is able to enact atonement. Simply put, the

---

93. See Aulen, *Christus Victor*. Smith (*Royce's Social Infinite*, 151–55) and Oppenheim (*Royce's Mature Ethics*, 144) recognize the options that Royce is rejecting, but do not discuss the Christus Victor option he seems to be affirming.

94. See, on the one hand, Gregory of Nyssa, "An Address on Religious Instruction"; on the other hand, recent liberationist, feminist, and Mennonite works, e.g., Jon Sobrino, *Witness to the Kingdom*; Darby Kathleen Ray, *Deceiving the Devil*; J. Denny Weaver, *The Nonviolent Atonement*.

95. Royce, *Problem*, 180.

96. Ibid., 202–5. Notice that, while in the Genesis narrative Joseph attributes the atonement to divine intention, he still had to perform his own, individual part to carry it out. That atonement is divinely willed does not exclude the participation of human intention.

creative deed of atonement can be understood as the present interpretation of an irrevocable past treason, addressed to the future community that will occupy the better world made possible by that treason. Someone must have the will to respond to past treason as the condition for future loyal acts, just as Joseph had the will to save and reunite his family rather than take vengeance. This will must be met and realized by the will of the traitors to have their treason responded to in this fashion, just as the brothers had the will to accept Joseph's superior position and his offer of reconciliation. These must ultimately be met and realized by the will of the reconciled family to live together in these new, better circumstances, just as Jacob's family did. The resulting interpretation of this process is the stronger union of the traitors with their community than could have existed before. In this way, without the interpretive process, there is no atonement.

Just as interpretation is inextricably temporal, so is atonement: both are oriented toward the future, though conditioned by the past. The future of interpretation opens toward endless novelty, but only in relation to past interpretations; similarly, the future of atonement opens to a new world, but only in relation to past treason. This past-conditioning is significant, for it shows that the creativity of atonement refers not only to the creation of a new, better world, but also to the transformation of a past evil act into the condition of possibility of such creation. The creativity of atonement is thus contingent: the possibility of a better world actualized by atonement is rendered by the irrevocable past evil, and so cannot be some utopian vision of the destruction of evil itself. Arguably, Royce's entire understanding of human creativity can be understood as that of contingent rather than absolute creativity.[97] Human creativity is always a response to past deeds and events, so that the truly creative action should be understood as *fitting*, rather than iconoclastic. An interpretation is fitting to the extent that it is constrained by its object and its receiver, just as atonement is fitting because constrained by the treason to which it is responding and the community it is reconciling. Atonement is a "fitting deed" because it is "the creation by somebody of a definite individual good on the basis of a definite previous evil," or more specifically, the creation of *this* reconciled community on the basis of *this* previous treason.[98] The fittingness of atonement does not render it less creative, only more concrete.[99]

97. On the theme of creativity in Royce's thought, see Smith, *American's Philosophical Vision*, chapter 9.

98. Royce, *Problem*, 186, 205.

99. Niebuhr also connects fittingness and interpretation, but his account is crucially different than Royce's. Oppenheim's rather disparaging account of Niebuhr's relation to Royce in *Royce's Mature Ethics*, 208–10, fails to appreciate this.

Of course, the creativity of atonement does require purposive activity. To describe atonement as interpretation is *not* to say that atonement simply consists in understanding or narrating the past treason in a way that allows community members to cooperate with the traitor in their future-oriented present activity. Rather, atonement accomplishes community-reconciling interpretation as a practical deed: the atoner's interpretation of treason as the condition for a better world is instantiated in an action, just as Joseph's interpretation of his brother's treason as such a condition is instantiated in his reconciliation with them. While Mead gives an explicit account of how an action that responds to another's prior action is an interpretation of that prior action, Royce's work is suggestive. Recall that Royce calls the love that binds a community together in the present (charity) an *interpretation*, and then explains that it consists in "*acting as if we could survey*" the entire nexus of cooperation in which we participate. Interpretation and action are bound together: to act cooperatively *is* to interpret the entire activity in which we participate as a cooperative endeavor, and so to interpret the actions of others, whether proximate or remote, as cooperating with ours. Similarly, to atone for treason with reconciling action as Joseph did *is* to interpret the past treason as the condition for a better world. To atone is to act *as if* past treason could render an even better world, and in so doing to bring about that better world. We can say that the atoning act incarnates the charitable interpretation of treason.

In this way, to say that atonement is an interpretive act is another way of saying that atonement is an idealizing act. Recall that idealization is that response to lost or historically failed causes, which requires specific forms of grief and imagination. A community torn apart by treason can certainly be understood as lost in the sense of historically failed. Atonement is thus a manifestation of loyalty to this lost community, accompanied by grief—which spurs the loyal servant to creative activity—and imagination—which provides a vision of a better world made possible by this treason to guide that creative activity. In this way, atonement instantiates the loyalty training described in *The Philosophy of Loyalty*, for it includes: a personal example in the person of the atoner; idealization, since atonement is occasioned by the failure of community itself; work on our part, in the sense that we must will to accept the atoner's charitable interpretation of treason, though this may involve giving up the vengeance that might release certain psychological and emotional pressures. If Royce had considered loyalty training in *The Problem of Christianity*, he might have identified its highest form as atonement, called it community training, and articulated it as Christianity's paradigmatic form of moral formation.

Regarding this last point, the three essential Christian ideas that Royce articulates can be understood as three essential ideas for understanding moral formation. The idea of the Lost Individual characterizes the problem that constitutes the need for moral formation; the lost individual is caught in a dynamic in which individualism and collectivism mutually reinforce each other, thus promoting stunted forms of both individuality and community. The idea of the Beloved Community serves as the norm of moral formation: socialization into any community is only good insofar as it promotes the individuality of those socialized, and the ideal of the Beloved Community, which should orient community life, demands such individuality. The idea of the Atonement describes the highest moral act, the act that most expresses the ideal of the Beloved Community, since it involves the reconstruction of a community that has been ruptured from the inside out, *on the very basis of that rupture*. In this sense, forming individuals to be able to participate in the interpretive process that constitutes atonement becomes the aim of moral formation.

If atonement is the aim of moral formation, and if it is understood as an interpretive process that requires irreducibly individual and personal acts, then moral formation must come to completion in some sort of individual development, the purpose of which is to better the community. The social training that leads to social chaos pits individual and society against one another; any community training that would lead to atonement must ensure the mutual co-working of individual and community, such that the highest expression of individuality serves the community without simply replicating or conforming to it. The interpretive acts that compose atonement literally recreate the community, so the shape and consequences of such acts cannot be determined in advance. Obviously, the capacity to atone requires socialization, in the sense of induction into the social mind that characterizes the community. At the same, such socialization necessarily under-determines how one can atone, since atonement is a creative venture into a future imagined for the community beyond treason. Individual imagination is doubtless shaped by the social mind, but once the community is torn apart by treason, that social mind becomes de-stabilized, requiring the individual work of imagination to re-orient it, and in the process, to renew it. Socialization is necessary but insufficient; a community that recognizes this should learn to promote individual development. Unfortunately, Royce does not give an account for what this might look like. In the final chapter of this book, I attempt such an account.

CONCLUSION

I trust that this chapter has given a portrait of Royce that belies Miller's. Loyalty and its instantiation as charity require much more than conformity to a fixed, external order. Because Royce does not understand the "Eternal" or the Beloved Community to be some pre-established substance that we are meant to simply copy, loyalty ultimately expressed as charity is consistent with creativity to the extent that it permits and demands the particular and unique deeds of individuals. Indeed, it is precisely such creativity in which the atoning process consists. The very notion of atonement as a process that humans can participate in reflect that, for Royce, not only are our social and moral systems open to revision, but also, insofar as atonement results in a better world, such revision can consist in directing and changing social processes. Royce thus advocates a form of community that is open rather than closed, and this openness is grounded, not occluded, precisely by the recognition of a moral order that transcends whatever particular communities we occupy. Moreover, while Royce certainly understands meaning in terms of signs expressed by minded beings that must be interpreted, it is not the case that he ignores the responsive aspect of meaning. Interpretation according to Royce is a process in which one person responds to another person's sign by interpreting it to yet another person. While such a sign must be expressive of mind, it can also be part of the interpreter's environment: consider the US Constitution, a collection of signs that is part of America's ideal environment, the interpretation of which can significantly affect our social environment. Simply put, and underlined by understanding atonement as an interpretive process, interpretation according to Royce is creative of meaning within human life, rather than simply representative or reproductive of some external meaning system. In this way Royce, while certainly an idealist of some sort, also betrays the sort of progressive and pragmatic elements that Miller attributes exclusively to Mead.

This is not to say that there are not crucial differences between Royce and Mead. The difference between them is not that between social conformism and individual creativity, but rather between models of individual creativity and transformation of social processes. For Royce, individual creativity is paradigmatically expressed as the healing of a fractured community, and so as the response to the disruption of community. For Mead, as we will see in the next chapter, individual creativity is paradigmatically expressed as the disruption of community, in response to a perceived waywardness and narrowing of communal life. Because in Royce our primary moral socialization is negative, leading to the chaotic dialectic of individualism and collectivism, and because community membership is the way out of this, community is somewhat put on a pedestal; only an evil act like treason can seriously threaten it. Royce is to be commended for articulating a social form that is not merely conventional, but his sharp distinction between society and community leads him to distribute conventionalism and personal satisfaction between them exclusively. The result is that Royce seems to have no sense that community life may become conventional, that participation in the interpretive process that drives community, despite its fundamental novelty-producing character, may become rigid and determinate for the sake of comfort or security. Stated otherwise, Royce considers the possibility that finite communities may fail to realize the Beloved Community because of treason, but not the possibility that finite communities may turn their back on the Beloved Community as their ideal and choose to defend the present shape of their communities. In this sense, there is a residual conservatism in Royce's position. Niebuhr joins Mead in confronting the possibilities that Royce does not: the narrowing and rigidifying of previously open communal life and the necessity for individual creativity to disrupt rather than heal such a narrow and rigid life, or better, to transform in an ultimately healing way by disrupting it.[100] Ultimately I aim to show that Niebuhr's use of Royce is embedded within a larger framework indebted to Mead. In order to do this, I must first provide an account of individual and community in Mead's thought.

---

100. Regarding the recognition of disruption, Tunstall levies a Levinasian critique at Royce, complaining that Royce's temporalism remains too egological, reducing others to the same temporal horizon, rather than being open to the possibility that others live within a different experiential time that, in situations of encounter, will disrupt our own time. See Tunstall, *Yes, But Not Quite*, chapter 7. Disruption by a different temporality is precisely what Niebuhr offers, I will argue, as a form of individual creativity.

— 3 —

Democratization through Novelty
Individual and Community in George Herbert Mead's Social Psychology

LAST CHAPTER ILLUSTRATED THE crucial place of individual creativity in Josiah Royce's account of moral development. In situations of treason, when one's community threatens to rupture due to some act of betrayal, what is required to repair the community is some individual to interpret that betrayal, through an act of grieving imagination, as an opportunity to make the community stronger than it could have been without the betrayal. In order to succeed, this interpretive act needs to be accepted by the members of the community *and* the traitor, which acceptances are themselves individual acts of grieving imagination. This is the atoning process, carried out through the "Will to Interpret," which requires each term—the atoner, the traitor, and the other community members—to fulfill their irreducibly individual tasks, all the while (given Royce's account of the divine) inspired by God who is (somehow) both the ultimate Community of Interpretation and its Interpreter. On this account of Royce, Miller's contention that the difference between Royce and George Herbert Mead turns on that between conservative idealism and progressive pragmatism is off target. Royce is certainly an idealist, but his version of it is much more progressive than Miller allows: there is an objective moral order in Royce's thought, but it does not stand as something external to humans demanding mere conformity, but rather as the ideal of ideal environments realized in and through the individual human creativity that constitutes atonement. This chapter intends to demonstrate that the true difference between Royce and Mead turns on their models of individual creativity, and it will do so, again, through an interpretation of those works by Mead that Niebuhr references or quotes, *Mind, Self, and Society*, and *The Philosophy of the Present*. My argument is that Mead's model of individual creativity is more disruptive than reparative of communal life. For Royce, the individual creativity of atonement manifests as the reparation of a broken community; the problem is rupture, the solution is repair. For Mead, individual creativity, expressed through figures of social genius, manifests as the disruption of a community too narrowly focused on preserving a particular version of itself from change; the problem is conservatism, the solution is critique and challenge. Of course, as in Royce, the function of individual creativity in Mead is to develop communal life. The crucial difference is how they conceive the mode of that development.

Methodologically, their approaches are significantly different. Mead, though philosophically trained, including having Royce as a teacher, stood at the forefront of the developing fields of sociology and social psychology. While Royce's impact has been more philosophically diffuse, Mead's major contribution is thus far to sociological theory, e.g., symbolic interactionism,[1] interaction ritual theory,[2] and the pragmatic turn in recent German social theory.[3] In order to prepare the reader for the rather abrupt shift, I will briefly illustrate this methodological difference through two crucial, shared commitments. First, both thinkers insist that the individual self is socially constructed. When Royce identifies interpretation as the only cognitive mode of access that humans have to each other because we are minded beings who express ourselves through signs, one implication is that self-constitution depends on others. To participate in the interpretive process requires receiving others' interpretations of our own signs, which shape our subsequent interpretive activity. During self-interpretation, when our present self is interpreting our past self to our future self, those various selves are constituted by how others interpret them. Thus, the individual self is constituted in and through larger interpretive processes. Mead affirms that the self is constituted in and through larger processes that are interpretive, but he articulates these processes differently. He identifies his approach as *social behaviorism*, meaning not only that the self is socially constituted, but that such constitution works paradigmatically through observable interactive conduct rather than the reception of mindful expressiveness. Mead's social behaviorism works from the outside in, in two respects: first, it begins

---

1. Blumer, *Symbolic Interactionism*.
2. Collins, *Interaction Ritual Chains*.
3. Joas, *G. H. Mead* and *Pragmatism and Social Theory*.

with an analysis of observable conduct, and only from there derives "inner experience"; second, it begins with an analysis of "a given social whole of complex group activity," and from there derives individual conduct.[4] Meanwhile, Mead's social behaviorism is a bottom-up approach, concerned with the emergence of the mind and self from such social activity. Mead contests the notion of the "substantive soul endowed with the self of the individual at birth," insisting that "minds and selves are essentially social products, products or phenomena of the social side of human experience."[5] In this respect, Mead is more of a naturalist than Royce. For both, the individual self is rendered by its social interaction with others, but while Royce pursues this theme through a predominantly idealist inquiry, Mead pursues it with newer conceptual tools.

Second, both thinkers affirm the irreducibility of the self to its constitutive social relations. Royce's account of loyalty, ultimately expressed as atoning charity, demands the individual creativity of those involved in the atonement process in order to repair their broken community. Those participating in the atoning process must somehow stand outside of the brokenness of their community, and so outside of current social relations, in order to imagine a healed community, transformed for the better by the inclusion of the traitor. Mead's approach leaves little room for appeals to religious or Christian categories, but he agrees that the individual self is irreducible to its social relations and so able to reflectively and creatively respond to its social inheritance, thus reconstructing her community. However, while Royce's atoners have an ideal according to which to repair their own broken community—the Beloved Community—Mead's creative self is reconstructing her own community by taking up latent or neglected elements from its social inheritance in order to critically broaden and deepen its communal bonds. As I have suggested, the result of this difference is that individual creativity in Mead is more disruptive than reparative. In this regard, Miller may be right that the crucial difference between Royce and Mead turns on the former's acceptance of an objective moral order, even if his characterization of what that acceptance entails is misleading. For Royce, because the Beloved Community functions as an ideal, and given its panentheist character, the process of atonement realizes that ideal by ensuring that one's community fits into that ideal community. Such fitness is not mere conformity to some external standard, but it is unclear how truly novel post-atonement community actually can be. For Mead, individual creativity exerts a critical force on one's community, and so calls for transformation

---

4. Mead, *Mind, Self, and Society*, 7–8.
5. Ibid., 1.

precisely when there is not a perceived need for it within the community; here, individual creativity tends more to cause than to respond to social trauma. This is exacerbated by Mead's account of reality as constituted by emergence, the continual occurrence of novelty that cannot be predicted in advance. The point of this chapter is to show how Mead articulates this model of disruptive individual creativity and its ramifications for establishing social life and understanding reality itself.

Again, a straight comparison of Royce and Mead is inessential for the purposes of my argument.[6] Both thinkers receive relatively isolated attention because the point is to bring them into conversation through Niebuhr, rather than directly. Next chapter will offer a reconstruction of Niebuhr's account of faith and responsibility by interweaving it through its explicit and implicit engagements with Royce and Mead. There I intend to show that Niebuhr contextualizes Royce's work on loyalty within a broader theological framework of trust and responsibility that leans heavily on insights taken from Mead. This leads Niebuhr to engage Mead and neglect Royce at crucial points in his account. Part of my reconstruction will involve showing how Niebuhr could have used Mead in a more sophisticated way than he explicitly does. Ultimately, I will offer a more Mead-indebted rendering of Niebuhr's thought than is apparent on its surface, which includes but qualifies Royce's contribution. To this end, an independent exposition of Mead's account of human development is necessary.

Before diving into this exposition, a few comments on textual sources are in order. As mentioned above, the bulk of my analysis of Mead's thought engages his major work, *Mind, Self, and Society*. This needs to be justified given the scholarly consensus that focusing on this work is limited due to the fact that it is cobbled together from student notes on his lecture course in social psychology, as well as from Mead's own unpublished manuscripts.[7] First, since the point of examining Mead is a reconstruction of Niebuhr's theological ethics through his implicit and possible dual engagement with Royce and Mead, I focus on the works that Niebuhr had available to him. While my reconstruction will go beyond strict intellectual history, I do want to map out a position that Niebuhr could have taken, based on what I

---

6. Mead's responses to Royce are not generally illuminating for my project. Mead's first response to Royce comes prior to *Loyalty* and *Problem*, when Royce leaned heavily on the notion of imitation, an emphasis dropped in the latter work; see Mead, "Social Psychology as Counterpart to Physiological Psychology," 99–101. Mead's eventual response to Royce's latter thought is summary and dismissive; see Mead, "Philosophies of Royce, James, and Dewey," 378–83.

7. Mead, *Mind, Self, and Society*, vi. All of the secondary literature I cite in this chapter notes the insufficiency of this work.

understand to be the inner logic of the texts I discuss in this and the prior chapter. In other words, I am interested in articulating what could have been, rather than what we can do now with more reliable texts available. Second, I do not believe that my interpretation of *Mind, Self, and Society* violates the accounts of the social development of the self given in other essays by Mead, though I will not take pains to demonstrate this. It bears mentioning here that those commentators who do point out the insufficiency of *Mind, Self, and Society* nevertheless refer to it in their accounts of Mead's thought. The problem is not that the work is misrepresentative, but rather that it is under-representative of Mead's contribution to social thought. For those engaged in constructive projects that use Mead (such as Niebuhr and myself) rather than purely exegetical projects about Mead, there is plenty of food for thought within the covers of the work. Obviously, this is not to disparage the sort of work that attempts to adjudicate precisely Mead's influences and contributions. I am simply using Mead for the purpose of advancing a constructive position, as I am all of the thinkers discussed. The point is not to give an exhaustive account of Mead's thought, but rather to give an account of those aspects of it that are salient for my own argument.

My argument proceeds in four sections. The centerpiece is the second section, which delineates Mead's anthropology as understood through his accounts of the I/me distinction within the self and of individual creativity as social reconstruction. The first section prepares for this by delineating Mead's account of how mind emerges from the development of language from physical gesture. Here we will see a different account of response and interpretation than that offered by Royce. The third section argues that Mead's notion of democratic community is that of a community that is able to value and promote the disruptions of individual creativity. The final section interprets Mead's metaphysical vision of time as rooted in the I/me distinction, while also developing the temporal dimensions of the distinction itself.

RESPONSE AND INTERPRETATION: FROM GESTURE THROUGH LANGUAGE TO MIND

This section examines Mead's account of the emergence of the form of consciousness that must obtain if socially constituted but reflectively intelligent selves are to be understood.[8] While the next section discusses Mead at his most theoretically provocative, articulating an anthropology that strains

---

8. For a good, concise account of the material discussed in this section, see Silva, *G. H. Mead*, chapter 3. He mostly depends on Mead, *Mind, Self, and Society*.

the naturalist limits set by his Darwinian turn, in this section we will see Mead operating well within these limits. In particular, Mead is concerned to show how consciousness, commonly understood to be essentially personal and private, is nevertheless the deliverance of social interaction. Moreover, such interaction is primordially gestural in an embodied, physical manner, becoming linguistic and conscious through the increasing vocalization of gestures. Mead's aspiration is to demonstrate that phenomena usually understood to be ideal, such as meaning and consciousness, are in fact real features of the world naturalistically understood, if not materially so. The dynamics that lead to the emergence of mind fund the development of the self in its critical and creative interaction with others and larger social processes.

If human minds and selves are understood to be emergent products of social interaction, an account must be given of *whence* they emerge. Following psychologist Wilhelm Wundt,[9] Mead begins with the notion of *gesture*. Gestures are the "phases" of a larger social act or process "which bring about the adjustment of the response of the other form."[10] One's gestures evoke the *fitting responses* of others within a common social endeavor. Mead uses dogfights, boxing, fencing and child-care to illustrate what he calls 'conversations of gestures': one's act is a stimulus for the other to respond to it, which response is in turn a stimulus to which the first must respond back, and so on.[11] One attacks in a particular way, the other must respond with an act that successfully defends that attack, to which defense the first one must respond fittingly in order to successfully re-attack; the child cries, the parent responds by feeding, to which the child responds by calming down or crying even louder, to which the parent must respond by continuing to feed or trying another form of placation. The result is a continual mutual readjustment between the one and the other, so long as the common social endeavor lasts.

For Mead, this notion of gesture demonstrates that imitation is *not* the impulse or instinct that leads to the emergence of the human mind and self. Gestures "call out acts different from themselves," *not* acts that reproduce these gestures.[12] To posit an imitative impulse or instinct is to presume that "we have in our nature already all of these various activities," which are evoked from us by seeing others do them.[13] This presumption implies a

9. Recall that Royce also appealed to Wundt, though not the same material.
10. Mead, *Mind, Self, and Society*, 45.
11. Ibid., 42–44.
12. Ibid., 52–54.
13. Ibid., 58.

substantive and predetermined self that *reproduces mechanically* what others do, rather than an emergent and relational self that *responds fittingly* to what others do.[14] Of course, Mead does not deny that humans have the capacity to imitate, to take over the processes or mannerisms of others. His point is that the imitative capacity cannot account for how humans come to interact.[15] Rather, the notion of gesture initiates an account of how the processes of others come to be taken over by the self in social interaction, and it is this dynamic that accounts for imitation. Insofar as Royce's view of the self as portrayed in *The Philosophy of Loyalty* and *The Problem of Christianity* is not substantive but process-based, the consonance between his and Mead's anthropologies should be apparent.

If gestures evoke different rather than similar responsive actions, supporting a conversation in which the participants play different roles, the question arises of how humans come to take over the processes of others such that we are able to imitate others. For Mead, the answer lies in language, which emerges from gesture once gestures become vocalized. He explains that a vocal gesture functions as a "significant symbol" "when it has the same effect on the individual making it that it has on the individual to whom it is addressed or who explicitly responds to it."[16] When one gestures vocally, one "hears its own stimulus just as when this is used by other forms, so it tends to respond also to its own stimulus as it responds to the stimulus of other forms."[17] Thus, when a conversation of gestures that are significant symbols is successful, the one "takes the attitude of the second individual toward that gesture, and tends to respond to it implicitly in the same way that the second individual responds to it explicitly."[18] Simply put, symbolically mediated conversations require each participant to take on the role of the other. When I ask you a question, I expect you to answer it, for by hearing my own question, I implicitly take on your role as answerer, I *imaginatively anticipate* your response.[19] Similarly, when you answer my question, you expect a counter-response because you implicitly take on my role as questioner, imaginatively anticipating my counter-response, as you hear your own answer.

---

14. For a discussion of Mead's rejection of imitation as fundamentally explanatory in his early essays, see Joas, *G. H. Mead*, 99–101.

15. Mead, *Mind, Self, and Society*, 59.

16. Ibid., 46.

17. Ibid., 65.

18. Ibid., 47.

19. Silva (*G. H. Mead*, 32) points out the imaginative and anticipatory character of taking on another's role.

Two comments. First, by role Mead does not mean some determinate social position within a stratified set of other such positions, but rather the practical position of the other vis-à-vis the self. A role refers to a set of expectations and attitudes attributed to a practical position responsive to our own; note that in the quotes above, Mead uses "role" and "attitude" interchangeably.[20] Obviously, this is not to deny that determinate social positions are occupied as roles taken between selves, but to affirm this with Mead is to affirm that such positions are constituted by interactive expectations and attitudes. Second, while Mead does not explicitly assert it, the facet of expectation built into this stimulus-response model presumes a certain level of *trust* between the one and the other. There would be no taking on the role of the other if the one does not somewhat trust the other to fulfill that role. Granted, such trust may not be robustly moral, in the sense of recognizing the other whose role is taken on as responsible to and for the self's well-being, but that is not to say that it is amoral or merely pre-moral.[21] This significance of the theme of trust will become clear in next chapter's discussion of Niebuhr's account of faith. For now, it is important to note that this is the first stage in humans taking on the other, and so in becoming a self.

The importance of arguing that language emerges from gesture lies in understanding the function of language to derive from that of gesture. Language and the taking on of the role of the other it requires, make the mutual readjustment between one and the other, which is constitutive of any conversation of gestures and supportive of any common social endeavor, "much more adequate and effective."[22] For Mead, language is "just a part of a cooperative process," leading "to an adjustment to the response of the other so that the whole activity can go on."[23] Language has the social function of coordinating human individuals' physical responses to each other in order to keep our common social endeavor going.[24] This *social* understanding of language implies a *social* understanding of meaning: "meaning is given or stated in terms of response." Meaning arises within the field of social experi-

---

20. Cook, (*George Herbert Mead*, 79, 83) discusses the interchangeability of role and attitude; Joas (*G. H. Mead*, 118) notes that a role is a pattern of behavioral expectation.

21. On the moral significance of trust, even on a natural level, see the work of Annette Baier, particularly *Moral Prejudices*. For a comparison of Baier and Mead on the theme of trust, see Daniel, "Cultivating Trust."

22. Mead, *Mind, Self, and Society*, 46.

23. Ibid., 74.

24. Hence, Joas's insistence (*G. H. Mead*, 13–14) that the root of Mead's thought is "practical intersubjectivity," a concept that connotes communicative relations without reducing them to linguistic relations, thus keeping language and action joined.

ence constituted by a triadic relationship: (1) the gesture of one evokes (2) the response of the other and indicates (3) the "resultant" or completion of the social act of which that gesture is an early phase. The response separates the gesture from the result of the social act it indicates, but the response also indicates that result.[25] Using Mead's example, the mother hen clucks to her chick to indicate food or danger, and the chick responds by running to his mother hungrily or by fleeing to a place of safety, which response is an indication of that food or danger.[26] Meaning arises from this response: the mother hen's cluck does not mean food or danger in the sense of representing them; rather, it means her chick running toward food or fleeing from danger by stimulating these actions as responses. The idea is that, unless her chick responds appropriately, the meaning of her cluck is not conveyed. Meaning, like language, is not primarily a matter of mental representation or states of consciousness, but rather has the social function of keeping common social endeavors going, and so depends on the response of others.

This understanding of meaning is also *hermeneutic*. Mead explains that "the adjustive response of one organism to the gesture of another is the interpretation of that gesture by that organism—it is the meaning of that gesture." The chick's running toward food or fleeing from danger *interprets*, and so *means*, his mother's cluck. Consonant with the social nature of language and meaning, such interpretation "is not, basically, a process going on in a mind as such, or one necessarily involving a mind; it is an external, overt, physical, or physiological process going on in the actual field of social experience."[27] This explains how action can be understood to be interpretive: insofar as an action responds fittingly to a prior gesture by continuing or completing the social act indicated by that gesture, that action *is* an interpretation. While this binding of action and interpretation is a point of contact between Mead and Royce, the difference is stark. For Royce, interpretation is the distinct cognitive process by which minded beings expressively communicate; for Mead, interpretation is a social process by which organisms respond to other organisms. Of course, interpretation is a social process for Royce as well, for whom it is specifically human (as well as divine), but for Mead interpretation is generally organic. Mead does not deny that interpretation can take on a mental or cognitive aspect, but simply insists that such an aspect must emerge from its social, organic background.

---

25. Notice the triadic structure of meaning here. This will be significant next chapter because it suggests that Niebuhr may be engaging Mead rather than, or as well as, Royce when he formulates his triads of faith.

26. Mead, *Mind, Self, and Society*, 76–77, 79.

27. Ibid., 78–79.

The emergence of consciousness from organic responsiveness is rendered by the emergence of language. Mead asserts that humans are distinct from animals in our capacity to indicate which aspects of an object evoke our response to it, our power "to pick out one stimulus rather than another and so to hold on to the response that belongs to that stimulus, picking it out from others, and recombining it with others" in order "to build up another act."[28] Language renders this capacity to pick out stimuli and hold our responses to them in order to control our conduct through significant symbols, rather than vaguely react.[29] Mead explains that significant symbols "pick out particular characteristics of the situation so that the response to them can be present in the experience of the individual."[30] Once we have heard or read a set of symbols, the various responses they evoke "can organize themselves into a form of action."[31] If someone rounds the corner screaming, "There's a bear coming after me!," an organized set of responses is (hopefully) evoked in us: "bear" evokes the response "avoiding claws and teeth," and when combined with "coming" evokes the response "avoiding claws and teeth very soon," and when finally combined with "after me" evokes "avoiding claws and teeth very soon in the direction away from which this screaming person is fleeing." That screamed sentence *means*, is *interpreted* by, our running away with the screamer. Importantly, this is only possible if we can take on the other's role: because the screamer can take on our role as relaxed loiterers who would spring into action if we only knew a bear was coming, he can scream with the expectation that we will join him in fleeing; and because we can take on the role of the screamer, we can join him in fleeing with as much gusto as if we had seen the bear ourselves. Again, note that the scenario works out only if there is some implicit trust between the screamer and the loiterers (e.g., trust that the screamer is not crying wolf, trust that the loiterers are not calmly enacting a part in some big plan that involves a loose bear). Also, this *active-hermeneutic* understanding of meaning applies to objects. Mead asserts, "The meaning of a chair is sitting down in it, the meaning of the hammer is to drive a nail."[32] Sitting down in a chair *interprets*, and so *means*, that chair; driving a nail with a hammer *interprets*, and so *means*, that hammer.[33]

28. Ibid., 92, 94.

29. Ibid., 97. Mitchell Aboulafia points out, "Mind itself must be understood as a social phenomenon that depends on communicative interaction for its development," specifically *linguistic* interaction, in Aboulafia, *Cosmopolitan Self*, 11.

30. Mead, *Mind, Self, and Society*, 120.

31. Ibid., 123.

32. Ibid., 104.

33. Not only does social interaction with objects constitute their meaning, it also

To fully comprehend this notion of meaning, the step between the chick example and the bear example must be clarified. The scream can evoke fleeing because "there is a certain body of more or less standardized responses that remain unchanged," organized sets of responses, whose meaning is *universal*. Now, universality here is socially derived rather than abstractly conceived: meaning is universal in the sense that there can be an identical, habitual response to diverse, particular stimuli.[34] Whether in Chicago, Denver or Cuzco, whether in the morning, afternoon or at night, whether it is an elderly man, young women or child screaming about a brown, grizzly or spectacled bear, our response is still likely to be fleeing, such that the meaning of these various screams remains basically the same. Certain vocal gestures, evoked by diverse and particular stimuli, "crystallize" into significant symbols that in turn evoke specific responses: the significant symbol "chair" crystallized from the vocal gesture meant to evoke sitting down in chairs and can be uttered to evoke diverse, particular others to sit down in diverse, particular chairs. When Mead states that any "universe of discourse is simply a system of common or social meanings," he is asserting that meaning is universal in the sense that there is a set of significant symbols that evoke, in others and ourselves, habitual responses to various stimuli, which are used to keep common social endeavors running.[35] "Chair" is not universally meaningful because it represents some abstract object known to all, but rather because it evokes the identical, habitual response of sitting down in all those who use and hear it.

Once significant symbols are used, mind has emerged. Mead explains, "Mentality is that relationship of the organism to the situation mediated by sets of symbols," which emerges "when the organism is able to point out meanings to others and to himself."[36] In other words, mind is that organic response to the environment that emerges with the use of language. As one scholar points out, "the mind should be confused neither with the brain nor with some speculative notion of 'pure substance,'"[37] that is, the mind should not be reduced to matter, nor elevated to some ideal realm. According to Mead, mind has both *holistic* and *reflective* dimensions. First, "Mind

---

constitutes them *as* objects in the first place. On this, see Cook, *George Herbert Mead*, 76, 171–72, and Joas, *G. H. Mead*, chapter 7.

34. Mead, *Mind, Self, and Society*, 125–26. Aboulafia (*Cosmopolitan Self*, 44, 72–73) points out that universality for Mead is a matter of "the potential generalizability of a response to a specific symbol," and so regards "shared experience" rather than disengaged reflection.

35. Mead, *Mind, Self, and Society*, 89–90.

36. Ibid., 125, 132.

37. Silva, *G. H. Mead*, 41.

arises in the social process only when that process *as a whole* enters into, or is present in, the experience of any one of the given individuals involved in that process." To become minded the individual must somehow experience the common social endeavor in which she is participating: as we have seen, it is the use of the significant symbols of language that allow the individual to take on the roles of others, and so ultimately to take on the *entire* social endeavor. Second, once this appropriation has occurred, the individual "becomes aware of *his relations* to that process as a whole . . . he becomes aware of that process as *modified by the reactions and interactions of* the individuals—including *himself*—who are carrying it on."[38] To be minded, the individual must also be reflective: while the individual is part of a larger social process, once this process is taken on by the individual, she becomes aware of her own unique place within it and, ultimately, of the possibility of somehow standing outside of it. It is precisely this tension between the common social endeavor in which we participate and our unique individual relations within and to it that underlies Mead's understanding of the self.

Before moving on, I would like to anticipate my ultimate argument. Notice that Mead's account of primary socialization is cooperative rather than chaos-producing as in Royce. Even though Mead uses combat metaphors (boxing, fencing) to illustrate the conversation of gestures, the implication is that participating in such matches requires some measure of cooperative agreement if the endeavor is to continue. A boxer who begins spitting in the eyes of his opponent in order to gain an advantage is someone who has been insufficiently socialized into the boxing endeavor or someone who has come to reject the conclusions of that socialization and is beginning to express an alternative direction for the endeavor. Whether the spitting is an under-socialized act or one of individual creativity, they occur against the background of fundamental cooperation. That primary socialization for Mead is cooperative partially accounts for why he articulates a disruptive model of individual creativity: the attempted transformation of fundamental agreements must take a disruptive form. The emergence of mind contributes to this. Because a minded individual is able to reflect on her social constitution holistically, she is able to disrupt it on a more sophisticated level than if she were only able to respond to it bit by bit. Mead's I/me distinction enables him to account simultaneously for the cooperative character of primary socialization and the disruptive character of individual creativity.

---

38. Mead, *Mind, Self, and Society*, 134; emphasis mine.

THE SOCIAL SELF

Mead's I/me distinction, particularly the character of the "I," is perhaps the most provocative aspect of his work, but also one of the most problematic aspects.[39] One commentator discusses it so briefly and dismissively, that he all but declares that Mead's usage of it was a mistake and distraction from his larger project.[40] However, most others have taken the allusive character of Mead's discussion as a challenge, both exegetical—attempting to determine what Mead means precisely by the "I"—and constructive—supplementing Mead's account with insights from other fields or recalibrating the distinction, in order to be plausible in our own social context.[41] Given the concerns of my own argument, my challenge is to reconstruct the distinction theologically, as an account of our relations to human others and to God; this will occur next chapter in dialogue with Niebuhr. Still, since my aim is to reconstruct rather than violate Mead's distinction, it is essential to give a worthwhile account of the material to be reconstructed. In the course of this section I will take a side in a recent debate concerning Mead's account of the "I," and that stance turns on the model of individual creativity I discern in Mead. The "I" contributes to communal life by reconstructing it according to its own-most possibilities, but that contribution first manifests as disruption.

The self, according to Mead, is a social self, constituted in and through the common social endeavor in which it participates. This self, as distinguished from a body or mere organism, is *reflexive* in the sense that it can be an object to itself, and *socially* reflexive because it views itself as an object from the standpoint of its common social endeavor.[42] As noted above, the first stage of taking on the other occurs in the use of significant symbols in a conversation, when one takes on the role of the other because the symbol one uses has the same effect on oneself as on the other, such that one implicitly responds to oneself as one expects the other to. The second stage occurs when, beyond taking on the roles of particular others within the same social group, one somehow takes on the interrelated set of roles that constitute the social group as a whole, what Mead terms the *generalized*

---

39. Mead's project, like Royce's, was a response to the work of William James. In particular, Mead's usage of I/me was taken over from William James work in psychology. For discussion of the influence of James, as well as John Dewey, on Mead's account of the I/me distinction, see Markell, "The Potential and the Actual," 114–19. For a fuller account that discusses the many influences, see Joas, *G. H. Mead*, chapter 4.

40. Cook, *George Herbert Mead*, 54–55, 62–66.

41. These projects will be mentioned throughout this section.

42. Mead, *Mind, Self, and Society*, 136–37.

other.⁴³ The self emerges insofar as the human organism passes from taking on the particular roles of other participants in a common social endeavor, to taking on that common social endeavor in its entirety. This can be understood as a development of trust: the self passes from trusting particular others to fulfill their particular roles, to trusting a common social endeavor to sustain oneself and others in the fulfilling of these interrelated roles.

Mead illustrates this development from taking on particular others to taking on the generalized other, by way of the transition from playing to participating in a game. When children play "at being a mother, at being a teacher, at being a policeman," they are "taking different roles." This involves responding to certain stimuli such that they become organized into a particular whole: when children play at being, or take on the role of, a parent, they are responding to, interpreting, and finally enacting, stimuli they have received from their parents. When children participate in a game, they "must be ready to take the attitude of everyone else involved in that game" so they can respond fittingly to contingent events. Here the child must take on, respond to and organize, not simply the stimuli of a particular other, but the roles of all the others participating in the game.⁴⁴ In baseball, if a batter hits a ground-ball to third base, the first baseman must take on the role of the third baseman fielding and throwing the ball if he is going to catch it for an out, just as the third baseman must take on the role of the first baseman if he is going to execute an accurate throw. If there is already a runner on first base before the ground-ball, the first and third basemen must take on more roles—those of the other fielders involved, the runner—if they are going to execute their own roles in a successful double play. To participate in a game is to perform a particular role *in relation to* all the other roles such that victory is won through the successful execution of these interacting roles. To play at a particular role is to perform a particular role *in isolation from* many of the other roles related it. Thus, while children may *play at being* a parent well, they could not successfully *be* a parent because they do not have full access to their parents' interactions with others (e.g., siblings, extended family members, teachers, neighbors, etc.) that are crucial to being a successful parent. In other words, children do not have access to the entire social endeavor of parenthood, only to a few of its roles. Participating in a game like baseball ideally helps children participate in later social endeavors like parenthood because it provides participation in a social endeavor in which children have access to all of the roles involved.⁴⁵

43. Ibid., 138, 158.
44. Ibid., 150–51.
45. Cook (*George Herbert* Mead, 97) notes that Mead's account of the development

When Mead defines the generalized other as that "organized community or social group which gives to the individual his unity of self," the terms that are especially significant are *organized* and *unity*.[46] A self takes on a generalized other, not simply because she is a member of a particular social group, but more precisely because she participates in the common social endeavor which the roles and attitudes of that social group are *organized* to perform; to use a distinction from Royce, the generalized other is expressive of a community, rather than a society. The generalized other is neither a mere collection of roles and attitudes nor (and the significance of this will be seen next chapter when I discuss Niebuhr's misinterpretation of Mead) a singular abstracted figure, but rather a coherent *whole* of interrelated roles and attitudes, which is precisely how it provides *unity* to the self. By taking on the generalized other, the self takes on the particular others with which it interacts in a unified way that interrelates them, such that the self gains integrity rather than dissipating into a variety of isolated roles and attitudes. Once the self is unified, reflexivity becomes possible: by organizing the self into a unit of integrated roles and attitudes, the generalized other enables the self to perceive its particular unique place within the common social endeavor that constitutes the generalized other.[47] The *organization* and *unity* dimensions of the self obviously parallel the *holism* and *reflexivity* dimensions of the mind. Thus, despite the structure of *Mind, Self, and Society*, Mead understands the mind and self to develop together, not as separate stages.

Inasmuch as an individual is a member of various social groups and participates in their common social endeavors, she takes on a number of generalized others and so is composed of a number of selves. Mead recognizes this when he remarks that in "most highly developed, organized, and complicated human social communities," there are two kinds of "socially functional classes or subgroups of individuals" with their own common social endeavors, and thus their own generalized others. The first are concrete subgroups "such as political parties, clubs, corporations," in which members directly interact. The second are abstract subgroups "such as the class of

---

of taking on roles, from the particular to the general, depends on a distinction that Mead does not discuss, between rudimentary role-taking that does not require language and self-consciousness, and more sophisticated role-taking that depends on these capacities. I think Mead's use of the chick and hen example at least suggests this distinction. Taking on the role of particular others occurs on both levels, but taking on the role of the generalized other can only occur on the sophisticated level.

46. Mead, *Mind, Self, and Society*, 154.

47. Ibid., 201–2. Aboulafia (*Cosmopolitan Self*, 46) asserts that the generalized other is Mead's version of the philosophical notion of *sensus communis*.

debtors and the class of creditors," in which members interact indirectly. At the same time, these latter provide "unlimited possibilities for the widening and ramifying and enriching of the social relations" within and between communities, since, insofar as they are abstract, they are capable of "cutting across functional lines of demarcation which divide different human social communities from one another." In other words, abstract subgroups are able to unite individuals who belong to different, and perhaps opposing, concrete subgroups (e.g., political parties) *and* to different communities (e.g., nations). For Mead, the "most inclusive and extensive" of such abstract subgroups is "the one defined by the logical universe of discourse," the total human community that participates in "the general human social process of communication."[48] The sense of calling such an entity an abstract *sub*group is puzzling, but it does indicate Mead's methodological presumption that the self does ultimately develop within a single whole community, which organizes these subgroups such that the unified self remains singular.

Mead's account of the "I" and "me," insofar as the latter term is used in the singular, presumes that self-development occurs within a singular community, but it is important to note that the account does provide resources for understanding how self-development could occur within multiple communities, since I exploit these resources next chapter. The "me" is that aspect of the self that is an object to itself from the standpoint of the common social endeavor in which it participates. Mead defines the "me" as "the organized set of attitudes of others which one himself assumes," or as "a definite organization of the community there in our own attitudes."[49] Simply put, the "me" is the generalized other internalized: "that self which is able to maintain itself in the community, that is recognized in the community in so far as it recognizes the others . . . a conventional, habitual individual."[50] The "I" is that aspect of the self that *actively responds* to the "me," this internalized socially organized set of responses and attitudes. Crucially, such a response is *uncertain* as it occurs, in the sense that it is *not specifically evoked* by any of our internalized social attitudes. Mead explains, "There is a moral necessity but no mechanical necessity for the act" of the "I," for such an act is "never entirely calculable" and "always something different from what the situation itself calls for." The "I" represents the self's *novel* activity toward the future, and so provides the self its "sense of freedom, of initiative."[51]

48. Mead, *Mind, Self, and Society*, 157–58.
49. Ibid., 175, 178.
50. Ibid., 196–97.
51. Ibid., 175–78. Aboulafia (*Cosmopolitan Self*, 61) aligns the I/me distinction with a spontaneity/system distinction, while Joas (*G. H. Mead*, 118–19) insists that the "I," besides referring to a principle of spontaneity and creativity, must also refer to "the

The elusiveness of the novel activity of the "I" is paralleled by the character of our access to it. While the "me" is always already internalized in our experience, and so always accessible, the "I" is only grasped in retrospect: Mead describes the "I" as an "historical figure," always only present in our memory as the "me" of the next moment.[52] While the active, novel response of the "I" to the organized social attitude that constitutes the "me" changes that attitude, such a change can only be registered once that response has settled into the new "me."[53] Aboulafia explains, "[A]n 'I' transforms a 'me,' but we become aware of the work of the transforming 'I' only through the new (social) 'me' that arises" from the transformative work.[54] Such elusiveness leads Mead elsewhere to describe the "I" along the lines of "the transcendental self of Kant," a "presupposition" or "implication" of the self's experience of responding to itself.[55] Now, Mead is not positing some transcendental faculty; the description is intended to mark our indirect access to the "I." As commentators have noted, the I/me distinction is functional rather than ontological: the "I" and the "me" are phases of the self as process.[56] The "me" refers to that phase of the self that is always presently available because it is the presently structured generalized other internalized. The "I" refers to that phase of the self that can only become available as its novel responses become part of some new, presently unpredictable generalized other.

This account of the "I" and "me" entails that taking on the entire common social endeavor in which we participate is neither the final step, nor the aim, of our self-development. The irreducibility of the self to social processes works on two levels. First, the self's reflection of the social endeavor as manifest in the "me" is unique because the position of each self within

---

endowment of the human being with impulses." I read this less as a disagreement than a specification on Joas's part: for Joas, our spontaneous creativity is motivated by presently unsatisfied yet socially satisfiable impulses. I will discuss a different specification, but I do not think it competes with Joas's.

52. Mead, *Mind, Self, and Society*, 174.

53. Ibid., 196. At times, Mead's portrayal of the I/me distinction seems co-extensive with the active/passive distinction. Next chapter's theological reconstruction of the I/me distinction will complicate this.

54. Aboulafia, *Cosmopolitan Self*, 25.

55. Mead, "Mechanism of Social Consciousness," 141, and Mead, "Social Self," 142.

56. Aboulafia, *Cosmopolitan Self*, 14–15; Aboulafia, *Mediating Self*, 25–26; Silva, *G. H. Mead*, 6. J. David Lewis points out that "I" is used equivocally in *Mind, Self, and Society*: sometimes it is a response, and sometimes it is that within the self which makes a response, in Lewis, "A Social Behaviorist Interpretation of the Meadian 'I,'" 114. Hopefully my account has made clear what Aboulafia and Silva realize, that Mead's total position obligates him to hold the former, despite sloppy articulation.

a social endeavor is unique. Second, the self's holistic response to its social endeavor, as manifest in the "I," is unique because it refers to the self insofar as it has gained a critical reflective position on its social endeavor.[57] Thus, the self is social, not only in the sense that it arises from a prior social process, but also because the self should be understood as "essentially a social process" itself, occurring as the interaction between the "I" and the "me."[58] Insofar as thinking is understood as an internalized conversation of significant symbols, the conversation partners are the "I" and "me."[59] Moreover, the "values" of both the "I" and "me" are essential to the fully developed self. The "me," our taking on of the social endeavor in which we participate, provides recognition of our rights and dignity as members of a community. The "I" provides the "freedom from conventions, from given laws" that allows us to appeal to a future, enlarged community when the conventions and laws of the current community are found to be wanting.[60] Mead even tips the balance of values towards those of the "I," where the self finds "the most fascinating part of our experience" and "our most important values," aspects of the self which "we are continually seeking" to realize.[61] If we presume that the self's "me" is plural insofar as it participates in a variety of social endeavors (e.g., family life, university life, church life, etc.), it is precisely the "I" which is able to integrate these endeavors so that the self has some unity, for the "I" is that aspect of the self which is able to achieve critical purchase on the social conditioning that constitutes the "me." The aim of our self-development thus lies in the fullness of expression and realization of the "I," the seat of our free creativity.

It is important to note that, while the "I" and "me" may often be in tension, they are never in irreconcilable opposition; the "I" is never an antinomian rebel. In other words, the development of the "I" never occurs at the expense of the "me." Mead explains that it is coherent to think the self both as a reflection of a larger social process *and* as having a peculiar individuality: each self "is differently or uniquely related to that whole process, and occupies its own essentially unique focus of relations therein," and so reflects that process differently than all other selves participating in the process.[62] In this way, the "me" provides form or structure to the novel activity

---

57. Aboulafia, *Mediating Self*, 12; Aboulafia, "Introduction," 13.
58. Mead, *Mind, Self, and Society*, 178.
59. Ibid., 182.
60. Ibid., 199.
61. Ibid., 204.
62. Ibid., 201–2.

of the "I."⁶³ This begs the question of how the response of the "I" to the "me" can change the latter when the "I" is formed or structured by it. What is the extent to which the "I" is formed or structured by the "me"? In what does or can the novelty of the activity of the "I" consist, given that it is structured by the "me"? The answers lie in Mead's understanding of the *social genius*.

Before turning to a discussion of the social genius, I want to note the current debate regarding the character of the "I." In Mead's attempt to be naturalistically plausible, he abandoned a substantial notion of the self as composed of separate faculties with particular functions, and so adopted a processual, functional anthropology. As implied at the beginning of this section, this provocative move raises more questions than it settles. Commentators appear to agree with Mead that the self can be understood as socially constituted ("me") yet somehow able to stand outside of that constitution ("I"). The question is how to characterize this second horn. Critical theorist Axel Honneth suggests that the "I" be aligned with the unconscious, as psychoanalytically articulated. The interaction between the "I" and "me" within the self is understood as the "interplay between unconscious surge and conscious, linguistically mediated experience." On this reading, the "I" is the source of *potential* social transformations that the self attempts to actualize by reconstructing society to meet its unconscious demands.⁶⁴ Political theorist Patchen Markell contests this interpretation, insisting that, according to Mead's texts themselves, the "I" is better understood as an actual response that actively takes place, rather than a reservoir of potentialities: "present, ongoing, and as yet incomplete activity," rendering the "I" "a site of uncertainty and novelty."⁶⁵ I agree with Markell on this point; the potentialities for social transformation reside in the community's social inheritance, and the "I" is the actual activation of these. The reason for my agreement is Mead's account of the social genius.

Social geniuses are those historical personages who have "strikingly changed the communities to which they have responded" and of which they are members. Such persons create "a form of society or social order which is implied but not adequately expressed" in their current community, by expressing "the principles of the community more completely" than others. For Mead, the new social order is always an *enlargement* of the current community because geniuses take "the attitude of living with reference to

---

63. Ibid., 209.

64. Honneth, *Fragmented World of the Social*, 266–67.

65. Markell, "Potential and the Actual," 122. Silva (*G. H. Mead*, 106), while endorsing Markell on this point, has his own reasons for contesting Honneth's aligning of the "I" with the unconscious.

a larger society."⁶⁶ This enlargement is not territorial, but *attitudinal*: it involves the sense "of having an intimate relationship with an indefinite number of individuals," of taking a familial attitude toward those beyond the current community, "of breaking down the walls so that the individual is a brother of everyone," all of which Mead likens to the experience of conversion. The social genius leads her fellow members in their current community to experience an enlarged community through attachments to others beyond the current community. The new social order created by the social genius is thus a type of abstract subgroup within the current community that has no explicit institutional structure, more akin to the "logical universe of discourse" than the class of debtors and creditors. Moreover, just as the novel activity of the "I" is future-oriented, so the novel activity of the "I" of the social genius refers to a future community: social geniuses "become representative of the community as it might exist if it were fully developed along the lines that they had started."⁶⁷ The social genius does not create the new social order whole cloth, but rather initiates an enlarged community that is yet to come.⁶⁸ This suggests that the new community can only be fully realized by those who respond to the social genius. The social genius is thus a necessary but not sufficient condition for the realization of a new social order.⁶⁹

Now it becomes clear how the "I" can transform, while being formed by, the "me." It is obvious that the "I" of the social genius is formed or structured by the "me" that represents the organized social attitude of the current community, for the novelty of the social genius consists *not merely* in opposing the current community, but rather in explicitly expressing what is implicit or latent within the current community, and thus within the "me." The social genius's unique relation to the common social endeavor in which it is participating consists in its focus on those implicit, latent elements of the endeavor that will enlarge it if explicitly expressed. In other words, the novel activity of the "I" is the attitudinal enlargement of the "me," insofar as the "I" is formed and structured by the "me" whose latent elements the "I" expresses through its novel activity. Thus, if the aim of self-development is understood to be the full expression and realization of the "I" through its enlargement of the current community, then the development of the "I" occurs in direct proportion to the development of the "me." In this sense,

---

66. Mead, *Mind, Self, and Society*, 216–17.
67. Ibid., 217.
68. Cook, *George Herbert Mead*, 134–35; Aboulafia, *Cosmopolitan Self*, 70.
69. Aboulafia (*Cosmopolitan Self*, 120–21) likens the novelty of the "I" to a mutation introduced into an ecosystem, which may or may not survive.

individual self-development ultimately grounds and contributes to, rather than threatens, communal development, insofar as the latter is understood to consist in the enlargement and extension of attitudinal attachments.

It is important to note that the social genius is on a continuum with the ordinary individual, lest we think that Mead is simply making some Nietzschean point. Mead asserts that what the social genius accomplishes in and for her current community, carries "to the nth power" what any member of that community does by participating in it.[70] The social genius may initiate a dramatic communal change, but every self changes its community somewhat through the novel activity of its "I": "To the degree that we make the community in which we live different we all have what is essential to genius."[71] Thus, the account of general self-development derived from Mead's account of the social genius is illuminative of the ordinary individual. This should be stressed, since the social genius only initiates the enlargement of her community and ultimately relies on the response of others to realize it. In fact, the novel activity of ordinary individuals could be understood to consist in their accepting response to the novel activity of the social genius, in their recognition of the meaning and value of what the social genius discerns as the latent future of their common social endeavor. Just as one must have the freedom of the "I" to discern what is only implicit in the current community as meaningful and valuable, so one must have the same freedom to recognize meaning and value in the latent as well as overt elements of that community. To use a term that Mead does not in this context, the social genius's initiation and the ordinary individual's recognition of the new social order are novel *interpretations* of their current community: for both, the current community implicitly *means* the new social order. Following this, the "I" is well understood as the interpretation of the "me," whose activity is the responsive completion of what the "me" evokes from it. This characterization suggests again that individual expression and development ground and contribute to the future of the community in an ultimately preservative, rather than destructive, fashion.

Still, Mead recognizes that the social genius's current community will often respond to her as an opposing force rather than a loyal vanguard. This is because, in expressing the community's principles more completely, the social genius will likely diverge from the community's prejudices: e.g., Jesus discerned the recognition of all other humans as our neighbors as a latent

---

70. Mead, *Mind, Self, and Society*, 216. According to the note on the bottom of this page in Mead's text, the genius is distinguished by her originality and uniqueness. However, since Mead's position insists that each individual is somewhat unique, I'm reading the distinction as a matter of degrees.

71. Ibid., 218.

principle of his own Jewish community, which opposed that community's explicit prejudice towards Samaritans, and for which he was crucified.[72] Obviously, the social genius's ordinary followers will encounter the same opposition, as did Jesus' disciples and many early Christians. This is why I have characterized Mead's model of individual creativity as disruptive rather than reparative: the novelty of the "I" less repairs broken communal bonds, and more provokes its social companions to stretch its current bonds, to deepen and broaden them. Such provocation, I wager, must be experienced as a disruption of the current operations of the common social endeavor, even if (or especially since) the purpose of the provocation is to develop that social endeavor. My point is that communal development in the sense of enlarged and extended attachments does not follow automatically from the novel interpretative activity of the social genius and her followers; novelty only results in new routines by upsetting old routines. At the same time, it is important to recognize that Mead does not believe that novelty and critique follow automatically from achieving reflective distance on one's communal life, a theme which will be significant in the next chapter. While the "I" is always an active interpretation of the "me," it "may be a process which involves a degradation of the social state as well as one which involves higher integration."[73] Since the "I" is the seat of unpredictable responses, there can be no guarantee, no *mechanical* necessity, that it will not narrow or isolate itself and its community, instead of enlarge them. Thus, the relation between "I" and "me" is *not* that between progressiveness and conservatism, but simply that between an individual self and a given situation.[74] Still, my main point holds. It is in the community's interest to ensure that it promotes the development of its members' "I's," because it is only the through the novelty of individual selves that communal life will thrive rather than stagnate and die.

So, the individual self is constituted in and through communal life, particularly through participation in shared endeavors. At the same time, communal life becomes reconstructed through the novel activity of its individual members. Importantly, such novelty is not disconnected from socialization: the social genius and her followers provoke social reconstruction by invoking latent and neglected elements within the social inheritance passed on in socialization. Mead is suggesting something rather paradoxical. Communities are likely to under-socialize their members precisely because they cannot help over-socializing them: communities are likely to be

---

72. Ibid., 217–18.
73. Ibid., 218.
74. Ibid., 280.

unable to form their members as mere mechanical cogs in a social process invulnerable to change, because they will, willy-nilly, pass on elements that can be exploited for communal transformation. This is especially the case for communities with rich inheritances, such as religious communities.[75] One historical example would be the form of Christianity articulated by slaves, which concentrated on freedom and liberation, despite the form of Christianity they were given by their slave-masters, which concentrated on obedience and submission.[76] It is within such a gap that the "I" works, disrupting present communal life for the sake of a future communal life that is broader and deeper. Despite the fact that the "I" can reflectively and critically respond to the "me," the "I" remains formed and structured by its communal socialization. In this regard, the character of the community conditions the manner and degree of the individual self's response to it. Mead's wager is that a communal life can be articulated that promotes individual creativity, a form of community that can bear disruption for the sake of future progress. To that wager we now turn.

UNIVERSAL SOCIETY: DEMOCRACY AS DIFFERENTIATION AND PARTICIPATION

Mead scholar Silva notes that, despite the priority expressed in the title *Mind, Self, and Society*, the explanatory order of Mead's characterization of the self is, "Society first, and then mind and the self."[77] By turning to Mead's account of society now, I would seem to be beguiled by the order of his title. However, the account I am turning to is his *normative* account of society, his articulation of democratic community. The individual self, characterized by the dialogical combination of the "me" and "I," is both a social participant and a novel actor. When Aboulafia notes that, for Mead, participating in a democratic community "entails a capacity for both universalism and pluralism, in particular, for locating the common and appreciating the different,"[78] he is attesting to an analogy between democratic community and the character of the human self. If the self is simultaneously bound in social relations and able to respond to them creatively, then a community committed to

---

75. This condition of richness of inheritance leaves open the possibility that there are in fact social bodies that can turn their participants into mere mechanical cogs, if the purpose of such social bodies is so narrow and restricted that they have no social inheritance. This is the possibility of bureaucratic society, as opposed to community.

76. See Mathews, *Religion in the Old South*.

77. Joas, *G. H. Mead*, 13.

78. Aboulafia, *Cosmopolitan Self*, 2.

the development of selves must learn to support both aspects of the self. According to Mead, such a community is democratic. Though Niebuhr does not take on Mead's account of democracy, it is worth attending to because it is an account of the sort of community that promotes individual creativity, and any theological reconstruction of individual creativity would need to be completed in some account of theological community, or church, that would promote it. So, the following is material that deserves to be reconstructed.[79]

Mead describes the ideal of the human community as "functional differentiation and social participation in the full degree," presently exemplified in the "ideal of democracy." Rather than the elimination of difference, democracy implies that "the individual can be as highly developed as lies within the possibilities of his own inheritance, and still can enter into the attitudes of the other whom he affects."[80] The social ideal of humanity demands that we individualize ourselves in a particular manner while continuing to remain members of our community. This ideal dovetails with the nature of the self, understood as the interaction between the "I" and "me," suggesting that the social "ought" derives from the social self's "is." This is important to note lest there be confusion over the term ideal. As will be shown below, Mead does not mean by "ideal" some substantial, fixed goal to be attained: there is no final form for either individuals or communities. Instead, by ideal here is meant "proper method," the continuation of a social process by which differentiation and participation, or individualization and communal attachment, increase in direct proportion.[81] The nature of the self as itself a social process grounds the social process that constitutes the social ideal.

The implication of this grounding is that functional differentiation somehow aligns with the novel activity of the "I." This may be counterintuitive insofar as functional differentiation suggests the distribution of individuals into fixed roles and tasks, rather than the development of individual peculiarities. Mead's notion of genuine superiority shows how such distribution and development are not necessarily mutually exclusive. Mead notes that, due to the social nature of the self, the realization of the "I" requires recognition by others if its free creativity is to have value for it.[82] This was alluded to above vis-à-vis the social genius requiring the positive response of followers if her vision of the future of the community is to be realized.

79. For discussions of Mead's earlier work on democracy and community, as well as his social participation and activism, see Cook, *George Herbert* Mead, chapters 7 and Joas, *G. H. Mead*, chapters 2–3.
80. Mead, *Mind, Self, and Society*, 326.
81. See Mead, "Philanthropy from the Point of View of Ethics," 404.
82. Mead, *Mind, Self, and Society*, 204.

Here though, Mead draws another lesson: the "I" "realizes itself in some sense through its superiority to others," for beyond the recognition of our rights and dignity as community members, "we want to recognize ourselves in our differences from other persons." Such superiority is not necessarily expressive of "the egoistic or self-centered person," or "the disagreeable type of assertive character" that gains self-recognition through others' inferiorities or misfortunes. This form of self-assertion in manifest in patriotisms, nationalisms and sectarianisms that require the exclusion of others as inferior in order to feel valuable. On the other hand, *genuine* superiority "rests on the performance of definite functions . . . it is a superiority which [one] makes use of." Such superiority loses any egoistic elements because it involves the excellent exercise of our peculiar, effective capacities in service to the community's social endeavor, capacities that others simply do not have or cannot exercise as well. For Mead, this entails the possibility that nationalism can take on a "functional expression," such that its superiority would consist in its unique contribution to the social endeavor of a community of nations, and so be consistent with, and even require, the recognition of other nations' unique superiorities.[83]

It is crucial to appreciate here that *definite function* in this account refers not to a fixed social role but to particular effective capacities. When Mead mentions good surgeons and lawyers to illustrate superiorities, the point is not to identity specific jobs that can be filled be anyone, but to indicate that individuals have peculiar capacities the exercise of which, in order to be recognized and realized, must be expressed as functions within a common social endeavor.[84] The superiorities of surgeons and lawyers, if genuine, are thus complementary. By mapping the exercise of peculiar capacities onto the novel activity of the "I," and then insisting that this exercise is best realized when socially functionally expressed, Mead is claiming that the realization of the "I" requires that its activity be functionally expressive of some "me." This is simply another way of saying that the novel activity of the "I" settles into a subsequent "me," and must do so in order to be recognized; any novel activity that fails to so settle, necessarily fails to be socially functionally expressive. In this sense, the alignment of functional differentiation with the novel activity of the "I" accounts for the social genius as well. The novel activity of the social genius may be socially functionally expressive for a community that is yet to come and only implicit in the current community, and so remotely rather than immediately functional, but its realization still requires that it ultimately become functional. Insofar as the social

83. Ibid., 204–9.
84. Ibid., 208.

genius's followers respond positively to her novel activity and begin building the community it explicitly expresses, they render it functional.

If the ideal of the human community is fullness of both functional differentiation and social participation, then participation within a particular community's social endeavor should not hinder but support the development and exercise of individual capacities. On Mead's account, the development from primitive to civilized human society consists in the "progressive social liberation of the individual self" from given social types within a fixed social activity, such that "individuality is constituted rather by the individual's departure from, or modified realization of, any given social type than by his conformity, and tends to be something much more distinctive and singular and peculiar."[85] In this way, the ideal form of social participation is one that permits *and values* individual development and expression, so that common social endeavors become ideal when they demand peculiar, novel responses, not conformity to given tasks. For Mead, this ideal form is expressed in *democratic* communities. He defines democracy as the combination of "the attitude of universal religion" with "widening political development," and as the combination of "the sense of brotherhood and identity of different individuals in the same group" with "the dominance of the individual or group over other groups." His point is that democracy combines social participation in the fullest sense with functional differentiation.[86] At the same time, Mead's account of the social genius should make it clear that participation and differentiation are not simply compatible, but also mutually supportive. The broadening of our communal attachments to be progressively inclusive of all human beings is initiated by the novel activity of the social genius and completed by the novel following of her disciples. This broadening and deepening of social participation is rendered by the creative exercise of individual capacities, which can be released by functional differentiation.

Two comments, which look ahead. First, in earlier sections I suggested that Mead has a fiduciary understanding of social relations: the self's development from taking on the isolated roles of particular others to taking on the integrated roles of a common social endeavor in their entirety presumes a sense of trust between self and others that must develop as well. If this interpretation is plausible, than the social participation aspect of the democratic ideal can be understood as an ideal of trust; a democratic community would be a community where members trust each other like (ideal) family members. Second, if, as I have been suggesting in this section, the

---

85. Ibid., 221–12.
86. Ibid., 286–87.

functional differentiation aspect aligns with individual creativity, than to insist that social participation and functional differentiation can be mutually supportive is to insist that trust and creativity can be as well. This binding of trust and creativity will be significant in the next chapter. For Niebuhr, it is precisely the self's trust in God that releases her creativity to transform her communities, and so transform her capacities for trusting human others as well. On my reconstruction of Niebuhr through Mead, such theocentric trust and radical creativity are attributable to the "I," understood as a direct but not immediate relation to God.

As noted, Mead includes the religious attitude of "universal neighborliness" as an aspect of democracy, but he also identifies another attitude with a universalizing tendency: the economic.[87] The idea here is that the process of exchanging our surpluses with each other can lead to the production of such surpluses for the purposes of exchange, and then to the transportation and other media necessary to execute the exchange. The economic attitude and the process it initiates thus "may lead to a social organization which goes beyond the actual structure in which individuals find themselves involved." The argument is not that the economic attitude and process create a social organization that is geographically bound yet encompassing of all the economic actors. Rather, this social organization is one of communication, uniting those who live in geographically separate communities because economic activity requires its participants to take on the role of the others with whom they exchange, for whom they produce, etc., and ultimately to take on the entire economic endeavor. The economic and religious attitudes share the tendency "to bring about the larger community even when the persons have not any ideals for its realization." Economic actors do not exchange and produce for the sake of some more universal community, even if they ultimately contribute to it. Likewise, Mead asserts that the person who comes to the "immediate assistance of another in trouble," as the Samaritan did in the famous parable, does not need to possess the ideal of "a form of society in which the interest of one is the interest of all" in order to so assist.[88] This raises the question of why the religious, and not the economic, attitude is integrated into the characterization of democracy itself, and answering it will deepen my account of Mead's notion of democracy.

There are two reasons, the first explicitly expressed by Mead, the second implicitly. First, Mead notes that the religious attitude "takes you into the immediate inner attitude of the other individual; you are identifying

---

87. On the importance of attitudes in Mead, and how this marks his position off from Kantian positions like that of Habermas, see Aboulafia, *The Cosmopolitan Self*, chapter 3.

88. Mead, *Mind, Self, and Society*, 289–97.

yourself with him in so far as you are assisting him, helping him, saving his soul, aiding him in this world or the world to come—your attitude is that of salvation of the individual." Identification with the other person is "far more profound" in this case than in that of the economic attitude, where identification is superficial because focused on the exchange of produced goods rather than on the person itself of the other participant.[89] In other words, while the economic attitude only broadens social participation, the religious attitude deepens it as well. This is significant because deep social participation more likely grounds relations of trust between individuals. Second, while Mead insists that the religious attitude does not necessarily entail the realization of an ideal of some future, enlarged community, his characterization of certain aspects of Christianity betray an emphasis on the kingdom of God, shared by Royce through his articulation of the Beloved Community.[90] Recall that Mead uses Jesus as an example of a social genius who discerned a universal human community to be implicit in his Jewish heritage and explicated it in, e.g., the parable of the Good Samaritan. Further, Mead insists, "Christian saints represented the sort of society to which every individual could conceivably belong," apparently following in Jesus' footsteps.[91] The point to be recalled and stressed here is that, in both cases, this discernment and representation of a future, enlarged human community is due to the novel activity of the "I" of both Jesus and his followers. Recalling that such novel activity is aligned with functional differentiation, it becomes clear that insofar as the religious attitude takes this particular Christian form and so is expressed in such novel activity, it not only broadens and deepens social participation, but it also supports functional differentiation. In this way, the specifically Christian religious attitude can contribute to both essential aspects of democracy.

Mead cannot discern this dual contribution because his explication of functional differentiation within democracy through the terms *dominance* and *wider political development* emphasizes the exercise of social power rather than individual novel activity. According to Mead, the specifically *democratic* form of dominance results from the development of the expression of political superiority. This development, discerned in the history of empires, is the movement from political superiority expressed in the destruction of other communities to that expressed in their maintenance. The first attitude is militaristic and self-assertive, while the second

89. Ibid., 286–87.

90. See ibid., 271. See Joas, *G. H. Mead*, 8 on "Mead's intellectual evolution, which consisted, in part, in the secularization of Christian themes." On Mead's developing relationship to his own Christianity, see Cook, *George Herbert Mead*, 6–8, 100–101, 115.

91. Mead, *Mind, Self, and Society*, 290.

is administrative and implicitly recognizant of the value of other groups. Administrative empires exercise "power to direct a social undertaking in which there is a larger co-operative activity." Of course, such empires are not sufficiently democratic, for an even larger (that is, broader and deeper) international community would be "organized in terms of function rather than in force." Mead has in mind the League of Nations, "where every community recognizes every other community in the very process of asserting itself."[92] While administrative empires and democratic communities share a concern to participate in a larger cooperative activity with other communities, they differ in their recognition of other communities entailed by this cooperation. The administrative empire recognizes the value of other communities as functional within a social endeavor it forces on them. The democratic community recognizes that value as functional within a social endeavor in which it is participating as an equal member alongside other communities. Thus, democratic communities are committed to a common social endeavor that is larger than each, the outcome of combining functional differentiation based on peculiar superiorities with the ideal of a universal human community. The point to be stressed here is that democratic communities have access to such an ideal through the individual novel activity of social geniuses and their followers.

Is it possible for a particular democratic community to be understood as a universal community, if that community's democratic nature is due to its recognition of its own and others' peculiar functions within the universal human community? One way to approach this is to recall that Mead's notion of universality refers to something socially derived rather than abstract or transcendent. Following this, the question about the universality of a particular community becomes less how it relates to other communities, and more how functional differentiation and social participation operate jointly within it: are they mutually supportive, increasing in direct proportion, or does individualization lead to withdrawal from or antagonism toward communal attachments? Mead locates ethical problems in the failure of integrating these two aspects of democracy. When the distinctiveness of the individual self, whose seat is in its "I" aspect, is not "carried over" into its "me" aspect, when the self's novel activity does not find some recognition or appreciation in its community, then the genuine sense of superiority based on function is replaced by the egoistic sense, which can only further fracture the individual from the community.[93] Simply put, a community that strives to be universal must be responsive and open to the novel activity of

---

92. Ibid., 284–87.
93. Ibid., 320–24.

its members.⁹⁴ At the same, it is precisely this responsiveness and openness which permits the appearance of a social genius and her followers to open the community itself, to make it more broadly and deeply responsive to other communities, and ultimately to the universal human community. In this way, a particular democratic community that is internally universal will tend toward participation in the universal human community.

The operation of this sort of particular universality of specific communities is explicated in other writings. Mead defines the democratic ideal as wider access to the reconstruction of values accomplished by removing those restrictions brought upon by, e.g., "economic, feudal, and cultural class distinctions." In other words, the democratic community's dedication to the progressive liberation of individuals from socially determined types or roles, and to the recognition of the novel activity of those individuals, entails that the resolution of conflicts between different individual values proceed, not by choosing some to the exclusion of others, but by taking account of all values in question. Such a resolution involves reconstructing—that is, creatively transforming—these values so that they are recognized by all, which itself involves the appeal to a community wider than that of the current one in which the value conflict arose, and so wider than the subcommunities dedicated to the conflicting values.⁹⁵ While Mead refers to the importance of reason in this regard, it is essential to realize that he is not referring to some transcendental realm completely exterior to the particular community, but rather to the enlarging of that community from the inside out. Reason abstracts the values from those situations in which they conflict *in order to* reconstruct them. In this way, reason does the preparatory work for the novel activity of individual community members.⁹⁶ The model of universality expressed here is not rational consensus abstracting from our particular communal attachments, but rather community reconstruction so that those attachments are broadened and deepened.⁹⁷

Thus, the democratic community is that social form that conditions its individual members to engage in novel activity through the exercise of their peculiar capacities, in order that the community be broadened and deepened. Importantly, this community reconstruction is not accomplished

---

94. On the connection in Mead between symbolic universalism, discussed in the first section, and political universalism, in conversation with Arendt and Habermas, see Aboulafia, *The Cosmopolitan Self*, chapters 2–3.

95. For a rich discussion of Mead's ethical method in this respect, see Joas, *G. H. Mead*, chapter 6.

96. Mead, "Philanthropy," 404–6.

97. In this respect Mead departs from Kant, and appreciating this has ramifications for judging Habermas's use of Mead.

by formulating and then conforming to some utopia, but rather by removing restrictions for the novel activity of individual members on a case-by-case basis, which Mead calls 'charity.'[98] Such removal of restrictions, again, suggests that the democratic community is marked by a prevailing climate of trust. Since democratic reconstruction has no determinate end, rather responding to specific obstructions as they occur and so always having the potential to lead the community in a novel direction, it must involve trust in the novel activity of individual members. Insofar as democratic reconstruction takes place through the novel activity of individual community members, such potentiality for novelty is unsurprising.

I have argued that Mead's model of individual creativity is that of disruption rather than reparation, yet my account of his notion of democratic community, which is meant to promote such creativity, has not discussed disruption. On the one hand, this is the point. The ideal of a social form committed to the promotion and recognition of individual creativity is the ideal of a communal life that experiences such creativity as enriching rather than disruptive. In reality, given the fact that most actual human communities have a threshold for novelty beyond which they begin to demand conformity, individual creativity is likely to manifest as a disruption. The resulting concern is whether initially disruptive novelty will come to be accepted as an expression of communal life, or rejected as a violation of it. In short, the crucial issue is time, specifically whether or not the community can take the time necessary to discern the value of novelty. Thus, the final section rounds off my account of Mead by examining his philosophy of time. On the other hand, from a theological perspective that understands individual creativity to be tied to a relation to God who finally transcends all finite communities, communities that under conditions of sin tend to narrow and restrict themselves and so reject such creativity, the sufficiency of the democratic ideal is questionable. From this perspective, the point is not to imagine a community that ceases to experience creative disruption as disruption, but rather one that learns to cope with such disruption, with the recognition that in time, novelty often settles into tradition. Articulating this will come in the final chapter, but its way is paved by next chapter's theological reconstruction of Mead through Niebuhr.

TIME: RECONSTRUCTION AND SOCIALITY

Implicit in Mead's account of the social self and the democratic community is the appreciation that humans are temporal beings. That human life

---

98. Mead, "Philanthropy," 405–6.

consists of responding to and interpreting each other and our current community in an anticipatory way, reaching towards a different future, demonstrates that human life takes time. That democratic community requires the resolution of presently conflicting values by imagining a future in which these values are reconstructed so as to cohere, also suggests the intrinsic temporality of human life. Moreover, since human action is creative, human life can be understood to *make* time in a particular sense. This emerges in *The Philosophy of the Present*, one of Mead's later works, and another that Niebuhr quotes, which shows how human creativity is inextricably tied to human temporality, which reveals a temporal notion of sociality. Hans Joas contends, "Mead's philosophy of time is certainly the least intelligible and least well elucidated part of his work."[99] I believe this is the case because, at least in *The Philosophy of the Present*, Mead waxes metaphysical. Still, examining it will enable me to pull together my account of Mead's anthropology, articulate how disruption works within a larger progressive process, and anticipate the crucial role that temporality plays for Niebuhr and for my ultimate argument.[100]

Mead's account of the connections between human temporality, creativity and sociality is grounded in a claim about reality. He posits, "reality exists [*only*] in a present," that dimension of time characterized by "its becoming and its disappearing." The world we live in "is a world of events."[101] Events here are not properly understood as parts or sections of the passage of time, but rather as unique occurrences, what Mead calls *emergents*.[102] Reality itself is composed of the continual emergence of novelty in the passing present: "novelty is part and parcel of a world of events and not merely the result of the activity of an ego taken with its own creative powers."[103] This implies, as Mead notes, that the past and future are somehow unreal. The sort of reality that Mead denies to the past and future is the sort he denies to the mind and self (and to the present): substantial. Just as the mind and self are understood to emerge with the development of the human organism rather than to be fixed entities given in the beginning, so the past and future are understood to exist relative to the present event rather than to be absolute history and destiny. The past "is expressed in irrevocability," but is in fact revocable: the past can only be regarded "from the standpoint of the

---

99. Joas, *G. H. Mead*, 167.

100. For fuller discussions of Mead's philosophy of time that reference earlier works as well as the influence of Alfred North Whitehead, see Cook, *George Herbert* Mead, chapter 9 and Joas, *G. H. Mead*, chapter 8.

101. Mead, *The Philosophy of the Present*, 35; intervention mine.

102. Ibid., 62

103. Aboulafia, *The Cosmopolitan Self*, 121.

emergent." Since the emergent, by definition, is always different from whence it emerged, the past always changes "with the passing generations."[104] The past is irrevocable in the sense of "the necessity with which what has just happened conditions what is emerging in the future," but revocable in the sense that, since such conditioning is never total determination, it can lead to a variety of possible futures, and so is vulnerable to being reconstructed in light of the emergent event.[105] In other words, it is necessary *that* the past conditions the future, but *how* that conditioning occurs changes with each present event. Meanwhile, if the past cannot be substantially fixed, neither can the future. To say that human action is oriented to the future is *not* to say that there is some fixed ideal formulated in some absolute past to which the present must be made to conform, but rather that human action is concerned with resolving those problems arising in our situation perceived through our present account of the past.[106] Such resolutions will change as the past changes with each present event.

The present is not only the locus of reality, but also of creativity, or to use Mead's term from this text, *reconstruction*. Humans make time in the sense that we continually remake the past and future in light of the present event. The temporal structure past-present-future is rendered by the occurrence of unique events: each present establishes a past and future that are its boundaries, its conditioning factors (past) and possible resultants (future).[107] Because humans are minded beings, we can extend these boundaries, the past by memory and history and the future by anticipation and forecast.[108] In this way, history is neither an absolute, fixed past, nor the human inquiry into such a past, but rather the active reconstruction of what has occurred as leading up to what is occurring now, in order to resolve the problems we are encountering and expect to encounter.[109] Mead describes the mind in this context as a *field*, the "temporal extension of the environment" of the human organism accomplished by characterizing the past and future with aspects of the present.[110] As with the novel activity of the "I," so our creation of past and future is not *ex nihilo*: while the new, future community is created from the implications of the current community (and now

---

104. Mead, *The Philosophy of the Present*, 36.
105. Ibid., 46–47.
106. Ibid., 108
107. Ibid., 53, 62
108. Ibid., 53
109. Ibid., 56–59. A similar conception of history animates Niebuhr's *The Meaning of Revelation*, a work that I do not discuss because of its focus on theological method.
110. Mead, *The Philosophy of the Present*, 54

it is clear that such a creation would also render a new communal history), the past and future are created from the implications of the present. Hence, Mead's term for contingent creativity, *re-construction*, a term that presumes existing elements.

If the present is the locus of reconstruction, the re-creation of past and future in light of the present emergent event, then it must also be the locus of the "I," that aspect of the self responsible for the novel activity that changes its environment (its current community) and so the other aspect of the self, the "me." It is important to highlight this connection, which Mead does not, though his notion of *sociality* enables us to discern the connection. For Mead, the present has an essentially social nature because it consists in the process of readjustment that is concomitant with emergence: the advent of the new within the old requires that both mutually adjust to each other if they are to endure. Sociality then refers to "the stage betwixt and between the old system and the new . . . between the ordered universe before the emergent has arisen and [. . .] after it has come to terms with the newcomer."[111] The present is social in the sense that it is the passage of the past into the future through the emergent event, "the situation in which the novel event is in both the old order and the new which its advent heralds." In this way, sociality also refers to "the capacity of being several things at once."[112] The present is social because it includes both its conditioning factors and its possible resultants, and this capacity grounds the continual reconstruction of past and future in the present. Mead uses the example of a revolution to illustrate the point. When a particular community's order is replaced by a new one, "(t)he old system is found in each member and . . . becomes the structure upon which the new order is established."[113] As with social revolution, so with individual creativity: it is not the advent of the new *ex nihilo*, but the reconstruction of existing, though probably ignored or neglected, elements. The old order is retained, but must adjust to the advent of the emergent event, whose own adjustment renders a new order. Such an understanding of sociality entails that a community is truly social only insofar as it changes over time, hopefully by broadening and deepening attachments.

This notion of sociality provides another perspective on the sociality of the self. Mead explains that the self "is what it is only so far as it can pass from its own system into those of others, and can thus, in passing, occupy

---

111. Ibid., 73
112. Ibid., 75
113. Ibid., 77

both its own system and that into which it is passing."[114] Humans are selves because they are minded beings, which means reflective beings: to take on the roles of particular others and a generalized other and see oneself from those perspectives *is* to be at once our own self and the selves of others. That the self has the capacity of being several things at once is implied in the notion that the self is composed of an "I" and "me." The "me" refers to the self insofar as it occupies the systems of others, in the sense of internalizing their roles and perspectives. The "I" then refers to the self insofar as it passes from one system, one role or perspective, to another, and so occupies both.[115] This is best seen if we recall the social genius and her followers. Here, the "I" is responsible for the transformation of the current community into a new, enlarged community, and insofar as the "me" refers to the community internalized in the self, the "I" is responsible for the transformation of the current "me" into a new, enlarged "me." In other words, the "I" is the self in passage from the old "me" to a new "me" through its active response to and interpretation of that old "me." This novel activity of the "I" must be located in the present, which is itself the passage of the old into the new through the emergent event. Again, such activity is only accessible in retrospect, and so only discernible as past action, but it must be understood to have occurred, or better *emerged*, in what was a passing present.

Questions must remain about the coherence of a basically metaphysical account of temporality as continual novelty with a behaviorist account of the human self in its relations to other selves and to its communal environment. Still, this account of time does enable us to understand how Mead's account of individual creativity can be both disruptive and progressive. If individual creativity emerges as a disruption of presently constituted communal life, as time passes and others respond to the disruption, continuities between the novel activity and the social inheritance of the community may begin to emerge, such that the individual creativity becomes less novel and so less disruptive, eventually becoming part of the common wisdom, which will be disrupted by future individual creativity in turn. Communal development works by a sort of cyclical progressiveness, progressive in the sense that reconstruction rather than preservation is understood to be the life of communities, and cyclical in the sense that there is never an appeal to a time in which there will not be the need for such reconstruction. If this vision is grounded metaphysically in Mead's philosophy of time, the engine that makes it move is the activity of individual selves, creatively responding

---

114. Ibid., 102–3

115. Aboulafia (*Mediating Self*, 16) contends that Mead's notion of freedom is the capacity to take multiple perspectives.

to their social inheritances and each other. We will see next chapter that Niebuhr articulates reconstruction as permanent revolution: the self experiences conversion to God precisely by ceaselessly reconstructing its social inheritances, religious and otherwise, in light of her irreducibly individual relation to God. Moreover, this relation to God turns on the interpretation of time as either death-bound or life-promoting. This theological reconstruction of Mead will be put to work in the final chapter.

CONCLUSION

I trust that the last two chapters have shown that both Royce and Mead have a progressive model of communal development, but depend on different models of individual creativity to advance it. Both thinkers hold that communities develop, that is, improve their present constitution, whether reintegrating at a stronger level, or broadening and deepening communal bonds. In fact, Royce would probably understand atoning creativity to result in a better community precisely to the extent that it broadens and deepens communal attachments, since the ideal of the Beloved Community includes universality. But whereas for Royce communal development is a response to some act of treason that has broken the once-whole community, for Mead such development is apparently part of the fabric of reality itself, an exemplification of the novelty by and through which time proceeds, which is to say that such development appears to be the rule rather than the exception. For Royce, individual creativity is exercised as atonement, repairing the community so that it is stronger and thereby turning the act of treason into a condition of communal development. For Mead, individual creativity is exercised as the disruption of communal life, pushing the community to follow the trajectory of its best, if neglected, elements. In this case, social reconstruction is not a response to broken community, but rather to a narrowed, prejudiced community, complacent in its routines and foreshortened possibilities. The difference between Royce's and Mead's models of individual creativity thus turns on the communal problems that each was attempting to solve. In Mead's vision of the interrelation between individual and community, an appeal to unity and reparation would be dangerous, potentially foreclosing the possibilities of social reconstruction. The social genius's creativity is provoked by the present state of a unified community that, in order to broadened and deepened, must have its present unity disrupted.

The next chapter will show that Niebuhr is in agreement with Mead on this issue: the problem with finite human communities is that, under conditions of sin, their unity is achieved at the expense of spurning God, whose created community, the entire universe of existing beings, should be our field of care and concern. Niebuhr articulates treason, not as an individual act that breaks some community, but rather as the form that communal life takes when it attempts to secure its existence in the face of God who it interprets as fundamentally hostile and evil. In other words, treason connotes a perverted form of faith. The solution to this predicament is a true form of faith, what Niebuhr calls radical faith, accessed through the risen Christ, which is true because it interprets God rightly as fundamentally friendly and good, despite the evils that occur. This radical form of faith grounds and promotes a form of individual creativity, what I will call radical creativity, that must be disruptive because its activity is the emergence of radical faith into perverted faith. Meanwhile, radical creativity is still a contingent form of creativity: not only is it responsive to particular expressions of perverted faith, as Royce would affirm regarding atonement's response to treason, but it also uses available elements from within the treasonous form of life, as Mead would affirm regarding reconstruction. Radical creativity is transformative. This will all be articulated through a theological reconstruction of the I/me distinction, which intends to demonstrate how Niebuhr uses Royce within a larger conceptual context that is heavily indebted to Mead.

— 4 —

Radical Faith and Responsible Transformation

Locating Individual Creativity in H. Richard Niebuhr's Theological Ethics

Having argued in the last two chapters that Josiah Royce and George Herbert Mead both appreciate the social constitution of the human self while recognizing the significance of individual creativity within and for human social life—namely that it is through the capacity of individual selves to think and act beyond the presently explicit traditions and norms of their social inheritances that communities are expanded and deepened—I now turn to the theological ethics of H. Richard Niebuhr, who I will refer to as Niebuhr. As noted, the point of discussing Royce and Mead was less to compare them directly, than to provide the requisite material for discerning how Niebuhr integrates insights of both thinkers into his own position. Specifically, I will argue that Niebuhr uses Royce's notion of loyalty within a larger conceptual structure of *faith*, a structure that Niebuhr articulates in a way that is indebted to Mead's vision of the self in her relations to various communities. Moreover, I aim to show that it is precisely the use of Royce within a wider framework indebted to Mead that accounts for why Niebuhr utilizes Royce's philosophy of loyalty but not his Christian interpretation of it as love. To argue that Niebuhr ultimately favors Mead over Royce as his determining influence is seemingly belied by Niebuhr's own critique of Mead, so I will suggest that this critique is due to a misreading of Mead, which is especially odd because what Niebuhr proposes as his own alternative to Mead is in fact deeply indebted to Mead. Finally, I will, in the spirit of Mead, reconstruct Mead's own account of the I/me distinction within the self through Niebuhr's account of responsibility, so as to illuminate these particular ideas from both thinkers. This will enable me to locate individual creativity within Niebuhr's theological ethics, and show that it aligns more with Mead's disruptive model than Royce's reparative model. My argument turns on discerning a crucial place for the individual self's direct relation to God—that is, a relation irreducible to its social mediation—within Niebuhr's account of faith. Recognizing and valuing such a relation requires a model of moral formation that, understanding the necessity of socialization, nevertheless must culminate in the development of individual capacities.

The portrait of Niebuhr that emerges should be simultaneously unfamiliar and familiar. On the one hand, I am reading him against a background that has yet to be discussed extensively in Niebuhr scholarship, the American intellectual background. The point is not to argue that the American intellectual influence is more significant than the European intellectual influence,[1] though I agree with Douglas Ottati that there is a need for more scholarship on Niebuhr's American theological background,[2] but simply to articulate constructive possibilities rendered by an American interpretation. Moreover, my reading of Niebuhr emphasizes individuality, which is seemingly in tension with what Niebuhr is usually understood to take from Mead, as well as with how Niebuhr places himself theologically. Mead's enduring insight is reputed to be his understanding of the self as socially constituted, supported by his importance for the field of sociology; when commentators point out examples of Niebuhr's thinking beyond his intellectual generation, it is usually to such insights. Meanwhile, Niebuhr's robust appreciation of divine sovereignty and the theology of Karl Barth, and consequent wariness toward the theological trajectory of Friedrich Schleiermacher and Albrecht Ritschl as intrinsically tempted toward a sort of anthropocentric solipsism whereby God becomes answerable to human values and value-relations, would seem to argue against the notion that there is a strong sense of human individuality in Niebuhr's thought.[3] Of course, Niebuhr's Barthianism is complex: from the beginning it was bal-

---

1. On Niebuhr's German theological background, see Frei, "Niebuhr's Theological Background," 9–64.

2. Ottati, "Meaning and Method," 327. William Clebsch notes that Niebuhr "summarized a great legacy of American religious thought," but gives no extended analysis of the influence of earlier figures on him, in Clebsch, *American Religious Thought*, 187. See Byrnes, "H. Richard Niebuhr's Reconstruction," which includes a scant discussion of Royce and Mead.

3. Niebuhr, *The Meaning of Revelation*, 12–18.

anced by an appreciation of Ernst Troeltsch,[4] and later in life he expressed worries that the theological momentum initiated by the criticism of liberal theology by figures like Barth was an overcorrection, resulting in an account of faith as right belief, the deification of Scripture and church, and the reduction of theology to Christology, ultimately endorsing "a greater kinship with all theologians of Christian experience."[5] Still, neither Troeltsch nor the "theologians of Christian experience" that Niebuhr lists are best understood as theorists of human *individuality*. My hope is that my particular reading of Niebuhr, integrating insights from both Royce and Mead, will add another dimension of Niebuhr's thought to appreciate.

On the other hand, the portrait of Niebuhr I offer should be familiar to those acquainted with his most infamous work, *Christ and Culture*.[6] In this work, Niebuhr attempts two things: first, he aims to offer a typologically exhaustive account of how Christian theologians have related their understandings of Jesus Christ to their surrounding cultural context; second, commentators agree that he endorses a particular type, "Christ transforming culture." I take it that my articulation of individual creativity in Niebuhr exemplifies this type. That is, I will argue that radical creativity, my term for the theological account of individual creativity I derive by mutually reconstructing Niebuhr and Mead, operates by transforming presently available cultural dynamics, processes, and products in order to loyally serve the divine cause. Because *Christ and Culture* is a typological account of the history of Christian ethics rather than a constructive account of the human self in faith relations, and because he does not engage Royce or Mead in it, it is not illuminative for my argument. At the same time, avoiding it does serve an intervention into current reception of Niebuhr. On my reading of recent theological ethics, it has become axiomatic to criticize Niebuhr's *Christ and Culture* typology for being rigid and misleading, failing to give an adequate account of either Christ or culture, and so necessarily reducing rich theological thinkers and movements as exemplifications of preordained positions.[7] I am not interested in defending *Christ and Culture*, though I do think its problems are overstated.[8] Still, Niebuhr's other works have been read, currently are read, and will continue to be read, through the critical

---

4. Ibid., xxxiv. Niebuhr wrote his dissertation on Troetsch. For discussion, see Fowler, *To See the Kingdom*, 17–34.

5. Niebuhr, "Reformation: Continuing Imperative," 142–43.

6. Niebuhr, *Christ and Culture*.

7. Paradigmatically, see the essays in Stassen et al., *Authentic Transformation*, especially Yoder, "How H. Richard Niebuhr Reasoned."

8. For a recent defense of the work, see Hunsinger, *The Eucharist and Ecumenism*, chapter 7.

response to *Christ and Culture*, given the historical significance of the work and the supposed havoc it has created in American Christian ethics. I hope to show, if only by implication, that an adequate understanding of everything Niebuhr intended to articulate with the idea of "Christ transforming culture" requires attention to his entire body of work. This chapter focuses on two established classics, *Radical Monotheism and Western Culture* and *The Responsible Self*, as well as the recently available but still neglected work, *Faith on Earth*. The next chapter will discuss other recently available works.

Methodologically, I read all of Niebuhr's works that I discuss as offering a unified account of the Christian moral life. In *Radical Monotheism* and *Faith on Earth*, Niebuhr argues that a radical form of faith available through Jesus Christ transforms the social forms of faith we participate in, and I argue that it is Niebuhr's discussion of responsibility in *The Responsible Self* that accounts for how such transformation occurs. While I will note differences between the works, I am not concerned to show how Niebuhr's thought developed. Also, this is a thematic interpretive intervention; I am interested in what Niebuhr has to contribute to an understanding of the relationship between individual and community in and through his theological ethics. As a result, I am not interested in whether Niebuhr's thought is christologically concrete enough, orthodox enough, or actually and sufficiently abandoning of the theologically liberal trends that he explicitly rejects. In this respect, my approach to Niebuhr's thought is confessional rather than defensive, and thus methodologically aligned with Niebuhr.[9] Finally, as stated previously, my reading of Niebuhr with and through Royce and Mead is more conceptual than intellectual-historical. Whether or not Niebuhr ever expressed worries about Royce's reinterpretation of his own philosophy of loyalty in *The Problem of Christianity* matters less than the plausibility of my interpretation of Niebuhr's account of faith as entailing those worries. Similarly, the reasons for Niebuhr's misreading of Mead matters less than the plausibility of my interpretation of Niebuhr's account of responsibility as deeply indebted to Mead. Moreover, since I intend to contribute to theological ethics constructively, not only exegetically, the point of my reconstruction of Mead's I/me distinction through Niebuhr's accounts of faith and responsibility is to show how Niebuhr could have used Mead, in order to advance my own argument that moral formation should culminate in the development of individual creativity, even and especially for religious communities. In this respect, my approach to Niebuhr's thought through

---

9. See Niebuhr, *The Meaning of Revelation*, for the distinction between confession and self-defense as methods of thought and inquiry.

Royce and Mead follows the contours of Mead's account of creativity as reconstruction.

My argument in this chapter proceeds in four major sections. The first section exposits Niebuhr's typology of faith in *Radical Monotheism* in order to show how his use of Royce's notion of loyalty is contextualized within a larger structure, that of faith, in which transformation plays an essential role. This contextualization is suggestive in terms of accounting for why Niebuhr engages Royce on loyalty, but not on love and community. The second section deepens Niebuhr's account of faith through an interpretation of his neglected work *Faith on Earth* as indebted to Mead while it develops a more specifically Christian account of the transformation of faith. The constructive significance of this section underscores an exegetical implication: there can be no full understanding of Niebuhr's account of faith and responsibility without engaging *Faith on Earth*. On my reading, this work forms a crucial bridge between *Radical Monotheism* and *The Responsible Self*, and I believe that convincing my readers to take it more seriously is an important collateral success of my argument. The third section includes an interpretation of *The Responsible Self* as also indebted to Mead, as well as the reconstruction of Mead's I/me distinction through Niebuhr's theological-ethical vision of human life before God. This is where I articulate Niebuhr's account of the self as occupying both an irreducibly individual relation to God and a socially mediated relation to God. This clears the ground for the final section, where I conclude my theological reconstruction of Mead's I/me distinction, showing how it grounds a distinction between kinds of creativity. Here I introduce the notion of *radical creativity* as that form of individual creativity that is grounded in and promoted by radical faith, our irreducibly individual relation to God. Such creativity is more disruptive than reparative, and so closer to Mead's model than Royce's, because the point of it is to open up communities that are turned in on themselves to the radical activity of God, which works through surrounding finite agencies. A fuller, more concrete portrait of such radical creativity and recommendations for how to promote it, are the tasks of the next chapter.

NIEBUHR'S THREEFOLD TYPOLOGY OF FAITH

According to Niebuhr, "Our human dilemma is this: we live as selves by faith but our faith is perverted and we with it."[10] This prognosis contains two claims that require examination: first, the human self is constituted by faith; second, this constitution is warped, and so warps us. Once these claims

---

10. Niebuhr, *Faith on Earth*, 83.

are clarified, it will be possible to locate moral formation and individual creativity in Niebuhr's thought. This section begins such clarification by examining how Niebuhr uses Royce's notion of loyalty within his own account of faith in *Radical Monotheism*. According to this account, faith constitutes the self as a double relation to some reality that confers value and provides a life-plan. Meanwhile, Niebuhr distinguishes different types of faith, two of which (pluralistic and social) are mal-formative of the self and in which we necessarily participate, and the last of which (radical) reforms the self by transforming the perverted forms of faith into expressions of true faith. Faith and a contingent form of creativity are implicitly aligned, and by the end of the chapter I hope to have shown how individual creativity theologically construed is grounded in and promoted by radical faith.

Niebuhr describes faith as "the attitude and action of confidence in, and fidelity to, certain realities as the sources of value and objects of loyalty." The binaries in this description indicate faith's double movement or relation. Faith has a passive aspect: *trust* in centers of value that confer worth on the self. Faith also has an active aspect: *loyalty* to causes that shape and unify the self's practical moral life. Faith constitutes the self because through faith the self gains worth and, in Royce's terms, a life-plan. Though faith is comprised of this double movement or relation, it is not oriented to two separate realities: what we trust provides the cause to which we are loyal.[11] The influence of Royce is explicit here, but it is important to see how the contextualization of loyalty in the larger structure of faith changes its function in the moral life. Recall that in *Philosophy of Loyalty*, loyalty to a cause provides an end for our moral autonomy. In line with Royce's voluntarism, we must choose which cause to give our autonomous loyalty. By tying loyalty to trust in faith, Niebuhr is claiming that loyalty relies, not on a cause of our own choosing, but rather on a reality that values us first (or stated biblically, elects us). Loyalty now becomes a *response* to the reality we trust, a reality that, for Niebuhr, ultimately demands our service to *its* cause. This changes the function of loyalty in the moral life.

The account in *The Problem of Christianity*, where loyalty to a cause is interpreted as love for the community, is closer to Niebuhr's position. Here, Royce appeals to divine intervention and grace in the form of the risen, ascended Christ who is identical with the spirit of the Community in order to account for the love that first pervades the Beloved Community and only then provokes our love for it. Our love for the Beloved Community is understood as a response to Christ's constitutive love for it. Significantly, Niebuhr does not reference this discussion in any of his accounts of faith.

---

11. Niebuhr, *Radical Monotheism*, 16–22.

This could simply be due to the fact that Niebuhr's theological virtue of choice is faith rather than love,[12] and loyalty is part of the conceptual complex that includes faith and trust.[13] At the same time, Niebuhr theological position of radical monotheism might have led him to be dissatisfied with the account in *The Problem of Christianity*. Royce's identification of the risen Christ with the spirit of the Beloved Community without clearly delineating the place of God the Father would have raised Niebuhr's suspicions, given his view that ecclesia-centrism and Christo-centrism are the most frequent and inextricably linked perversions of Christian faith in God.[14] In order to understand these suspicions and the reasons why Niebuhr uses Royce's concept of loyalty but not his Christian interpretation of it, it is essential to examine Niebuhr's account of the three types of faith in *Radical Monotheism* and of the structure of human faith in *Faith on Earth*.

For Niebuhr, faith is not restricted to religion, but is expressed "in all our other social decisions, actions and institutions."[15] Faith is a human phenomenon, pervading "every area of human existence."[16] Niebuhr repeatedly insists that science and philosophical positions that pit science against morality and religion are both inquiries that express trust in and loyalty to some center of value. This is important, for when Niebuhr distinguishes the three forms of faith and formulates them as "theisms," he is not (necessarily) referring to faith in gods that are to be understood religiously or theistically. Following Luther, Niebuhr conceives of gods as the practical, moral necessities of human life: "To be a self is to have a god."[17] Such gods are those of human faith, the centers of value and the causes that constitute the self. Thus, each type of faith can be understood to instantiate a particular moral formation of the human self.

The first type of faith Niebuhr calls henotheism or social faith. Here, the self finds its center of value and cause in a closed society or finite community. Such faith is not necessarily empiricistically, materialistically or

12. Despite the Protestant insistence that faith is a relation rather than a virtue, a gift rather than a habit, Niebuhr understands the theological virtues as given relations that provoke active responses. See Niebuhr, "Reflections on Faith, Hope, and Love," 151–56. This material will be discussed in the next chapter.

13. Niebuhr, *Faith on Earth*, 47–48.

14. Niebuhr, *Radical Monotheism*, 58–60; Niebuhr, *The Meaning of Revelation*, 78–79.

15. Niebuhr, *Radical Monotheism*, 11.

16. Niebuhr, *Faith on Earth*, 1.

17. Niebuhr, *The Meaning of Revelation*, 40–42. Luther asserts, "A 'god' is the term for that to which we are to look for all good and in which we are to find refuge in all need . . . Anything on which your heart relies and depends, I say, that is really your God." See Luther, "Large Catechism," 386.

anthropocentrically reductive, for one's society may admit of what Royce might call ideal members, such as the dead, the unborn or supernatural entities, as well as animals and other natural phenomena. Accordingly, social faith can take a specifically religious form, as it does in Christianity when the church becomes the center of value and cause. The distinguishing quality of social faith is its derivation of the self's worth from its "position in the enduring life of the community," and its identification of its cause with that community's "continuation, power, and glory." Social faith is trust in and loyalty to one's finite community. For Niebuhr, the most pervasive modern form of social faith is nationalism, which he was particularly attuned to after the Second World War, though he notes smaller (classism) and larger (civilization-ism, humanism, nature-ism, life-ism) forms as well.[18] The second type of faith is polytheism or pluralistic faith. While there is no absolute chronology between them, Niebuhr notes that pluralistic faith tends to follow social faith. Because of internal strife or conflict with other communities (or both), one's finite community is bound to break apart or dissipate into a larger society. The result is a restless search for recognition and worthiness: because the self no longer has a community to value it, it is forced to seek centers of value, haunted by "the feeling that it is justified in living only insofar as it can prove its worth." Causes that previously required "unified fidelity" become mere "interests that from moment to moment attract vague potencies resident in the mind and body." The self becomes "a bundle of functions," and any society can only be understood as "an assemblage of associations devoted to many partial interests."[19] Once one's finite society ceases to serve as center of value and provide a cause, the self becomes its own empty center, its cause the acceptance of value from any source. Pluralistic faith is trust in and loyalty to whatever interests attract us at the moment.

Radical monotheism is the third type of faith. While the first two are perennial, analyzable human phenomena, radical monotheism is known "more as hope than as datum, more perhaps as a possibility than as an actuality." Radical monotheism is the ideal of human faith, and when historically actualized "has modified at certain emergent periods our natural social faith and polytheism."[20] In other words, radical monotheism does not stand alongside the other types of faith, and so cannot override or abrogate them, but is somehow expressed through them, just as Royce's universal loyalty is served through particular loyalties, and his Beloved Community

---

18. Niebuhr, *Radical Monotheism*, 25–27, 35–37.
19. Ibid., 28–30.
20. Ibid., 31.

is realized in particular human communities. Though Royce is clear that universal loyalty is the norm of particular loyalties, Niebuhr is clearer about the relation of radical monotheism to henotheism and polytheism: radical monotheism *transforms* or *converts* them. Of course, Royce understands universal loyalty to transform particular loyalties: that universal loyalty is the moral standard for particular loyalties suggests the transformation of the latter by the former in specific cases. However, unlike particular loyalties in Royce, social faith and pluralistic faith are inherently mal-formative of the self. While loyalty is a problematic *solution* for Royce, social faith and pluralistic faith are *solely* problems for Niebuhr. At the same time, the relation of radical monotheism to henotheism and polytheism is not the same as that of loyalty to social training. As we will see, social faith and pluralistic faith are inherently mal-formative of the self because they are *perversions* of faith. Social training is also mal-formative, not because it perverts loyalty, but because it is incomplete formation: though it renders the moral self-consciousness necessary for loyalty, it leaves the self in oppositional relationships to others. Henotheism and polytheism can be understood as forms of treason, but whereas Royce understood treason to consist in individual acts for which communal acts atone, for Niebuhr treason manifests as forms of human life, treasonous formations of the self that can only be redeemed by radical monotheism. In other words, treason here manifests as the shape of communal life itself, rather than a rupture of such life. Thus, the form of creativity that radical monotheism promotes must be disruptive rather than reparative of such communal life.

Radical monotheism finds its center of value in the "One beyond all the many, whence all the many derive their being, and by participation in which they exist," in "the principle of being which is also the principle of value." Radical monotheism means that trust and loyalty are placed in God, who is beyond all being because the creator of all beings, and beyond all value because the lover of all beings. For Niebuhr, the radicality of such faith consists precisely in its identification of the principle of being with the principle of value, or theologically stated, the identification of the creator with the redeemer. As trust, "radical monotheism depends absolutely and assuredly for the worth of the self on the same principle by which it has being; and since that principle is the same by which all things exist it accepts the value of whatever is." The suggestion is that, insofar as the self recognizes that its value is bound to its being, and that its being is bound to that of all beings, the self is led to value all beings and affirm that "whatever is, is good." To trust in God is to be assured of the value of all beings because God values them. As loyalty, radical monotheism "is directed toward the principle and the realm of being as the cause for the sake of which it lives."[21] The principle of being and the realm of being are not truly distinguishable causes, for the realm of being *is* God's cause. To be loyal to God is to be loyal to God's cause, the realm of being.

Loyalty to the realm of being as God's cause is universal loyalty qua radical monotheism. Niebuhr explicitly contests Royce's definition of universal loyalty as loyalty to loyalty, asserting that universal loyalty is "loyalty to all existents as bound together by a loyalty that is not only resident in them but transcends them." In other words, what unifies the realm of being is not the loyalty of existents to each other, but rather "the loyalty that comes from beyond them, that originates and maintains them in their particularity and their unity."[22] Insofar as Niebuhr implies that loyalty to loyalty unifies loyal humans *only* through their loyalty to each other, he is reading Royce incompletely: loyalty to loyalty unifies loyal humans *also* through the shared cause to which they are loyal, in this case the "Eternal." Still, Niebuhr is fair to suggest that loyalty to loyalty orients us only toward beings that can be loyal, rather than beings *qua* being. However, the more significant difference signaled here is Niebuhr's contention that universal loyalty is grounded on divine loyalty: radical monotheism demands loyalty to the realm of being *because* God is loyal to the realm of being. Radical human faith is thus a *response* to divine faith. I argue that it is precisely here, where Niebuhr departs from Royce, that he begins utilizing insights from Mead. In order to validate this claim, I must turn to Niebuhr's still-neglected *Faith on Earth*.

FAITH AS A HUMAN PHENOMENON

Since *Faith on Earth* consists of material that Niebuhr wanted to be published with *Radical Monotheism*,[23] it would seem that Niebuhr himself thought that a full understanding of his account of faith required both texts. I believe the work is still neglected,[24] though there are exceptions.[25] Perhaps

---

21. Ibid., 32–33.
22. Ibid., 34.
23. See Fowler, *To See the Kingdom*, 203–4.
24. Shriver, *H. Richard Niebuhr* for the Abingdon Pillars of Theology series includes no discussion of *Faith on Earth*. A series meant to introduce a new generation of students to major theologians ought to command up-to-date accounts. Also, I find it odd that Beach-Verhey, *Robust Liberalism* does not engage *Faith on Earth*, since Beach-Verhey's covenantal approach to Christian political engagement could only benefit from the work's discussion of faith as responsive relations of trust and loyalty.
25. Fowler (*To See the Kingdom*, chapter 5) devotes an entire chapter to its manuscript form, analyzing its contribution to our understanding of Niebuhr's understanding

its publication in 1989 means that generations of theologians and ethicists articulated a compelling, fruitful account of Niebuhr's contribution that continues to pay dividends, without engaging this particular work. I do not wish to make the exaggerated claim that the key to understanding all of Niebuhr's thought resides in *Faith on Earth*, but it does deserve more attention. More immediately, it is significant for my particular project. I argue that in this work we see more acutely Niebuhr's use of Royce within a larger conceptual structure indebted to Mead, which suggests more reasons why Niebuhr uses Royce on loyalty, but not on community. In particular, I will show that Niebuhr's disarticulation of cause and community enables him to articulate the self's direct or irreducibly individual relation to certain realities that are also socially mediated. Theologically, this means that individual selves have direct relations to God along with their socially mediated relations, and for Niebuhr, both of these relations must be mediated through the risen Christ if our constitutive faith is to be true rather than perverted, and if our faith is be transformed and so transformative. This will serve as preparation for the next sections, where I show that this direct relation to God characterizes radical faith, which then grounds and promotes a radical form of individual creativity.

In *Faith on Earth*, Niebuhr describes faith as a relationship between selves. Noting that the Latin for *belief*, *trust* and *loyalty* are variations of the same root, he asserts that these "are not three different meanings of the word faith but three parts of one interpersonal action in which *fides* (believing) is the phenomenal element which is largely based on the fundamental interaction of *fiducia* (trust) and *fidelitas* (loyalty or fidelity)."[26] In Mead's terms, faith is a social act, a common social endeavor with different roles. However, faith so understood is not a distinguishable social act among others, such as child-care, but one that underlies all human social endeavors. Niebuhr devotes a chapter to showing how the social act of faith undergirds our knowing. According to him, belief constitutes "by far the major part of our intellectual furniture and of the basis of our daily actions" *only* insofar as it is mediated through our trust in others. Beliefs that we take for granted because of upbringing, that we take on authority and that we are persuaded of, are obvious examples of "holding for true on the ground of

---

of the task of theology. Stassen, "A New Vision," uses it as a jumping off point to provide an account of "Christ transforming culture" that is more explicitly christological and ecclesiological. Since my concern is neither Niebuhr's theological method nor defending him against a particular sort of criticism, their treatments do not contribute much to my own projects. Moreover, I am fairly certain that Stassen would be worried about my focus on individuality.

26. Niebuhr, *Faith on Earth*, 47–48; see Godsey, *Promise*, 22.

trust in another." For Niebuhr, this discloses the social character of knowing and believing, which occurs only "in a social situation in which a self in the company of other selves deals with a *common* object." Self, other and common object constitute the "triad of knowledge."[27] For some commentators, the presence of a triadic structure indicates Niebuhr's dependence on Royce rather than Mead. But recall Mead's chick example and my bear example from last chapter: the mother hen's cluck and the chick's response, the runner's scream of "Bear!" and our response, are *about* a common object. These responses are based on our trust in the runner regarding the bear and the chick's "trust" in the mother hen regarding food or danger. Niebuhr's implicit contention in describing faith as a social act underlying all human endeavors is that participation in any such endeavor by taking on the roles of others is based on trust: to take on the role of another is to trust her, to some degree.

In fact, *all* knowledge, not just indirect, is based on social trust. Niebuhr notes, "Language and knowledge are inseparably woven and language is received in trust and belief." We trust that the very words and concepts we use to communicate our understanding of objects are meaningful to others *and* disclose specific "features in our experience."[28] Niebuhr thinks of languages along the lines of conceptual schemes.[29] Mathematics and poetry are distinct languages that enable us to know different *aspects* of reality because they are relative to different communities. Niebuhr's point here is less an analytic one about the relationship of language and reality, than an epistemological one about the relationship of faith and knowledge: "an element of believing, of acceptance of the reports of our companions, of the tradition of our society about encounters with nature, enters into all our knowing at the very beginning."[30] This tying together of language, knowledge, and community resembles Mead's claim that language enables the human self to take on the role of an entire social endeavor. Niebuhr's implicit contention is that it is some measure of trust that grounds our socialization into communities, or in Mead's terms, our taking on of those roles whose relations constitute our communities.

In a rather classically pragmatist move, Niebuhr uses the cooperative practice of science as the model to show how even direct knowledge, where the self has unmediated access to the object of knowledge, requires trust in others. Direct knowledge must be socially verified, requiring "not only

27. Niebuhr, *Faith on Earth*, 32–34, 47.
28. Ibid., 36–37.
29. See Davidson, "On the Very Idea of a Conceptual Scheme."
30. Niebuhr, *Faith on Earth*, 37–38.

that the same subject shall find the same consequences in an experiment or in an encounter with the same objective order in repeated instances, but that other subjects find similar or identical results in similar encounters and that *these other subjects be trustworthy.*"[31] We must trust others regarding objects we have no direct knowledge of *and* regarding their subjective experiences of and encounters with shared objects.

Belief and trust are bound together because all of our knowledge is based on trust of others, and loyalty completes the social act of faith. Niebuhr asserts that there is a form of knowing intrinsic to belief, the *acknowledgment* of others as persons or selves. Acknowledgement involves recognizing the other as a co-knower or co-believer regarding a shared object. More significantly, it involves recognizing the other as a "moral self," one "who has bound himself to us by explicit or implicit promises not to deceive us but to be faithful in telling us the truth about what he knows." In other words, to trust others is to acknowledge them as "beings who live as self-binding, as promise-making, promise-keeping, promise-breaking, covenanting selves and never merely as knowers." The relationship between believing, knowing selves is thus a covenant relationship.[32] This gives a deeper sense of the relationship between trust and loyalty in faith. Not only does our own trust render our own loyalty, but also our "trust is a response to and acknowledgment of [another's] fidelity."[33] The self's trust is the acknowledgment of another moral self because it is the response to that other's loyalty. It is precisely on the basis of this response that the self comes to recognize its own moral nature: "As I trust and distrust the other loyal-disloyal self I become aware of myself as one trusted or distrusted by the other in my loyalty and disloyalty."[34] To trust another is to take on her loyalty, and so to discover my own loyal character from the perspective of her trust. Ultimately, to have faith, to be a faithful being, is to participate in a social act or common endeavor in which we take on the roles of trust and loyalty in response to others' loyalty and trust.

Directly relevant to the theme of moral formation is Niebuhr's claim that immaturity consists in acknowledging the moral personality of others without recognizing one's own self as a moral person. This occurs when the self trusts or distrusts others, expecting them to be loyal, without confronting its own capacity, willingness or obligation to be loyal to them. This is a developmental point: insofar as children must develop the capacity for

31. Ibid., 39.
32. Ibid., 40–42.
33. Ibid., 47; intervention mine.
34. Ibid., 49.

loyalty, there must be a time when they trust others without the expectation of their being loyal in return. This can also signal a form of moral failure: such immaturity in adults is an evasion of the obligation to be loyal that is entailed in trusting others, a refusal to fully participate in covenant relations because a refusal to regard oneself from the perspective of others' trust or distrust.[35] Such evasion and refusal is the failure to be a moral self.[36] For Niebuhr, following Royce closely here, moral selfhood emerges with loyalty, understood as a "mode of self-existence," the exercise of freedom "not only to attend to this or that reality as knowing self, not only to choose this or that good as desiring self, but to bind itself by promises, to choose goods that are not necessarily its own, to attend to beings in which it is not interested."[37] What distinguishes Niebuhr's account of loyalty is the emphasis on its promissory and covenantal nature: to be loyal is to bind oneself to others and to one's own future conduct in relation to them, in response to their implicit trust. Royce assumes autonomous, disconnected selves who become loyal in order to be in right relation with others. Niebuhr, following Mead here I am arguing, assumes selves already in relations of trust who become loyal in order to sustain these relations rightly. Niebuhr appears to presume that our primary socialization is more cooperative than chaotic.

There are two aspects to the freedom that constitutes loyalty. First, the self can choose *which* promises to make, *which* covenant relationships to enter and so *which* social endeavors to participate in. We can (eventually) choose whose trust to take on, whether that means sustaining our existent covenant relations or entering into new ones. Second, the self can "break promises and violate trust." This is the freedom to commit treason, which Niebuhr calls "the dark side of the freedom of fidelity. . . the dark possibility of selfhood." Though he does not use Royce's term "moral suicide," the effect is similar. Worse than moral immaturity, treason breaks those very conditions that make us moral selves: evoking distrust in others, the treasonous self has denied the fundamental fiduciary relationships that evoke its loyalty.[38] Niebuhr's explicit account of treason is less significant for his

---

35. Ibid., 49–50.

36. Niebuhr does not admit or confront the possibility of demoralization, that is, that the absence of trustworthy relationships within someone's life may render them profoundly incapable of trusting others and so of learning how to be loyal. On my interpretation of Niebuhr through Mead, he ought to admit this possibility, though whether or not traditional Christian visions can do so is an important question. For a discussion of these issues from a philosophical perspective, see Baier, "Demoralization, Trust, and the Virtues."

37. Niebuhr, *Faith on Earth*, 48.

38. Ibid., 49.

total position, due to the contextualization of loyalty in the larger structure of faith. For Niebuhr, the human dilemma is the perversion of the whole of faith, not only of loyalty. The human problem is thus not only disloyalty but also distrust. As will become clear below, just as loyalty is grounded on trust, so disloyalty is grounded on distrust. This is why Niebuhr's thought implies an account of treason as referring to an entire social life, not only voluntary acts.

Insofar as faith involves the knowledge of others as moral selves, and not just as co-knowers, another triadic structure comes into view. As knowing, self and other are related to a common object; as faithful, self and other are related to a common *cause*. Again, the influence of Royce is explicit, but there are differences. The first difference is that the cause here is not only an object of loyalty, but also an object of trust. In loyally serving our cause, we trust that it will not make our services futile.[39] The second, more striking difference is found in Niebuhr's appeal to forms of human society to clarify the triadic structure of the faith community. According to Niebuhr there are three such forms. First, he notes the famed distinction between *associations* and *communities*. While associations involve external relations between members based on common interests, communities involve internal relations between members sharing a form of life. Niebuhr himself makes a further distinction within the category of communities, between "communities of human individuals" who share customs and traditions, and "communities of selves" spiritually related in "common fidelity, respect and responsibility." What is stake in this distinction is the preservation of individuality: communities in the former sense result in "the merging of personalities into a kind of whole," while in communities in the latter sense members are "independent of each other yet bound to each other in trust and responsibility." For instance, a marriage of selves involves respect for the partner's divergent, and not just common, interests; a family of selves is egalitarian, involving less common life and more independence. For Niebuhr, the faith community is such a community of selves.[40] The implication is that self and other each have an *individual, unique* relation to their common cause, which is not coextensive with their relations to each other.

What is striking here is that Niebuhr's notion of a community of selves in relation to a cause is seemingly positioned against the Royce of *The Problem of Christianity*. Recall that Royce ultimately dropped the notion of cause in favor of community, understood to be a distinct level of human existence where social minds manifest forms of life expressed in languages and

39. Ibid., 59–60.
40. Ibid., 54–58.

customs. This account seems to align with the category of "communities of human individuals," especially as Niebuhr refers to such communities as relations 'of mind.'[41] I contend that Niebuhr is wary of this form of human society, and so of Royce's move from cause to community, because it tends to collapse cause and community. If a community of human individuals tends to merge self and other in a shared form of life, than that form of life, that community, will tend to become the cause because it is the only thing uniting self and other. This is social faith. The category "communities of selves" preserves the distinction between cause and community because self and other each have a relation to the cause that is not reducible to their relations to each other. Niebuhr explains: "the cause transcends the community. No matter how large the We-group of the loyal grows that which unites them in loyalty is always something beyond the community for the sake of which they are united in community."[42] In the triad of faith, self and other are not united with each other for the sake of their community, but for the sake of an object of trust and loyalty; and it is precisely their individual relations to this object that prevent their dissolution in community. Radical monotheism is oriented to the God beyond all being—more specifically, the God loyally devoted to all being—and so exemplifies such a triad of faith: self and other are united for the sake of God, and so for the sake of a 'community'—the realm of being—that is irreducible to the community of self and other. Moreover, as will be shown below, radical faith in God is always unique for each particular self, and so irreducible to the trust and loyalty that human selves have for each other.

This is not to say that Royce in *The Problem of Christianity* promoted a form of social faith or that his notion of community abrogated individuality. The argument of chapter 2 should dispel worries on these accounts. Nor is it to say that Niebuhr thought that about Royce: there are no explicit references to *The Problem of Christianity* or to Royce's notion of community. Still, the structural parallels between Niebuhr's category of social faith and Royce's notion of community, and the implications of these parallels, do explain why Niebuhr's use of Royce is restricted to the earlier work that focuses on loyalty.

By preserving the distinction between cause and community within the structure of faith, Niebuhr gives himself a reference point outside the community, a "horizon" of transcendence. He claims, "Behind the faiths and communities of faith in which we are united in family and nation and company of scholars there looms the grand structure of a community of

---

41. Ibid., 56–57.
42. Ibid., 60.

faith which is universal, in which all selves are involved as companions and in which the third, the cause and object of trust, is the transcendent reality"; moreover, "in this acknowledgment of a transcendent object there is included acknowledgment of an Absolute."[43] In short, the acknowledgment of God is constitutive of human faith. Niebuhr can be accused of taking a leap by moving from the notion of *transcendent to the community* to the notion of *Absolute*. A child transcends the community of her parents, excellence in football transcends the community of football teams, but neither children nor football excellence can sensibly be called *absolute*. The problem here regards Niebuhr's stance in *Faith on Earth*. As Fowler notes,[44] in the beginning of the work Niebuhr presumes an audience with a non-theistic, non-Christian interest in human moral life. In middle of the work, precisely where he moves from human faith in each other to human faith in God, he adopts "the method of confession and demonstration," the "effort to understand a faith that has been given."[45] Taking this stance means that one takes faith in God to be an assumed or posited part of human faith, rather than a derivative. In this way, the move from *transcendent to the community* to *Absolute* is not meant to be a derivation, but a location of human faith in God: whether trust or distrust, loyalty or disloyalty, such faith concerns something radically and not just laterally beyond the human community.

Niebuhr's stated aim when his attention turns to faith in God is to use his analysis of human faith in each other in order to more fully analyze the faith in God present in human faith.[46] One insight gained is that faith in God is a personal relation: we comport ourselves to the Absolute as to a self. Our belief in God is inextricably tied to trust and loyalty. For Niebuhr, our immediate awareness of this faith is negative: "Our natural faith, our ordinary human attitude toward the transcendent source of our existence, is one of disappointment, of distrust, and of disbelief," acknowledgement of the Absolute as someone who ought to be loyal to us, but does not appear to be. Niebuhr calls this the "natural religion of negative faith." Importantly, this does not simply describe faith in God prior to Jesus Christ, whether historically or individually, but also "something in our present life, an old relation that may be passing away but which is nevertheless present."[47] Natural, negative faith is always present. In *The Meaning of Revelation*, Niebuhr asserts that the relation between "natural religion" and "revealed religion"

43. Ibid., 60–61.
44. Fowler, *To See the Kingdom*, 243.
45. Niebuhr, *Faith on Earth*, 64.
46. Ibid.
47. Ibid., 67–68.

or "historical faith" is not one of mutual exclusion or developmental stages, but of transformation or conversion.[48] Revelation refers to the "conversion and permanent revolution of our human religion through Jesus Christ," such that Christianity itself is understood as "'permanent revolution' or *metanoia*, which does not come to an end in this world, this life, or this time."[49] Reading retrospectively, this suggests that positive faith in God, the trust in and loyalty to God accessed through Jesus Christ, is the continuous transformation of our natural religion of negative faith. Trust in and loyalty to God do not replace or succeed, but rather continually convert, our ineradicable natural distrust in and disloyalty to God.

Of course, this should remind us of the relationship of radical monotheism to henotheism and polytheism, also one of transformation or conversion. While it is unfortunate that Niebuhr does not connect his discussion of the three types of faith from *Radical Monotheism* to his discussion of negative faith and Christian faith from *Faith on Earth*, the structural similarities provide adequate clues. Before making these connections, an unspoken aspect of negative faith should be made explicit: the human response to *tragedy*. Though negative faith is natural, it is not fundamental: "Distrust is only possible where the conditions for trust have first been established." According to Niebuhr, "The self comes to awareness of itself, of its companions and of the common life with a sense of promise." Trust in the Absolute as the source of our existence as selves includes an *expectation* that the Absolute is loyal to that existence, that existence and all being are intended for "something glorious, splendid, clean and joyous." But then: "The odor of death, the feeling of betrayal, the sense of pollution, invades all our existence," and the self "awakes to a deception that is in it and all around it . . . learns to live in the midst of distrust and in the expectation of disloyalty."[50] Niebuhr is in agreement with Mead when he implies that *expectation* structures the faith relationship between self and God. When the chick responds to the mother hen's cluck, it *expects* that food or danger is imminent; when I respond to someone screaming, "Bear!" by following her, I *expect* to be running away from a bear or bear-like predator. Thus, to say that taking on the roles of others in a social endeavor requires trust, is also to say that it proceeds by expectations and succeeds by expectations met. This trust-expectation dynamic is clear in radical monotheism: faith in God as the principle of both being and value is constituted by the trust that God values all being, and so by the expectation that God will continue to so value. The occurrence of

---

48. Niebuhr, *The Meaning of Revelation*, xxxiii.
49. Ibid., 99, xxxiv.
50. Niebuhr, *Faith on Earth*, 78–81.

natural and social evils, or tragedy, frustrates that expectation, casting doubt on God's loyalty to us and leading to our natural, negative faith.

According to Niebuhr, our natural distrust takes three forms: hostility, fear and isolation. *Hostility*, based on "profound disillusionment" in the Absolute, arises when "a self bound to other human selves in loyalty raises its voice against Omnipotence on behalf of others." For hostility, tragedy demonstrates that God is our enemy, and so must be defied for the sake of our fellow humans. The hostile response to tragedy is the expression of our faith in other humans at the expense of our faith in God. Like hostility, *fear* or *anxiety* responds to perceived enmity between God and humans. Unlike hostility, fear is not courageously defiant: fear "is either more aware of the all-powerful character of what man confronts than Promethean defiance is, or it is less confident of human power to contend with the "Omnificent," or it is less loyal to fellowmen and simply more self-centered," so that "its approach is one of appeasement." Rather than defy God in response to tragedy, fear seeks to appease God so the self may be saved from God. Niebuhr clarifies the nature of this fear: "It is the fear of the loss of selfhood, not simply of life; it is the fear of exclusion from the community of selves." Fear may be a theological advancement over hostility, for it recognizes truly divine power and human powerlessness before it, but it is a moral regression insofar as it leads to self-obsession rather than loyalty to others. Niebuhr admits that fear allows the self to have concern for "those companions in and with whom it has its existence," but it is clear that fear generally leads to a narrowing of moral concern. Finally, *isolation* or *forgetfulness* responds to tragedy with "the defensive mechanism whereby men try to forget the presence of the ultimate reality while they construct for themselves an imaginary world in which they can pretend to be at peace." Isolation simply ignores both tragedy and God and "tries to live among the things that are close at hand with such peace of mind and such pleasure as one can extract from them."[51]

To repeat, Niebuhr does not connect this discussion with that of the three types of faith. Still, parallels can be discerned. Insofar as isolation motivates a turning away from God and toward the surrounding variety as a source of peace and pleasure, it resembles polytheism, pluralistic faith: distrust of God leads to momentary trusting in whatever attracts our interest. Neither hostility nor fear can be as easily aligned with a type of faith, though they would seem to tend toward henotheism, social faith. Insofar as hostility opposes God to humanity, so that distrust of God renders loyalty to humanity, it underwrites a form of henotheism. While radical monotheism demands loyalty to the entire realm of being, hostile distrust of God

51. Ibid., 68–77.

demands loyalty only to one's finite, human community. Moreover, if the tragedy that hostility responds to is social-political, if God the enemy is discerned in aggression against a smaller community, such as one's nation, university, neighborhood, city, family, etc., than hostility may easily underwrite narrower and narrower forms of henotheism. Insofar as fear is more self-centered than hostility, it may appear to be closer to polytheism than henotheism. However, Niebuhr intriguingly suggests that fear "is fortified, and perhaps also rooted in, the social life in which fear of the unknown power is used as an instrument by those responsible for the welfare of the group for the sake of maintaining its solidarity."[52] In this way, fearful distrust of God can also render trust in and loyalty to small, finite communities.

Niebuhr shows a remarkable disinterest in how we fall from trust to distrust in God, other than his appeal to our awakening to deception. He explains this disinterest by his stance, a problem noted above: "From the point of view of a reconciled faith we do not have much interest in asking how and why the fall into distrust occurred." He does note two aspects of this fall. First, "it is a genuine *fall* and cannot be the absolute beginning of our personal existence." As stated above, trust is the condition of distrust, for "(f)aithlessness does not eliminate the order of faith but perverts it." As Niebuhr notes, this means that distrust in and disloyalty to God *remain* relations, if antagonistic or neglectful, to God.[53] This also explains why distrust in and disloyalty to God render trust in and loyalty to finite things and communities: if the self is constituted by faith, than distrust in God cannot destroy faith, but can only orient it toward something else, something not God. *This* is the perversion of faith, and so of ourselves.

Second, the fall into distrust "is a complex interpersonal event in which the whole structure of faith is involved." In Mead's terms, the fall is a social act, and so "cannot easily be blamed in a mechanical or an individualistic manner on an isolated act or person." For Niebuhr, "disloyalty and distrust, self and neighbor, are so involved that the distrust of God is a response to the companion's deception or disloyalty and the self's disloyalty in the breaking of its own promise is another source of its distrust." Importantly, Niebuhr is *not* proposing the reduction of distrust in God to distrust in human others: recall that in the triad of faith, self and other each have relations to God that are irreducible to their relations to each other. Nevertheless, insofar as faith is a social act that does involve self, other and God, any change in the particular relations within the triad must reverberate to the other relations. As will be seen below, the self can only respond to God through responding

---

52. Ibid., 75.
53. Ibid., 78.

to others. Niebuhr's point here is to distribute rather than fix blame: "all have sinned . . . this does not mean that each has sinned by himself but that all have sinned together."[54] Though the fall into distrust is a social act, an interpersonal event, the individuals participating are not thereby acquitted. Niebuhr combines what Royce tore asunder. Recall that Royce distinguishes between original sin—the social training that forms the self to contrast itself with others and society—and voluntary sin—the treasonous act by which the self destroys its community and its own moral selfhood. In social training, *no* blame can accrue to the individual self since, despite its ill effects, social training is responsible for, and so not the product of, our moral self-consciousness. In treason, *all* blame accrues to the individual self insofar as it is a morally impossible choice without reason. Niebuhr's social notion of the fall into distrust combines these: each individual self is to blame for it, though it can only occur with others; it is a social process for which each participating self is accountable. This enables Niebuhr, unlike Royce, to keep original and voluntary sin connected.

Niebuhr calls our natural distrust in God "broken faith," and I have argued that social faith and pluralistic faith, henotheism and polytheism, are forms of broken faith. The faith of Jesus Christ discussed in *Faith on Earth* is thus to be identified with radical faith: to say that radical monotheism transforms our social and pluralistic faiths is to say that the faith of Jesus Christ qualifies our natural distrust. This means that radical monotheism is mediated to us through Jesus Christ. Both *Radical Monotheism* and *Faith on Earth* agree on this, but since Niebuhr takes a different stance in each work, the emphases of each work are different.[55]

In *Radical Monotheism*, Niebuhr notes that radical monotheism emerges historically, using the term *incarnation*: "the concrete expression in a total human life of radical trust in the One and of universal loyalty to the realm of being." Moses and the prophets are understood to be such incarnations, with Jesus Christ being one "to an even greater extent" because his faith is "unqualified by distrust or competing loyalty." This sounds supersessionist, but for Niebuhr the relevant comparison here is not between Judaism and Christianity, but between Old Testament figures and Jesus Christ as incarnations of radical faith. Jesus is the one "who single-mindedly accepted the assurance that the Lord of heaven and earth was wholly faithful to him and to all creatures, and who in response gave wholehearted loyalty to the

---

54. Ibid., 78–79.

55. For discussions of the promises and drawbacks of Niebuhr's Christology, see Frei, "Theology of H. Richard Niebuhr," 105–16, and Stassen, "Concrete Christological Norms."

realm of being," and by implication the others did not.⁵⁶ At the same time, a "continuous struggle between social henotheism and radical monotheism" is present in *both* Judaism and Christianity. In Christianity, henotheism takes the form of ecclesia-centrism or Christo-centrism. In the former, faith in one's finite church replaces faith in God so that one's God becomes the god of the church rather than the God of all being. In the latter, faith in Jesus Christ replaces faith in God so that the "person through whom Christians have received access to God" becomes a god himself. Niebuhr notes that Christo-centrism often becomes ecclesia-centrism "insofar as the community that centers in Jesus Christ is set forth both as the object of his loyalty and the Christian's loyalty."⁵⁷ The history of Christianity is thus a continuous struggle with the temptation to replace Jesus Christ and one's church for God as the objects of our trust and loyalty.

As suggested above, this may explain why Niebuhr avoided Royce's discussion from *The Problem of Christianity*. By so closely identifying the risen *Christ* with the Beloved *Community*, Royce combines the two temptations to radical monotheism as the center of his account of Christianity. This is not to say that Royce's account is ecclesia- or Christo-centric: he eschews making Jesus Christ the essence of Christianity and insists that the Beloved Community is not to be confused with the visible church. Still, it is plausible that Niebuhr might have been worried by Royce's discussion given his view that Christ and community are the two objects that Christians tend to idolize. Ultimately, Niebuhr's view that ecclesia- and Christo-centrism are the persistent temptations of Christians underlines his contention that radical faith is more of a hope and goal than an achievement, such that Christianity is understood to be a 'permanent revolution.'⁵⁸ At the same time, because faith is a pervasive human phenomenon, conflict between types of faith occurs, not only in religions, but also in all other cultural activities. Niebuhr devotes a chapter each to showing how this conflict manifests in politics and science.⁵⁹ This implies that Christian radical monotheism may constantly transform not only ecclesia- and Christo-centrism, but also the social and pluralistic faiths that appear in other cultural activities. How this works will become clear when we discuss Niebuhr's ethics of responsibility. Suffice it to say for now that, insofar as radical monotheism regards God to be the God of all being, its God must be the God of all cultural activities. When Niebuhr describes Judaism and Christianity as "efforts at the incarnation of

---

56. Niebuhr, *Radical Monotheism*, 40–42.
57. Ibid., 57–60.
58. Ibid., 63, 31; Niebuhr, *The Meaning of Revelation*, xxxiv.
59. Niebuhr, *Radical Monotheism*, 64–89.

monotheistic faith in total life," he means that radical faith transforms our entire cultural life.⁶⁰

In *Faith on Earth*, Niebuhr's discussion of Jesus Christ is strictly confessional. He approaches Christianity as "the interpersonal movement of faith that centers in the person of Jesus Christ . . . in such a way that he directs all trust and loyalty away from himself to the Transcendent and Circumambient," rather than as a set of doctrines or beliefs. This means that Jesus Christ is not understood as the founder of a religion, nor as the object of belief or doctrine, but rather as "personally present" now: "He is the personal companion who by his loyalty to the self and by his trust in the Transcendent One *reconstructs* the broken interpersonal life of faith."⁶¹ Richard R. Niebuhr asserts that the use of the term *reconstruction* here is an intentional use of Mead. Referring to Mead's *The Philosophy of the Present*, he contends that for Mead the reconstruction of the past, which is involved in all knowledge of the past, can only take place from the perspective of the present: to say that Jesus Christ reconstructs our past broken faith, requires locating Jesus Christ in the present.⁶² In this way, the resurrection becomes particularly significant, for the one who is personally present in Christian faith "is not a Jesus of history but the Christ of faith, not Jesus incarnate, but the risen Lord."⁶³ Jesus Christ is a necessary part of the social act of Christian faith, and as such cannot be a fixed historical figure. Rather, only the risen Christ can presently reconstruct our past broken faith.

It is essential to see that Niebuhr's appeal to the risen Christ is not a reference to Royce's discussion from *The Problem of Christianity*. For Royce, the risen Christ is identical with the Spirit of the Beloved Community, and while this certainly locates Christ in the present, it collapses Christ and the Spirit (and so also the Community). What Niebuhr calls his *binitarianism* does not allow this. According to this theological position, there are only two divine persons, Father and Son. The Spirit is not a third person, but "an attribute of the two persons in the Godhead and that which makes is possible for us to be selves with them." The triad of Christian faith is composed of the human self, Jesus Christ as our other, and the Absolute and Transcendent God as the common third; the Spirit serves as the "principle of community" given to us so that we may be bound to Jesus Christ and God.⁶⁴ This position raises its own problems, but for the task at hand we can see how it

60. Ibid., 56.
61. Niebuhr, *Faith on Earth*, 85–87.
62. Ibid., 88 n. 3.
63. Ibid., 87.
64. Ibid., 105.

allows Niebuhr to define the triad of Christian faith.[65] Despite appearances such Christian faith is *not* individualistic; to say that Jesus Christ is the other of the human self is *not* to say that the self has a relationship to Jesus Christ unmediated or uninfluenced by others. Niebuhr explains that Jesus Christ is "introduced into our personal-interpersonal existence by persons who trusted him, were loyal to him . . . by persons who were trusted by us." Our access to Jesus Christ is through our companions: "The Christ we see is the Christ reflected in their existence, the Christ who is hidden and yet pointed to in their devotion." While Niebuhr admits that through communication between self and others Jesus Christ "is born again into our minds" such that we ultimately each have a direct relationship to him, he insists that the relationship "is never a lonely one, without companions."[66] In this way, within the triad of self, Jesus Christ and God there appears to be a subordinate triad: self, others and Jesus Christ as common third. Insofar as Jesus Christ directs all trust and loyalty away from himself toward God, this subordinate triad opens out to the theo-centric triad.[67] Christo-centrism and ecclesia-centrism can thus be understood as stunted forms of Christian faith, ironically inattentive to Christ's own faith. Insofar as the self gains a direct relation to Jesus Christ through and with companions, Christian faith is individual, but not individualistic; in the words of *The Responsible Self*, it is unique but repeated.[68] The point of the resurrection is to secure Jesus Christ's unique status within the triad of Christian faith as the other whose faith mediates God to us.[69]

According to Niebuhr, Jesus Christ is the unique mediator of God because he *completely* trusts that God is "wholly loyal," and in turn is *completely* loyal to God's cause.[70] This follows Niebuhr's analysis of human faith, but also raises questions about its applicability. Recall that in human faith, our trust is a response to the other's loyalty, and our loyalty emerges as we take on the other's loyalty, considering ourselves from the perspective of the other's implicit trust. While Jesus Christ's trust in God is certainly a

---

65. For Niebuhr's own discussion of Trinitarianism, see Niebuhr, "The Doctrine of the Trinity." For a secondary discussion of Niebuhr's Trinitarianism, see Frei, "Theology of H. Richard Niebuhr," 98–101.

66. Niebuhr, *Faith on Earth*, 89–94.

67. Lonnie Kliever articulates this within a tetrahedron model. See Kliever, "The Christology of H. Richard Niebuhr."

68. Niebuhr, *The Responsible Self*, 115.

69. In this respect, for Niebuhr Christian faith is not faith *in* Christ, but rather our participation in Christ's own faith in God; that is, Niebuhr understands "faith of Christ" according to the subjective genitive.

70. Niebuhr, *Faith on Earth*, 94–95.

response to God's loyalty, it is less clear that Jesus Christ's loyalty to God's cause emerges in the eyes of God's trust. Can God be understood to trust, or does that compromise God's sovereignty since trust is a passive stance? Niebuhr does not answer this question, perhaps because his own change of stance to confession in *Faith on Earth* hinders him from explicitly connecting the earlier human account to the later theological account. Still, we can say that his binitarianism allows him to hold that God trusts Jesus Christ without compromising divine sovereignty insofar as Jesus Christ is understood to be the Son of God, the second divine person. In this case, God's trust in Jesus Christ would be a sort of divine self-trust. Again, this provokes further theological questions, but what should be clear is that Jesus Christ's faith in God can be understood to involve the mutual trust and loyalty that is involved in humans' faith in each other.[71]

However, Jesus Christ's faith in God as exemplified in his human life is *not* sufficient for the reconstruction of human faith. Jesus Christ's trust in and loyalty to God were distrusted by others, and so he was betrayed and executed, seemingly abandoned by God. Without some validation of Jesus Christ's faith, it would simply dissipate, having no reconstructive effect on our broken faith.[72] For Niebuhr, the resurrection serves as the validation of Jesus Christ's faith. While he insists, "The Son reveals himself as Son in his moral, personal character" of complete trust in God and complete loyalty to God's cause, he also insists that "he is not made known as Son of God in reality until he is established in power" by the resurrection: "The Father reveals himself as Father in the resurrection of the Son; the Son is revealed as Son by his life and resurrection." Prior to the resurrection, natural human faith distrusts God and so distrusts Jesus Christ's faith in God. With the resurrection, God is shown to be loyal, and so Jesus Christ's faith in God is validated.[73] Consistent with his confessional stance, Niebuhr does not mean the resurrection as a discrete historical event whose objective truth must be assented to, but rather as an experienced event in the interpersonal history of those who believe in God with Christ. The resurrection is the establishment of Jesus Christ in power "over our personal life," an "ever-repeated event" by which we gain "a little ability to trust." The resurrection validates Christian faith, not as an event that impersonally, objectively proves God's loyalty, but as an experience of being in present relationship to Christ: the resurrection explains how "our distrust of God is turned somewhat in the

---

71. A more explicit Trinitarianism would enable Niebuhr to articulate this theologically.

72. Niebuhr, *Faith on Earth*, 95–96.

73. Ibid., 99–100.

direction of trust . . . our hostility is turned slightly in the direction of a desire to be loyal . . . our view of the society to which we are bound in loyalty begins to enlarge." With the resurrection, in our present relation to Jesus Christ, "we are enabled to qualify our distrust" of God: "metanoia, a revolution of the personal life begins."[74] Resurrection is the beginning of the reconstruction of natural human faith.

In this way, neither is the resurrection sufficient for the reconstruction of faith, at least in the sense of the resurrection accomplishing such reconstruction once and for all. In Mead's terms, the resurrection is an emergent event, constantly and ever-presently reconstructing our natural human faith by turning it *away* from those finite communities and plural interests we turn to in distrust of God, and *toward* God and the divine cause. If the resurrection that renders Christian faith is an emergent event, then Christian faith is itself an emergent event. The emergence of Christian faith is the in-breaking of novelty into our natural life of faith: once the God of all being can be trusted, new possibilities become available for human loyalty. Mead's language of emergence parallels Niebuhr's language of transformation: if radical faith transforms social and pluralistic faith, but is itself a hope or goal rather than an achievement, then radical faith can be understood as an emergent event, and transformation can be understood as reconstruction. Thus, Christian faith as radical monotheism is creative. Again, such creativity is not *ex nihilo*, but contingent: radical faith can only reconstruct natural faith from the elements it finds. At the same time, insofar as such reconstruction is continual, those elements will continually change: the creativity of radical faith is conditioned, but not determined. These connections to Mead add content to Niebuhr's claim that the Christian life is a permanent revolution. Since radical Christian faith reconstructs our natural faith, it is revolutionary. Since radical Christian faith is an emergent event, the revolution it initiates cannot ever be finished, and so it remains permanent.

If Niebuhr's position follows Mead's model of emergence and reconstruction, we should expect Christian faith to be the transformation of natural faith toward a future that is not substantially fixed. According to Niebuhr, a "universal community of faith grounded in God and existing toward him as well as in mutual relations" arises with the reconstruction of faith as the end of human endeavor: "the community of faith is necessarily human work in response to the divine." Such a community is "both given to our present and promised to our future, as something which has been and is being established by the faithfulness of God"; it is both "historical and archaic" *and* "eschatological and teleological," lived both "in memory and in

74. Ibid., 97–99.

hope."[75] In other words, the universal community of faith is a social reality in Mead's sense of *sociality*: it emerges in the present as both rooted in past communities of faith and anticipatory of a future community of faith, as the passage from those past communities to the future community. In Niebuhr's context, the passage from past to future occurring in the present is the passage from natural faith to radical Christian faith. This means that the emergence of the universal community of faith in the present involves characterizing past communities of faith as distrusting in and disloyal to God so that it may become a trusting, loyal community.

Without using Mead, Niebuhr's earlier work *The Meaning of Revelation* demonstrates how such a passage from natural to radical faith takes place in the Christian community. While an in-depth analysis of this work would take us too far afield, it is worthwhile pointing out that integral to this passage of faith is the community's recognition of "all events, even though it can see most of them only from an external point of view, as workings of the God who reveals himself." This requires accepting external criticisms of the Christian community as divine judgments that are rendered "occasions for active repentance."[76] In other words, the emergence of the universal community of faith in the Christian community requires engagement with the non-Christian world as the means to confront its own natural distrust and disloyalty. *Faith on Earth* does not address the relationship between the Christian community and the non-Christian world, though Niebuhr does assert here, "The line between church and world runs through every soul, not between souls." Read in context—where "church" refers to the Holy Catholic Church of the creed—this is a denial that the sociological difference between Christian communities and the non-Christian world can be mapped onto the difference between the radically and naturally faithful. The Holy Catholic Church of Christian faith, which is the universal community of faith that is the work of radical faith, cannot be identical with any visible church because it is an emergent reality. Thus, the reconstruction of faith within the Christian community is itself a struggle between church and world. In this way, it is no accident that Niebuhr ends *Faith on Earth* by gesturing to the notion that the reconstruction of faith "modifies, transforms, corrects our constant tendencies to fear," not only in religious life, "but in our domestic and our total cultural life."[77] The transformation of the Christian community rendered by the emergence of the universal community of faith is an aspect of the transformation of the entire human world.

75. Ibid., 109–12.
76. Niebuhr, *The Meaning of Revelation*, 44–45.
77. Niebuhr, *Faith on Earth*, 116–18.

It is against this background indebted to Mead that Niebuhr re-introduces Royce, for *loyalty* is responsible for the human work of the emergence of this community of faith. Just as faith is the double movement or relation of trust and loyalty, so Christ's reconstruction of faith involves two moments: "What Jesus Christ does in the restoration of faith is not only to reconcile us to God so that we can trust in him, but to challenge by his fidelity to God and to God's cause, the creation, the response of our loyalty." Our trust in God is restored in order that we may be loyal to God's cause. Niebuhr insists that loyalty is not the automatic consequence of restored trust, since "a person, as a responsive being, is not a machine." Rather, restored trust is "a most vigorous challenge to the will to believe, that is, to the will to be faithful to the universal cause and to all our companions in it."[78] This position allows him to retain the voluntarism of Royce's philosophy of loyalty, but emphasize its responsive character. For Niebuhr, the human will chooses its own cause less than it responds to a cause demanded of it. Whether one's response is loyal or disloyal depends on whether one trusts or distrusts the one whose cause is demanded. As shown above, the self's trust is a response to the other's loyalty. We can now see that the self's loyalty is also a response to the other's loyalty, but *through* the self's trust of that other. Loyalty is no longer the self's solitary choice of a cause, but the self's responsive role in a social act of faith that depends on others.

The question that remains is how transformation or reconstruction occurs. How does radical faith transform social and pluralistic faiths? More specifically, how does Christian faith reconstruct natural faith? Niebuhr provides an initial answer by stating toward the end of *Faith on Earth*, "The restoration of faith is the challenge to a life of continuing responsibility."[79] Among other things, Niebuhr's classic *The Responsible Self* is an account of how such transformation occurs.

RESPONSIBILITY AND REINTERPRETATION

If *Radical Monotheism* and *Faith on Earth* describe radical Christian faith as the reconstruction of our natural, broken, social, faith, and then claim that the risen Christ is our access to such radical faith, then *The Responsible Self* articulates that this transformation occurs hermeneutically. That is, the reconstruction of faith concerns the reinterpretation of God and God's world, and it is the example and power of Christ, available to use through the resurrection, that enables us to reinterpret. While this section

---

78. Ibid., 110.
79. Ibid., 111.

traces some developments of Niebuhr's thought, pointing out differences and continuities between his earlier works and his turn to responsibility, its major contribution is to articulate the promised theological reconstruction of Mead's I/me distinction. This comes in two steps. First, theologically construed, the "I" refers to that aspect or phase of the self that it is in direct relation to God, irreducible to socially mediated relations. The "I" is not some substance or faculty in the self that possesses or controls this relation, but is simply the self as constituted by that divinely bestowed relation. In short, the "I" refers to the self as radically faithful. Second, as the direct relation to God, understood as the radical power that is responsible for all of the agencies that constitute the world, the "I" can take one of two forms, radical trust or radical distrust, the interpretation of God as radically benevolent or radically malevolent. The transformation of the self that is achieved through the transformation of faith, is the transformation of the "I," not the transformation of the "me" by the "I." On my theological reconstruction of the I/me distinction, it is not enough to recognize and promote the "I" over against the "me"; rather, the character of the "I" itself must be attended to. Ultimately, we will see that the reconstruction of natural, socially polytheistic faith into radical faith depends on the transformation of radical faith itself, from radical distrust into radical trust; only as trust will radical faith transform our social faiths so that they can serve the divine cause. The final section completes my reconstruction by articulating the form of individual creativity grounded in and promoted by radical faith.

The Responsible Self is subtitled, "An Essay in Christian Moral Philosophy," and given the problem of stance in *Faith on Earth* discussed above, it is worthwhile noting what Niebuhr takes the stance of Christian moral philosophy to mean. The stance is *Christian* because the "point of view is that of a Christian believer." This perspective is funded by a Christian faith in God, more specifically, by identification with "the cause of Jesus Christ." At the same time, the stance qualifies as *moral philosophy* because "the object to be understood is man's moral life" and "the method is philosophical." *The Responsible Self* concerns not simply the Christian life, but rather "human moral life in general." Niebuhr aims to develop "an instrument of analysis which applies to any form of human life including the Christian." This entails being "Bible-informed" rather than "Bible-centered": while a Christian perspective is bound to result in scriptural resonances, it does not require deriving its conceptual resources straight from scripture.[80] The idea is that the particularity of the perspective does not necessarily limit the area or method of inquiry. In this way, Christian moral philosophy can be

---

80. Niebuhr, *The Responsible Self*, 42–46.

understood as a combination of the confessional stance of *The Meaning of Revelation* and the second half of *Faith on Earth* and the general stance of *Radical Monotheism* and the first half of *Faith on Earth*. *The Responsible Self* thus serves as a fitting capstone to Niebuhr's work.

The point of *The Responsible Self* is to show that *responsibility* is the symbol that more adequately construes the moral life than *purposiveness* or *citizenship*. Niebuhr's notion of symbolism regards "the use of a *special* experience for the interpretation of *all* experience, of a part for the whole."[81] The argument is that the experience of responsibility and responsiveness better illuminates the entirety of human experience than the experiences of making and of living under a law: "All life has the character of responsiveness."[82] However, the other experiences and symbols have historical precedent. The symbol of purposiveness, intrinsically related to *making* or *fashioning*, grounds teleological ethics in various forms, e.g., "idealists and utilitarians, hedonists and self-realizationists." Here, the self is understood as "an artificer who constructs things according to an idea and for the sake of an end," living by "practical ends-and-means reasoning."[83] Purposiveness undergirds ethics of the *good*, motivated by the question: "What is my goal, ideal, or telos?"[84] The symbol of citizenship, on the other hand, grounds deontological ethics. Here, human life is understood to be more like politics than art: "We come to self-awareness if not to self-existence in the midst of *mores*, of commandments and rules, *Thou shalts* and *Thou shalt nots*, of directions and permissions." The self's agency is understood to be primarily "legislative, obedient, and administrative."[85] Citizenship undergirds ethics of the *right*, motivated by the question: "What is the law and what is the first law of my life?"[86] For Niebuhr, these two symbols have dominated our understanding of the moral life. The experience and symbol of responsibility is more illuminative because it includes the experiences of purposive making and being a citizen, while going beyond them.

The symbol of responsibility fronts "the image of man-the-answerer, man engaged in dialogue, man acting in response to action upon him." Here, all human action is understood to have the "character of being responses, answers, to actions upon us." Human agency is understood to be in constant interaction with natural and social environments. This means

---

81. Ibid., 52.
82. Ibid., 41.
83. Ibid., 48–50.
84. Ibid., 60.
85. Ibid., 52–54.
86. Ibid., 60.

that it depends on external stimuli: unlike purposiveness and citizenship, responsibility discloses the human self to be the sufferer of external forces *before* it is an actor. In this sense, responsibility does not deny the experiences of purposiveness and citizenship, but rather contextualizes them. Niebuhr is not denying that human agency makes according to an ideal or gives and follows laws, but rather insisting that such purposive and political activity is always responsive to prior agencies, and that the significance of such activity consists precisely in its responsive character. All human activity is responsive, but it is not all purposive or political. Unsurprisingly, the significance of responsibility is most keenly felt in situations of social emergency and personal suffering. Responsibility undergirds an ethics of the *fitting*, motivated by the question: "What is going on?" While teleology and deontology respectively subordinate the right and the good to the other, responsibility ethics accounts for both by insisting that the fitting action "is alone conducive to the good and alone is right."[87] Responsibility better illuminates the moral life and so provides a moral theory able to combine the insights of dominant and conflicting moral theories.

Niebuhr isolates four elements that compose the moral theory of responsibility. The first is *response*: "All action . . . is response to action upon us." The significance of this has been noted. Suffering, or *receptivity*, is the background of human action.[88] Though Niebuhr does not explicitly say so, this element of response highlights the self's dependence on others, and so implies the significance of trust in all human relations. The second element qualifies the manner of our response as "to *interpreted* action upon us." Humans are characterized by an "awareness" that "identifies, compares, analyzes, and relates events so that they come to us not as brute actions, but as understood and as having meaning." Action upon us is thus understood to be "symbolic of larger meanings," part of "large patterns of interpretation" that determine how we respond. Royce's influence, though unstated, is heavy in Niebuhr's examples: communities and individuals interpret others' actions in order to ascertain what they *express* about the agents' *minds*. In this sense, interpretation appears as the accompanying cognitive process that distinguishes human from non-human response. At the same time, Niebuhr roots interpretation in the entire human self, for it "is not simply an affair of our conscious, and rational, mind but also of the deep memories that are buried within us, of feelings and intuitions that are only partly under our immediate control."[89] While this reads like an appeal to the importance

87. Ibid., 56–61.
88. Ibid., 61.
89. Ibid., 61–63.

of the unconscious in our interactions with others, it also betrays Mead's influence. Recall that, for Mead, interpretation is fundamentally organic, language emerging from gesture and meaning emerging from social interaction. The large patterns of interpretation with which we respond are bequeathed, not only to our minds, but also in our entire selves. Our deep memories, feelings and intuitions, the result of our organic development, manifest in our interpretations of others' minded action upon us. In this sense, interpretation is more existential than purely cognitive, because it regards the whole self's felt response action upon it.

The third element in the moral theory of responsibility is *accountability*. Beyond responding to interpreted action upon us, our responsible actions must be "made in anticipation of answers to our answers." Responsible actions are dialogical, responding to another's past action and anticipating the other's future action as a reply. This means that responsible action is future-directed: the responsible agent "looks forward in a present deed to the continued interaction" with others. This dynamic announces the *timefullness* of the self, which as we will see below, sets the dilemma for faith. This also means that no responsible action can have meaning in and of itself, but only "as part of a total conversation" that has meaning "as a whole."[90] In Mead's terms, responsible actions are parts of larger social acts, aimed at keeping that social act going. This portrays the self as social, which in turn discloses the fourth element of responsibility, *social solidarity*. Responsible actions take place "in a continuing discourse or interaction among beings forming a continuing society." The self must have continuity, not only with "a relatively consistent scheme of interpretations," but also with "the community of agents to which response is being made."[91] In other words, interpretive response to action upon us takes place *with* others. The large patterns of interpretation with which we respond are *socially* bequeathed, arising from rather than given prior to social interaction.

The strong influence of Mead should be apparent in these four elements of the moral theory of responsibility, and I have highlighted them because Niebuhr is rarely explicit about which of Mead's conceptual resources he finds useful, and so rarely develops them. Niebuhr does describe Mead as an advocate of "the fundamentally social character of selfhood" that the idea of responsibility assumes and does quote him on the reflexivity of the self as arising through dialogue with others. At the same time, he notes that Mead is "following a long tradition," and then proceeds to draw parallels

---

90. Ibid., 63–64.
91. Ibid., 65.

with Martin Buber.⁹² This makes it difficult to discern how much of an influence Mead is compared to others. This is complicated by Niebuhr's criticism of Mead's idea of the generalized other. In his article "The Ego-Alter Dialectic and the Conscience," Niebuhr approves of Mead's notion that the self is "a social being which knows itself through the mediation of another," but accuses his theory of narrowness insofar as it depicts the self as living in only one society.⁹³ Last chapter I agreed that this depiction is present in *Mind, Self, and Society* and *The Philosophy of the Present*, the two works of Mead's that Niebuhr quotes, but also noted that the I/me distinction gives Mead a way to deal with a picture of the self living in multiple societies; Niebuhr never discusses or uses this distinction, but there is room for it in his position. In *The Responsible Self*, Niebuhr complains that the notion of the generalized other, like that of Adam Smith's "impartial spectator," is "unanalyzed and rather vague," needing more accurate definition.⁹⁴ Here, Niebuhr betrays a superficial understanding of this notion, and an analysis of his criticism will show that *The Responsible Self* is more deeply indebted to Mead than he admits.

Niebuhr understands the generalized other as the abstraction of "some vague general figure from all the particular individuals who together constitute my society." Such a figure is opposed to isolated and atomic others *and* to "members of a group in whose interactions constancies are present in such a way that the self can interpret present and anticipate future action upon it."⁹⁵ This second opposition is the problem: while Niebuhr differentiates the generalized other from those "constancies of behavior" that arise from social interaction, Mead himself understands the generalized other more as a set of interactive constancies than as an abstract figure, though the phrase itself implies the latter. Recall that the generalized other stands at the end of the development from playing to participating in a game: to play is to take on the roles of particular others in an isolated way, while to participate in a game is to take on all of the roles of one's teammates and competitors in order to successfully fulfill one's own role. Taking on the role of the generalized other *includes* taking on the roles of every particular other within a common social endeavor, but in a way that interrelates and integrates them. Simply put, the generalized other stands precisely for those constancies of behavior and interaction that bind the self to a set of particular others. Thus, to respond to the generalized other is precisely to "respond to the meaning

---

92. Ibid., 71–73.
93. Niebuhr, "The Ego-Alter Dialectic," 353–54.
94. Niebuhr, *The Responsible Self*, 77.
95. Ibid., 77–78.

of present action because such action is a part of a total action, something which means the total action or derives its meaning from that whole," to respond to an other "symbolic in his particularity of something general and constant."[96] Niebuhr's criticism is off the mark because his own position is in agreement with Mead's.

Like the structure of faith relations, the life of responsibility rooted in responsiveness takes a triadic form: self and other interact "always in the presence of a third" distinguishable from the self and other and to which they both respond. As in *Faith on Earth*, Niebuhr illustrates this morally and epistemologically. Just as faith as belief involves a triad of self, other and common object, so knowledge of nature arises "in a continuous dialogue" between "the self, the social companion, and natural events." While the self and other always only interact in response to a common object, the self's response to that object is always mediated by its interaction with its social companion, through which the self has gained those large patterns of interpretation and behavior that allow it to interpret objects and events at all. Moreover, the self's response to natural objects and events is itself responded to by others. Crucially, the self's social inheritance does not entirely determine the self's response to natural events. Admitting the impossibility of the self ever gaining complete exteriority from its social inheritance, Niebuhr nevertheless insists that the self has some independence "to the extent that I have a direct relation to these events and can compare the social reason or the dominant pattern of interpretation with my experiences." Social inheritance under-determines the self, leaving room for "all that is personal and all that is novel, in scientific theory or in poetic vision or artistic reconstruction of natural phenomena."[97] This would be an appropriate place for Niebuhr to utilize Mead's I/me distinction, but oddly he does not.

Niebuhr illustrates the moral triadic form of responsibility with explicit reference to Royce, describing loyalty as "a notion closely related to our notion of responsibility" and positioning Royce against teleological and deontological ethics. Niebuhr interprets loyalty as a continuous interaction between self, other and cause: "In reaction to the present action of his companions, he anticipates the action upon him of that third and does his fitting act, that is, makes a response that fits into this continuing triadic interaction."[98] I stress that this is an interpretation for two reasons. First, the notion of fittingness does not figure in Royce's philosophy of loyalty:

96. Ibid., 77–78.
97. Ibid., 79–81.
98. Ibid., 83–84.

in *The Philosophy of Loyalty*, the stress is on the autonomous self binding itself to a cause so as to gain an objective life-plan. Second, while this notion does show up in Royce's philosophy of Christianity, since atonement is described as a "fitting deed," the fittingness of atonement has more to do with its answerability to the single act of treason than to the totality of the community's life. This is not to argue that Royce's thought cannot bear this interpretation. Indeed, his account in *The Problem of Christianity* of interpretation as a communal process seems especially suited to being understood according to Niebuhr's notion of responsibility: making, receiving and bearing interpretations can all be understood as fitting acts that answer each other, keeping the interpretive process going and the community of interpretation bound together. Once again, though, Niebuhr does not reference this discussion. I have suggested that this is because he might be wary of Royce's focus on the community in *The Problem of Christianity* given his understanding of social faith; I believe this is borne out in what follows.

Niebuhr notes that the third reality in the triad of responsibility has a double character: "On the one hand it is something personal; on the other it contains within itself again a reference to something that transcends it or to which it refers." Niebuhr aligns the distinction between personal and transcendent with that between the community and the community's cause. The idea is that, while a cause defines a community by binding the self to others, that cause must also transcend that community. Just as in the knowledge of nature the self escapes the social determination of others through its direct experience with natural events, so in the life of loyalty the self has a "direct connection" with its cause, which enables it to interpret the actions of its companions within a larger context and "not be subject to the tyranny of the immediate instance and the present moment."[99] Again, the self gains some exteriority from its social inheritance through its direct contact with its community's cause; and again, Mead's I/me distinction becomes an appropriate point of contact. Recall that the "I" and "me" are two aspects of the self: the "me" is the self insofar as it is formed by its community, while the "I" is the self insofar as it reflexively responds to its own communal formation, and thus to its own community. Using Niebuhr's terms, the "me" can be understood as that aspect of the self that confronts natural events and moral causes with its social companions, through the large patterns of interpretation inherited from those social companions. Meanwhile, the "I" can be understood as that aspect of the self that has direct contact with events and causes, enabling it to reflexively respond to its social inheritance.

99. Ibid., 84–86.

Such a construal of the I/me distinction ultimately gives more definition to the "I." Recall that for Mead, the "I" is perennially elusive, always grasped in retrospect as what's responsible for the present state of the "me." For Niebuhr, the "I" must be defined as that aspect of the self that is in direct contact with God, while the "me" would be that aspect that confronts God with social companions, through the religious and theological traditions inherited from those companions. Just as for Mead the "I" is formed by the "me" yet able to creatively respond to it, so for Niebuhr the self's relation to God is mediated by socially inherited traditions yet irreducible to social relations with others; stated in the language of faith, the self's trust in God and loyalty to God's cause is socially mediated yet irreducible to trust in one's communities and loyalty to their causes. This parallel suggests that, if for Mead the novel activity of the "I" is responsible for the enlargement of the self's current community by initiating attachment to others beyond that community, then for Niebuhr the self's individual, unique relation to God must be responsible for its ability to transform its communities. Insofar as the self is related to the radically monotheistic God who is beyond all beings, it is able to struggle against the forms of henotheism that threaten not only its religious, but also its various other, communities. If the parallel with Mead holds, than such transformative struggle will not arrive as an exterior aggression against the self's communities, but rather will arise from within them. For Mead, this occurs through the self making explicit latent and neglected aspects of its social inheritance; for Niebuhr, this occurs through the self responding to God through its response to others, which would include the explication of latent, neglected aspects, if such explication were a fitting response to God. Notice how this construal of the I/me distinction recognizes that the self is formed in many communities, and so contains many "me's," while insisting that the "I" can creatively respond to all of them. This is because the "I" is defined by the self's direct relation to God, who is not only the one beyond the many, but also "the one who acts in and through all things."[100] In this sense, the "I" is that aspect of the self that is attuned to the presence of God in all of its communities and causes.

While my theological reconstruction may give more definition to the "I" than Mead does, I should make it clear that I do not intend to conceive of the "I" as some thing or substance in the self; nor do I intend to re-transcendentalize what Mead attempts to naturalize, though my own position is hardly naturalist. On my account, the "I" is best understood as a responsive relation, specifically, the self's direct relation to God. Because it remains responsive and relational, the "I" cannot be simply God within the self. The

---

100. Niebuhr, *The Meaning of Revelation*, 96.

directness of the self's relation to God through the "I" does not entail a collapse of self and God, but rather the elusiveness of that relation from our relations with finite others. Such a direct relation only obtains so long as God, by God's own divine prerogative and initiative, relates to the self, so that the "I" can be understood as constituted continually by divine providence. In this way, the "I" can never become substantial or self-possessed. This is the theological dimension of the elusiveness of the "I": it is our relation to an ultimately elusive reality. This theo-centric elusiveness corresponds well to the temporal elusiveness of the "I" that Mead articulates. Just as the novelty of the "I" cannot be recognized until it has settled into a "me," so the presence of God often cannot be recognized except in retrospect. Augustine's *Confessions* is an expression of precisely such retrospective recognition, and I would argue that it was only insofar as he was able to act upon, or better, in response to, the divine presence in his life *in particular presents when he was not sure what has happening to him and what he was doing*, that he was eventually able to reach a point from which he could recognize the divine presence. I will pick up the issue of temporal elusiveness in the next chapter. For immediate purposes, it is essential to see that the theological relation that constitutes the "I" also works spatially, enabling the self to transcends its communities.

It is precisely this theological relation that Niebuhr understands himself to be contributing to social theories of the self and the moral life. For Niebuhr, within the very dynamics of the responsible life there resides "a movement of self-judgment and self-guidance which cannot come to rest until it makes its reference to a universal other and a universal community." Human societies are caught up in a "process of self-transcendence" that propels them to recognize "the third beyond each third," God, and ultimately "the total community of being," God's cause. Such a process renders the notion of *universal responsibility*: "a life of responses to actions which is always qualified by our interpretation of these actions as taking place in a *universe*, and by the further understanding that there will be a response to our actions by representatives of universal community." Niebuhr admits that such a "movement toward universal community" is not evident to those who do not hold his monotheistic point of view, though he argues that this movement is present in science while reminding the reader of the work's stance. More significant for our purposes is Niebuhr's claim, "The responsible self is driven as it were by the movement of the social process to respond and be accountable in nothing less than a universal community."[101] This would seem to put the lie to my understanding of the "I" as in direct relation to

---

101. Niebuhr, *The Responsible Self*, 86–89.

God exterior to the self's social relations and inheritance, for here it is a *social* process that drives the self to that community which is God's cause. However, Niebuhr is clear that such a process does not secure the *character* of the universal community. How the universe is construed, whether as ultimately hospitable or hostile, is a function of the character of the "I," which interprets God as ultimately friend or enemy.

Recall that the responsible self is the accountable self, the self who is future-oriented, anticipating the actions of others. For Niebuhr, this means the self is time-full or historical: the self always resides "in the moment," in a present of which the past and future are extensions, as memories, habits, loves and guilt and as expectations, anxieties, anticipations, commitments, hopes and fears that affect the present.[102] The influence of Mead is clear, if not expressed. Present, past, and future have no substantial reality: the present emerges moment by moment, rendering the past and future as functions of it. For Mead, this view of time is metaphysical, tied to a vision of the world as composed of events rather than substantial entities. For Niebuhr, this view of time is existential, tied to a vision of the self as responsive and responsible. Time-full existence is "existence in encounter, in challenge and in response." Here, existence in time is identical with existence with others: "To be in the present is to be in *compresence* with what is not myself." This is most significant when the others we encounter are *foreign* others, for "we are most aware of our existence in the moment, in the now, when we are radically acted upon by something from without," by "those others or those actions that have not been in our past, at least not in the way they now are." In other words, time-full existence with others is most keenly felt, not in the routines of our life when we are responsive to and responsible for "familiar others and well-known actions," but rather "on the D-days of our personal and social life," when "we are *compresent* with a not-ourself in threatening or promising form."[103] While Mead's self is oriented to a future emerging by way of the self's reconstructive activity, Niebuhr's responsible self is oriented to an other who is ultimately death-dealing or life-giving, and so who acts within a "universal teleology" of entombment or resurrection.[104]

Just as the self's sociality renders a theological reference through the triad of responsibility, so the self's time-fullness renders such a reference through compresence. According to Niebuhr, "The self that knows itself in encounter with others, find itself to be absolutely dependent in its existence, completely contingent, inexplicably present in its here-ness and now-ness."

---

102. Ibid., 90–93.
103. Ibid., 94.
104. Ibid., 143.

Time-full existence with others, historicity, discloses our absolute dependence. The fact that we exist in this moment makes us aware of a "radical deed" that constitutes our very selves, but which is not identical with any specific actions that constitute particular elements of our existence. This radical deed or action is that "by which I am and by which I am present with *this* body, *this* mind, *this* emotional equipment, *this* religion."[105] This radical act constitutes our historical particular existence, but *not* our own particular*ities*: my mother may be responsible for my proclivity to drink coffee at night, but some radical other is responsible for my being existentially positioned so as to learn this habit from this parent. Moreover, this radical action is providential, "not one by which I was thrown into existence at some past time to maintain myself thereafter by my own power," but rather "the action whereby I am *now*."[106] It is precisely this experience of radical action that is the self's direct connection to God. God is the radical other whose creative and providential action is the radical action that constitutes us. Niebuhr explains that the experience of God's radical action "is unique, though it is repeated by millions of selves."[107] That it is unique emphasizes the irreducibility of this experience to our experience of finite others; that it is repeatable highlights its universality. Though the experience of radical action is "intensely personal," it is "not solipsistic," for God the radical actor acts in and through all things.[108]

Recall that essential to responsibility is interpretation. The self does not merely react to actions that impinge on it, but hermeneutically responds to them as significant. Radical action fits into this dynamic, if in a special way: the self interprets this radical action, thus qualifying its responses to all finite actions. The "chief ingredient" of this "primordial interpretation" is faith understood as "the attitude of the self in its existence toward all the existences that surround it, as beings to be relied upon or to be suspected." Such faith is "fundamentally trust or distrust in being itself," or for monotheists, trust or distrust of God understood as "the power by which I am and we are."[109] This marks an important shift in emphasis for Niebuhr. In *Radical Monotheism*, the question of faith regards how to connect being and value: if being and value are interpreted as coextensive, than our trust and loyalty should be oriented to the universal community of being and not merely to our own closed societies and private interests. In *The Responsible*

---

105. Ibid., 109–12; emphasis mine.
106. Ibid., 114; emphasis mine.
107. Ibid., 115.
108. Ibid., 112; Niebuhr, *The Meaning of Revelation*, 96.
109. Niebuhr, *The Responsible Self*, 118–20.

Self, the question of faith regards how to connect power and value: if power and value are interpreted as coextensive, than our comportment towards those finite beings who wield some form of power over us to the extent that their actions may and often do impinge on us, should be fundamentally trustful. In other words, if the God whose power creates, sustains and works through all beings is interpreted as good, as friend rather than enemy, than we have reason to trust those finite beings whose power impinges on us. Conversely, if such a God is interpreted as our evil enemy, than relations to finite beings become motivated by suspicion.[110] As we will see, it is precisely such fundamental trust or distrust that grounds our comportment toward foreign others as ultimately transformative or defensive.

Direct experience and interpretation of God's radical action upon us provide the means for the self to gain unity amid the diverse relations it has with others exercising power over it. Recall that Niebuhr is vexed by Mead's exposition of the I/me distinction because it seems to presume that the self emerges in only one society. Once we recognize that the self participates in "many systems of interpretation and response" and is subject to manifold powers, the question arises how the self maintains integrity. For Niebuhr, the self's unity is "the counterpart of a unity that lies beyond, yet expresses itself in, all the manifold systems of actions upon it." The self's unity is secured by the unity of God's radical action: "I am one within myself as I encounter the One in all that acts upon me."[111] To use Mead's terms through Niebuhr, the self gains unity amid the many "me's" that socially have formed and continue to form it through the response of the "I" who is attuned to God. Insofar as it is the self as "I," directly related to God, that is responding to others and not merely the self as the function of one of its "me's," its response to diverse others can be unified. The self accomplishes this by ensuring that its response to every finite action "takes the form of response to the One that is active in it."[112] In other words, the responsible self interprets every finite action upon it as an instance of God's radical action. This provides the ultimate answer to the primary question of an ethics of the fitting: what is always going on is that "God is acting in all actions upon you." The imperative follows from this indicative: "So respond to all actions upon you as to respond to his action."[113] The responsible self interprets every finite action upon it as an exercise of God's power and so responds to it, not only

---

110. For a discussion of power and value in Niebuhr's theology before *The Responsible Self*, see Frei, "Theology of H. Richard Niebuhr," 69, 95–96.

111. Niebuhr, *The Responsible Self*, 122.

112. Ibid., 123.

113. Ibid., 126.

as an exercise of finite power, but *sub specie aeternitatis* as an exercise of divine power.

The exposition so far has been mostly descriptive, characterizing the moral life through the notion of responsibility. The responsible self has direct experience of a God beyond, but radically acting through, all finite actions and communities, through which the self gains some independence from its diverse social inheritances, and the interpretation of which allows the self to qualify and unify its hermeneutical responses to diverse others. This fundamental interpretation hinges on the relationship between power and value: we either trust or distrust in God as one exercising divine power for good or evil. Since the quality of human life depends on the nature of this interpretation, it becomes essential to evaluate these interpretations. For Niebuhr, this task is made easier by the pervasiveness of distrust: "The natural mind is enmity to God; or to our natural mind the One intention in all intentions is animosity." Following his discussion in *Faith on Earth*, Niebuhr asserts that fundamental distrust is humanity's natural comportment toward God, rendering three specific ways of response: ignoring, fighting, appeasing.[114] But while in *Faith on Earth* this is understood to *result* from the occurrence of tragedy that destroys our inchoate sense of promise and expectation of life, in *The Responsible Self* natural distrust serves as the *explanation* for the pluralistic nature of human life. The human condition is "one of internal division and conflict" because we are "surrounded by many agencies, many systems of actions upon the self; these are diverse from each other, and to their actions the self makes unreconciled, ununified responses." Such agencies appear impersonal and "exercise dominion over us at least in this sense that we adjust our actions to them, do what fits into their action."[115] In Mead's terms, this suggests that the self's condition is one of dispersal among its various "me's" rather than groundedness in its "I." However, Niebuhr is clear that such unreconciled dispersal is rendered by our natural, fundamental distrust, and so precisely by the "I," though the "I" attuned to God interpreted as enemy.

Such a theological construal of the I/me distinction prevents us from reducing it to some moral distinction such as good/bad or good/evil aspects of the self. Niebuhr would agree with Mead that the "I," insofar as it is the self in direct contact with God, is the site of the self's greatest value and, as we will see, of the self's creativity. For Niebuhr though, this is because only through the "I" does the self gain access to its being-valued by God. Moreover, the self gains access to this only through the interpretation of

114. Ibid., 140–41.
115. Ibid., 137–39.

God rendered by the "I": if God is interpreted as friend, the self understands itself to be valued; if God is interpreted as enemy, the self understands itself to be devalued. In this case, the "I" is just as responsible for the perversion of faith and the self as it is for the reconstruction of faith and the self. The "I" is the site of the self's greatest value only insofar as it is also the site of it's greatest disvalue. Regarding the "me," neither Niebuhr nor Mead would argue that no value attaches to it; for both, social relations within finite communities are essential to the emergence and sustenance of the self. The question concerning the "me," or our various "me's," is the self's attitude toward them: should we simply fit ourselves into our various social endeavors and reproduce them, or should we exploit our reflexivity upon such endeavors to critique and improve them? Recall that Mead admits that there is no *mechanical* necessity that the "I" will improve (enlarge, integrate) its communities. At the same time, since he gives no account of how the "I" could fail at this, his position exudes a certain confidence in the moral possibilities of the "I" to improve its "me's." For Niebuhr, the "I" is more likely to reify its "me's" than to expose them to criticism and improvement. Reflexivity on our social inheritances is the condition, not only for criticizing them, but also for defending them against others.

Niebuhr explains the consequences of interpreting God as the enemy: "Hence the color of our lives is anxiety, and self-preservation is our first law. Hence we divide our world into the good and evil, into friends who will assist us to maintain ourselves awhile and foes intent on our reduction to beings of no significance or to nothingness."[116] Natural distrust drains the world of the various shades of gray that give it texture, leaving it subject to the stark opposition of frozen light and seemingly endless darkness. Natural distrust turns our ethics into "defense ethics," "ethics of survival," "ethics of self-maintenance against threatening power" that pervades our lives as "a movement or a law in the interaction of all things," guaranteeing only death. Such an ethics requires us to respond to all beings that act upon us as "either good or evil," and this distinction is made according to "the way they support or deny our life, whether this be our physical or spiritual or social existence." The result of this fixation on self-preservation is the isolation of humans "from each other, individual by individual, group by group."[117]

Niebuhr does not explicitly connect this discussion to that of the three types of faith in *Radical Monotheism*, a similar lack as in *Faith on Earth*; but again, connections can be made. If we interpret God as the enemy such that the threat of death saturates the horizon of our lives, we are forced to

---

116. Ibid., 140–41.
117. Ibid., 98–100.

turn to our private interests and memberships in finite societies to guarantee our worth and continued existence, that is, to become polytheists and henotheists. Niebuhr refers to this state as "polytheism," explaining that our isolated responsibilities to the various closed societies in our life mean irresponsibility to both God and self.[118] Here, Niebuhr aligns what he previously holds apart: responsibility-analysis, which insists on the social nature of the self, discloses that polytheism takes a henotheistic form inasmuch as the self trusts in and is loyal to *many* finite societies. Insofar as our family, church, profession and nation are understood to be our only life supports, we are loyal to them and will defend them against all criticism. Insofar as these finite societies appear to fail to support our life, we turn to other family members, churches, professions, hobbies, etc. We become henotheistic polytheists. By smuggling henotheism into the explicitly used term *polytheism*, Niebuhr foregrounds the irony of natural distrust. Interpreting the power behind all agencies that impinge on us as unified, as the action of one agent, seems to provide the means to a unified response to those agencies. Yet, when that power is interpreted as being exercised by an enemy, our response to all agencies necessarily fractures: though our responses are made according to a single evaluative framework, good/evil or friend/enemy, the responses themselves shift and are not integrated with each other. When the "I" is attuned to God as enemy, its responses to its various "me's" will split and shift. This suggests that we can achieve *true* unity, that the "I" can gain a unified response to its various "me's," only by interpreting God as friend, as good. Thus, the truly responsible life is radically monotheistic.

A fundamental attunement to God does not guarantee radically monotheistic responsibility. It should come as no surprise that the latter is achieved by transforming our natural fundamental attunement to God; the "I" must change its attunement to God from distrust to trust. Fittingly, Niebuhr first addresses this possibility within the context of the self's time-fullness, the same context in which he first addresses our being-toward-death rendered by natural distrust. The possibility of transforming our fundamental interpretation of God as enemy turns on the possibility of freedom. For Niebuhr, freedom concerns "the self's ability in its present to change its past and future and to achieve or receive a new understanding of its ultimate historical context," the result of which is "reinterpretation of present action upon the self" and "response that fits into another lifetime and another history." Niebuhr notes two ways freedom has been understood. The first way is *anti-traditionalism*, the method of radical doubt traceable back to Descartes. The point of this is to abandon the past and

---

118. Ibid., 137–38.

start afresh in the present.[119] Niebuhr's Mead-indebted account of time does not permit him to accept this method. The past can only be abandoned in favor of the present (and future) if each tense is neatly separable from the rest. For Mead and Niebuhr though, the tenses cannot be substantially fixed: past and future are extensions or functions of, and so included within, the present, which continually passing. On this view, there can be no abandonment of the past without abandoning the present and future.

The second way to understand freedom is *reinterpretation*. This method "recalls, accepts, understands, and reorganizes the past," or to use Mead's term, which Niebuhr uses himself here and elsewhere, *reconstructs* the past in the light of the present. Again, the influence of Mead is clear, but implicit. Niebuhr turns Mead's descriptive account of the temporality and sociality of the self into a normative account of freedom: the point of reconstructive reinterpretation of the past is to guide our present responses in a new way. Given the larger context of this discussion, the interpretation of God as enemy or friend, it is not surprising that Niebuhr uses the Civil War as an example. The reinterpretation of past animosities provides the possibility of guiding present interaction in a way that does not simply recapitulate these animosities, but rather begins to heal them. As I expand on below, this parallels Royce's view of atonement, in which a past treason is interpreted in the present as the condition for a better future for the community. At the same time, Niebuhr is following Mead and taking a more sociological approach: what needs to be reinterpreted is not simply a past act, but rather an entire social inheritance. Reinterpretation *frees* us to the extent that it liberates us from the *domination* of "inherited images" and "merely customary symbols and emotions," thereby enabling us to make novel responses in the present.[120]

Such reinterpretation is of the future as well. Niebuhr notes two aspects of this that are significant to his position. First, we can revise the "constancies in our predictions," a somewhat anemic way of saying we can revise our expectations. This is connected to the reinterpretation of our social inheritances, insofar as these embody expectations in their images and symbols: the North and South expect each other to behave in a particular way and act accordingly, and so will act differently if they expect different behavior. Second, we can "identify ourselves with different groups." Niebuhr seems to mean *larger* groups, since he claims, "[T]he future lengthens at the same time that the society broadens."[121] The point here is that reinterpretation

---

119. Ibid., 101–2.
120. Ibid., 102–3.
121. Ibid., 104.

can break open our fixation on self-preservation: to identify with more and different others is to make ourselves responsible to those who are not immediately supportive of our own selves. By reinterpretation, we become responsible to a future and community that includes but exceeds us.

Crucially, all of these reconstructive reinterpretations will not radically alter our socially inherited patterns of interpretation and response unless "our sense of the ultimate context" is reinterpreted as well.[122] Recall that interpreting God as enemy results in our distinguishing others as either good or evil, life-supporting or death-dealing. This evaluative framework permits the reinterpretation of specific others from hostile to friendly, and so allows for some expansion of one's community. Two factions of a single community may reinterpret their shared history of animosity so as to face the future as allies, but do so under the threat of an aggressive foreign community. In this case, natural distrust remains intact; the line between friend and enemy has simply shifted. Radical reinterpretation, the conversion from natural distrust to trust, consists in the reinterpretation of "our mythology of death into a history of life," redefining "what is fitting response in a lifetime and a history surrounded by eternal life, as well as by the universal society of being."[123] Such reinterpretation means we come to interpret and respond to all action upon us as occurring in a universal teleology of resurrection rather than entombment; all exercises of power that impinge on the self come to be interpreted and responded to as manifestations of God's life-giving power. The result is that the hostility and foreignness of others can no longer serve as reasons to deny or neglect relations with them, for self-preservation ceases to serve as the first principle of the moral life. Instead, we become responsive and responsible to the future of being itself, the divine cause that runs over any and all barriers—domestic, political, national, religious, etc.—we place between ourselves and others.

Reinterpretation is the *how* of transformation. We are able to transform our pluralistic social faith into radically monotheistic faith, our natural faith into Christian faith, because we are able to reinterpret not only specific others and their actions, but also the ultimate context of all existence. The life of radically monotheistic, Christian faith is the life of universal responsibility. Given the Christian perspective of *The Responsible Self*, it is no surprise that such reinterpretation is understood to come into the world through the "life, death, resurrection, and reign in power" of Jesus Christ.[124] Since Christology is scant in *The Responsible Self* proper, the editor added supple-

---

122. Ibid., 105.
123. Ibid., 106.
124. Ibid., 143.

mental material that is explicitly christological. Here, Niebuhr understands Jesus Christ to be a symbolic form, employed by Christians "as an a priori, an image, a scheme or pattern in the mind which gives form and meaning to their experience."[125] Jesus Christ the symbolic form can be distinguished from Jesus Christ the historical figure. The former is normative, that by which the self "guides and forms itself in its actions and sufferings," while the latter is descriptive. At the same time, there is no dichotomy between the two: history becomes symbolic once it is used to guide the present and future.[126] What is at stake is the same as in *Faith on Earth*: Jesus Christ must be located in the present if he is to guide and form our faith. In *Faith on Earth*, Niebuhr achieves this by confessing that the Christ of faith is the *risen* Christ. Here, he achieves it by arguing that the Christ of faith is the *symbolic* Christ. This is a shift in emphasis, but not necessarily in christological content. To say that the resurrection validates Jesus Christ's trust and loyalty so that we respond to them in the present, is precisely to say that the resurrection transforms Jesus Christ the historical figure into a symbolic form that we use in the present. To emphasize symbolic-ness over risen-ness is to fit the work of Jesus Christ in the context of responsibility: Christ's interpretation of the context of all existence enables our re-interpretation of that context as life-giving rather than death-dealing.

This relationship between Jesus Christ as historical figure and as symbolic form is a construal of Christ's double character: "In him man is directed toward God; in him also God is directed toward man."[127] As an historical figure he exemplifies the ethics of universal responsibility: "he interprets all actions upon him as signs of the divine action of creation, government, and salvation and so responds to them as to respond to divine action."[128] In this way, Christ is humanity directed toward God. Since the ethics of responsibility can be found in Jewish ethics—most notably, the Joseph story—and Stoicism, it does not distinguish Christianity from other religions and philosophies. Christianity is distinguished because Christ is also God directed toward humanity: Christ is not only an example for us of fundamental trust, but rather "accomplishes" that trust *within* us, "actualizing" us as children of God. Niebuhr is intentionally silent on *how* Christ does this, recognizing it demands a theory of atonement without offering

125. For a discussion of the theme of Jesus Christ as a symbolic form that utilizes unpublished material from student notes, see Keiser, *Roots of Relational Ethics*, chapter 6.

126. Niebuhr, *The Responsible Self*, 154–56.

127. Ibid., 163. For Jesus Christ as double mediator, see Niebuhr, *Christ and Culture*, 28–29, and Frei, "Theology of H. Richard Niebuhr," 108–16.

128. Niebuhr, *The Responsible Self*, 167.

one.[129] What is more important for his position in *The Responsible Self* is that the movement from God to humanity accomplished in Christ is the actualization of the ethics of responsibility historically exemplified in his life, just as in *Faith on Earth* the resurrection validated and initiated Christ's own faith for and in our lives. If Christ's humanity consists in his moral exemplarity, his divinity includes the endorsement and maintenance of that example in us. Jesus Christ transforms our faith by providing the example and the power to reinterpret the ultimate context of existence.

Faith as trust, the radical interpretation of God as friend and of the radical action upon us as ultimately life-giving, renders the radical monotheistic affirmation: whatever is, is good. Though Niebuhr shifts his emphasis throughout this work on the coincidence of power and value, in the end this coincidence grounds that of being and value: the goodness of all beings derives from the goodness of God whose power creates, sustains and redeems them. Niebuhr is clear that, according to trust, God is the standard of goodness, so that what is good for God *is* what is good for universal being. In Royce's terms, oddly absent as applied to God in *The Responsible Self*, this is simply to say that universal being is God's cause. The idea that divine power grounds the relation between God and being poses a challenge. The responsible self affirms, "there is no evil in the city but the Lord has done it; no crucifixion but the One has crucified." The naturally distrustful responsible self affirms that such evil and crucifixion is evil if befalling itself, but good if befalling its enemies. The radically trustful responsible self must affirm that such evil and crucifixion is good *tout court*, and good for it because good for God.[130] While this might seem to support a form of quietism in the face of evil and suffering, Niebuhr insists that the perspective of trustful responsibility is not fatalistic: "The God and Father of our Lord Jesus Christ is the loving dynamic One, *who does new things*, whose relation to his world is more like that of father to his children than like that of the maker to his manufactures."[131] On this view, evil and suffering are parts of God's *novel* activity, and inasmuch as our trust in that activity evokes our loyalty to it, than our own novel activity is a more appropriate response than mute acquiescence.

Royce's notion of atonement fits well in this context, but the context is ultimately indebted to Mead. To passively accept treason is to accept fracture as the fate of one's community. Instead, loyalty demands that we interpret

---

129. Ibid., 175–77. For discussion of the atonement, or lack of it, in Niebuhr's thought, see Frei, "Theology of H. Richard Niebuhr," 96–97, and Godsey, *Promise*, 54.

130. Niebuhr, *The Responsible Self*, 125.

131. Ibid., 173; emphasis mine.

this act of treason as the condition for the community's reconstruction and improvement. While Niebuhr does not refer to this discussion, it certainly aligns with what the trustful responsible self would do: by interpreting treason as a manifestation of God's good, novel, life-affirming activity, the self would be particularly motivated to respond in such a way as to reconstruct and improve its community. For Royce, such atoning interpretation is grounded in loyalty. For Niebuhr, this would be grounded in trust, understood as our hermeneutical comportment toward the world and the God who creates, sustains and redeems it. I discussed above how this difference influences Niebuhr's reception of Royce's philosophy of loyalty, chastening its voluntarism by emphasizing its responsive character and its dependence on trust. I also argued that this is due to Niebuhr's reception of Mead. In *Faith on Earth*, Niebuhr notes that trust is primary to and the ground of loyalty within the social act of faith. In *The Responsible Self*, his discussion of faith refers exclusively to trust; while he uses loyalty to illustrate the triad of responsibility, faith is no longer discussed as the combination of trust and loyalty. In this way, the turn to responsibility involves even closer adherence to Mead than to Royce.

For the Royce of *The Problem of Christianity*, the problem of evil regards treason, particular acts that destroy the community; the solution involves interpreting these acts in a way that recreates the community. For Niebuhr, the problem of evil regards our socially inherited mythology of death that compels us to interpret all action upon us as expressive of a hostile God; the solution involves reinterpreting that mythology into a story of life before a good God. Niebuhr states, "salvation now appears to us as deliverance from that deep distrust of the One in all the many that causes us to interpret everything that happens to us as issuing ultimately from animosity or as happening in the realm of destruction. Redemption appears as the liberty to interpret in trust all that happens as contained within the domain of life, that destroys only to re-establish and renew."[132] Such redemption does not result in a finished state, but rather initiates *metanoia*, "a great relearning which is never completed" in our lifetime.[133] In other words, redemption initiates the ceaseless reconstruction of our social inheritances so that we may increasingly respond to all action upon us in trust rather than distrust. Mead is more useful here given his analysis of how the self is in constant reflexive and reconstructive interaction with its social endeavors, an analysis that focuses on how the self negotiates large-scale social processes to which it is subject and dependant rather than on how it responds to acts that

---

132. Ibid., 142.
133. Ibid., 176.

threaten its chosen community. Because redemption in Royce responds to particular acts rather than to social inheritances, he does not discern that treason may be a form of life. For Niebuhr, pluralistic social faith is the animating attitude of forms of life that are treasonous because they deny the goodness of God by interpreting God as hostile; radical faith is the ceaseless transformation of such natural faith, the constant reinterpretation of God as friend rather than enemy. Niebuhr follows Mead's analysis in insisting that any community that aspires to embody radical monotheism and fundamental trust is dependent on while transformative of the primary social inheritances of its members; in other words, such a community is the reconstruction of other communities.

Part of the problem is Royce's social analysis. Recall that, for him, society is the site of social conflict that evokes self-consciousness and social and moral disciplines that provoke self-assertion, while community is the site of language, custom, religion, etc. Community is the redemption of the self from the original sin of social training, while atonement is the redemption of the community from the voluntary sin of treason. Oddly, this analysis divorces discipline from language, custom and religion, making it appear as though these communal elements cannot be disciplinary tools used to quash self-expression and self-assertion. This occludes the possibility that the self may need to be saved from the community, a possibility to which Niebuhr is keenly sensitive. Royce may respond that the redemption of the self from social training in community is recognition of this, that whereas Niebuhr discusses the transformation of pluralistic social faith by radical faith, Royce discusses the salvation of the self from society by the community. However, given Royce's characterization of society and community, he cannot see that it is precisely the social mind of a community with its language, customs, holidays, festivals, religions, and so on that can morally mal-form the self. Instead of addressing the possibility of a deformed community, a community that may save selves from their lost state only to deform them in turn, Royce only addresses the possibility of treason against a genuine community. In this way, he discusses treason as a kind of act rather than as a form of life.

Niebuhr's use of faith to analyze not only trust in God as the good power that sustains all being, but also the trust in finite societies and social endeavors that results from distrust in God as the evil power that destroys, allows him to see the perversion of the human self as the perversion of faith rather than its absence. Moreover, since forms of faith come with attendant communities, perverted forms of faith place us in perverted communities. Simply put, on Niebuhr's analysis, community itself cannot save us because faith unqualified cannot save us; what matters is the *character* of faith and its attendant community. Redemption lies in the ceaseless qualification of our perverted faiths by radical faith, and so in the ceaseless reconstruction of our perverted communities and their social inheritances. Because these communities are perverted precisely by distrust in God that results in the evaluation of beings as either good or evil, such communities will often be in conflict with each other. Part of the challenge of radical faith is learning to respond to those from other finite societies who attack our own finite societies as critical members of the universal community of being, rather than as hostile aggressors, as beings valued by God, and so valuable to all who trust in that God, rather than as enemies who can be dismissed or destroyed. The notion of treason is limited to the extent it suggests that the concern of redemption is the problem of internal enemies and not external enemies as well. The idea of radical faith is the idea that our responses to external enemies can be transformed from self-defensiveness to openness to other's criticism and correction because we are all in the hands of a life-affirming God. In other words, radical faith involves openness to external disruption, and this, I would argue, is the complementary side of radical faith's promotion of a sort of creativity that is necessarily disruptive, and only as such potentially reparative. I complete this chapter by articulating this sort of creativity and its relation to radical faith.

LOCATING CREATIVITY IN NIEBUHR'S THOUGHT: THE RADICAL CREATIVITY OF RADICAL FAITH

One question crucial to my argument remains: where can we locate individual creativity in Niebuhr if he contextualizes loyalty in, and eventually replaces it by, trust in his account of faith? If faith becomes solely trust, and if trust is understood as passive, individual creativity in the form of loyalty becomes separated from faith, and so separated from what constitutes us as selves. This problem is exacerbated by my theological interpretation of Mead's I/me distinction in which the "I" is construed as our direct access, and the "me" is construed as our socially mediated access, to God. Insofar as this interpretation understands direct access to be one of trust or distrust, it would seem to prevent the "I" from being the self's center of *active, novel* response, and so to drain it of creativity. One way to approach this problem is to see how both Niebuhr's and Mead's positions are transformed in interaction with other.

First, it is crucial that the I/me distinction is not mapped onto some active/passive distinction, something that Mead may seem to suggest by characterizing the "I" as active and novel. If the I/me distinction is understood as that between direct access and socially mediated access to God (or any other reality), than the distinction is a matter of *how* the self responds, not whether or not it is responsive. Thus, both the "I" and "me" can be understood as having active and passive aspects. The passive aspect of the "me" would be that aspect of the self that receives social inheritances, while the active aspect of the "me" would be the aspect that takes on its social inheritances and the various roles within them. This means that creativity can be found *within* social endeavors, not just insofar as the self escapes from them; position players in baseball can take on their roles in unique ways without transcending the game of baseball. Mead himself suggests this when, as noted last chapter, he claims that the self occupies a unique position within any social endeavor, and so reflects that endeavor uniquely; this unique position is *not* equated with the "I." This understanding of the "me" also entails that individual creativity does not depend on complete socialization, on entire "me's" to which to respond, but rather that it occurs from the beginning of socialization: we all make a creative contribution to our own socialization.

The passive aspect of the "I" would be that aspect of the self that experiences something beyond its social inheritances. Niebuhr's examples are nature and God, but we might include other social inheritances than our own, as well as any phenomena that appears or acts contrary to what our own social inheritances claim about them. The active aspect of the "I" would be that aspect of the self that responds to such phenomena. Now if trust or distrust are the self's fundamental response to God, then trust can longer be understood as the passive aspect of faith, if by that is meant the non-active aspect. Trust must now be understood as active, which is why Niebuhr aligns trust with the interpretation, rather than just the experience, of God as friend and God's world as hospitable. At the same time, loyalty can remain an intrinsic aspect of faith as that aspect of the self that is responsible for actions that embody and express trust's interpretation of God and God's world. Such an activist understanding of faith is not in danger of replacing human for divine agency because the activity of faith, both as fundamental interpretation and loyal deed, is responsive to prior divine action. The individual creativity embodied and expressed in such faith would be transformative of the self's social inheritances in light of its experience and interpretation of God. However, this would occur only insofar as that faith is trust, not distrust. Insofar as our faith in God is distrust, the self, in its endeavor to preserve itself in the face of others interpreted as hostile, would reify those of its social inheritances that support its own existence and defend them against criticism and correction. The result would be pluralistic social faith, and the self could only exercise creativity *within* its social inheritances, not *upon* them.

I will refer to the creativity that is exercised within social inheritances and supported by pluralistic social faith as *social creativity*, and the creativity that is exercised upon social inheritances and supported by radical monotheistic faith as *radical creativity*. This distinction concedes that human creativity is not restricted to those exercises of human agency that respond to God's redemptive action. If the human self is fallen and warped, its creative agency is more likely to express rejection of divine action and the consequent rejection of many of God's creatures. In short, humans can be creative in their destructiveness. At the same time, the distinction between social and radical creativity is intended to parallel that between social and radical faith. Just as radical faith is the ideal and hope of human faith, expressed as a transformation of social faith, so radical creativity is the ideal and hope of human creativity, and can only be exercised as a transformation of social creativity. Just as radical faith is *metanoia*, the repentant conversion of our natural distrust in God and faith in our finite social inheritances, so radical creativity is the repentant conversion of our social creativity away from self-defense and other-destruction and toward the sustenance of all creaturely life. In the language of responsibility, radical creativity is the reconstruction of our exercise of power from death-dealing to life-affirming. Such creativity will involve the transformation of our social inheritances, because these depend on social creativity to subsist. The point of radical creativity is to open up these creative reserves and orient them toward the redemption of being itself.

Because social faith and the social creativity it promotes are oriented toward the self-defense of its supporting community, the radical creativity that transforms communal life by transforming its sustaining social creativity must take the form of disruption rather than reparation. To take up Mead's language, the radically social genius must manifest as the enemy of her community: precisely because the genius imagines a future for her community that is not obviously presently accessible, not obviously supportive of its current form, her community's social faith will compel it to discern her as threat rather than opportunity. Of course, we will find the same tension here that we found in Mead, though theologically construed. Radical faith, which is a faith in God despite the failures of our human communities, would seem to demand that radical creativity not be experienced and interpreted as a threatening disruption, but rather as a welcome reminder that the destiny of created life is beyond our finite imagining. Thus, radical faith would seem to promote a sort of creativity that builds communities that subsist by remaining open to transformation rather then by controlling their borders, such that radical creativity would no longer have to take the form of disruption, but would rather appear as the reparation of the universal community of being. However, the reality of sin, of natural faith as radical distrust, ensures that radical creativity will always be disruptive to some degree. Self-defensive communities, precisely by defending themselves against outsiders, necessarily prevent themselves from participating in some wider community of created being. Radical creativity, whose end is the reparative building-up of such a universal community in the face of sin, will necessarily arrive as disruption.

Recall that for Mead, the "I" can only be grasped in retrospect, insofar as we recognize that our current "me" has changed. Radical creativity should be understood in the same way: it can only be recognized insofar as we discern that our exercises of social creativity have become transformed, serving not only our own finite societies, but the universal community of being as well. This ensures that radical creativity will remain an ideal and hope to be achieved and never become some ability or skill we possess. If radical creativity is a form of *metanoia*, it requires constantly repenting of the inevitable narrowness of our social creativity. Recall the role that grief plays in Royce's notion of 'loyalty training': in the face of the historical failure of our cause, grief spurs us on to the active recovery of what has been lost so that our loyalty remains intact. Here, repentance takes the place of grief as the spur to action, forcing us to discern in all of our exercises of individual creativity traces of distrust and self-defense so that we never become satisfied with what we do achieve, and so rendering radical creativity the perennial goal. Because these traces of distrust and self-defense can always be discerned, the radical transformation of our social creativity will always appear as free gift rather than as merited accomplishment. This is important to note, since the emphasis on human creativity may seem to make this position Pelagian. The elusiveness of the "I" in Mead is being theologically construed here as an index of the free gift character of radical creativity: radical creativity is graced human creativity. This preserves the primacy of divine action to human action and so discloses the contingency of human creativity, while grounding *metanoia* and so motivating the renewal of human effort rather than its abdication.

The tension between grace and human effort, between divine and human activity, and ultimately between divine providence and redemption, and human moral formation, has a long and varied history in Christian moral thought. While exhaustively discussing these debates is beyond the scope of my argument, it is important to notice that Niebuhr's position, as well as the theological understanding of creativity being offered here, insists that divine action and human effort are not mutually exclusive. For Niebuhr, God's creative, providential and redemptive activity is pervasive, working in and through all finite creatures and actions. Nevertheless, we are not automatons; God is construed along personal categories, addressing us as persons in and through all things and demanding our personal, free response.[134] The freedom that is granted through Jesus Christ is, like radical creativity, not some fixed skill or ability that we come to possess and exercise at will, but rather the initiation of our *metanoia*, "the never-ending pilgrim's progress of the reasoning Christian heart."[135] Such freedom is God's permission to be divinely reformed and reconstructed by progressively reinterpreting God's creation as hospitable rather than toxic in light of Christ's example and power, but *we* must do the work of reinterpretation, *we* must accept that permission and use it, not bury it and wait for such transformation to happen magically on its own.[136] As the next chapter will articulate, the waiting that attends Christian freedom is the waiting that regards the future of our presently creative actions: in retrospect, will such actions appear as truly transformative, or just a new way to shore up old defenses? That is, will they be actions we need to repent of, or actions to thank God for? In either case, the fitting response is new efforts of creativity, whether making our repentance fruitful, or keeping our creative achievements from solidifying into the sort of thing that we feel the need to defend. Again, Niebuhr's point in insisting that the Christ of faith is risen and symbolic is to insist that he is a person addressing us in the present and expecting a free, personal response. To use Mead's language, there is only a moral, and no mechanical, necessity that we reconstruct our lives according to Christ's.

CONCLUSION

Any understanding of the moral formation of communities based on Niebuhr's notion of radical faith must include the development of capacities for radical creativity, and such capacities, this chapter has argued, are irreducibly individual because grounded in the self's direct relation to God. Just as radical faith presupposes social faith, and radical creativity presupposes social creativity, so the development of these irreducibly individual capacities presupposes the socialization of these individual selves. However, Niebuhr enables us to see that to stop at socialization as the goal of moral formation is to stop short of radical faith and creativity, and so to be stuck in a teleology of entombment, seeing death and hostility everywhere and responding by shoring up the defenses of one's finite communities.

---

134. See Niebuhr, *The Meaning of Revelation*, 80–81.

135. Ibid., 72.

136. Godsey (*Promise*, 111) remarks that Niebuhr's "emphasis on fidelity or loyalty catches up the notion of active discipleship and places it squarely with an interpersonal understanding of faith." Niebuhr "makes it absolutely clear that the Christian is called in his faith not simply to enjoy God but also to serve him."

Communities whose moral formation stops at socialization are self-defensive, moral formation itself serving as a tactic of self-defense. On the other hand, communities whose moral formation leaves them open to the development of individual capacities beyond socialization, leave themselves open to reconstruction, to the re-orientation of their moral concern away from themselves and towards the universal community of being through the radical faith and creativity of their individual members. Christian communities achieve this through the present exemplarity of Christ, relation to whom leads individuals to that direct relation with God that grounds radical faith and releases radical creativity. Here, the emphasis is on Christ as an exemplar for individuals in community, not on Christ as exemplar for communities. We might say, the emphasis is on *how* Christ is political, not *what* his politics are, for Christ is understood more as transformer than founder. Christian communities whose final goal is growing and sustaining membership, or whose engagement with God's wider community is confined to the expression of communal norms, are likely to approach Christ as communal exemplar, as the giver of some particular social inheritance; in this way, Christo-centrism becomes ecclesia-centrism, and moral formation for such communities must stop short at socialization. Niebuhr offers an alternative to this, and the task of the next chapter is to articulate how this alternative might work. To this task we now turn.

— 5 —

The Transformation of Faith, to Transform Faith

Locating Radical Creativity through Christ

To this point, the self's *direct* relation to God has been a place holder for a divine-human relation that is understood to transcend, and so fund creative and critical reflections upon, *socially mediated* relations to God and the world. This dynamic was articulated through a theological reconstruction of Mead's account of the self, whereby these two relations (direct and socially mediated) align with the two aspects of the self, the "I" and the "me." The self's capacity to creatively respond to those social inheritances that have formed and continue to form it—the capacity of the "I" to respond to the "me"—is grounded in the self's direct relation to God. The self's relation to its social inheritances is filtered through its interpretive response to God. For Niebuhr, this interpretive response is a form of (radical) faith that has transformative effects upon our lives in finite societies, which themselves are expressions of a form of (social) faith. Crucially for Niebuhr, radical faith takes two possible forms: radical distrust, which interprets God as enemy and God's world as inhospitable, prompting individual selves to hunker down in their finite communities and defend them from external criticism; and radical trust, which interprets God, ultimately, as friend and God's world, ultimately, as hospitable, prompting individual selves to transform their finite communities so that they are open to criticisms *and opportunities* from other communities, all for the purpose of loyally serving God's own cause, the universal community of being. I have argued that radical and social faith fund two forms of creativity: radical creativity, the transformative work we accomplish *upon* our social inheritances; and social creativity, the transformative work we accomplish *within* our social inheritances. It is essential to see that radical faith funds both forms of creativity. Radical trust assures us that there is value beyond our finite communities, for according to it the object of God's valuing is the universal community of being, thus motivating the transformation of our communities so they are open to discerning that value. Radical distrust persuades us that the only real value is to be found in those finite communities that support our lives, since according to it God is always and everywhere against us, thus motivating the self-defense of those communities against others. The life of radical faith and creativity is not a life bereft of social faith and creativity, but rather a life of continually reconstructing our social faiths and creativities so that they express radical trust in God and service to God's cause. This is a theological reconstruction of Mead's account of the self's good life as the continual reconstruction of its "me" (or various "me's") by its "I."

What remains to be done is to discuss the character of our direct relation to God, the character of faith, of the "I" theologically construed. More specifically, the question is, in what does this directness, and the radical creativity it funds, consist? In what follows, I mine suggestions from Niebuhr's later work and propose the term *existential resonance* to describe our direct relation to God. Chapter 4 treated Niebuhr's classics and one neglected work as a singular position; this chapter continues that practice with his later works. Meanwhile, the burden of chapter 4 to demonstrate that the tension between individuality and community, which is so central to the works of Royce and Mead, also beats at the heart of Niebuhr's core works, is matched by the burden of this chapter to demonstrate how issues of the directness of experience and creativity, which animate the background of Niebuhr's core works, take front stage in his last writings. The aim remains conceptually reconstructive. My theological account of existential resonance is, in turn, meant to bolster my moral-pedagogical argument that being formed in and through social inheritances is necessary but insufficient for moral formation, since the moral development of communities—that is, the expansion and deepening of their moral care and concern—depend on their members to exercise their individuality, whether by being or by conscientiously following social geniuses. Thus, I argue in this chapter, from a Christian theological perspective, that we must attend to individuality in moral formation by discerning the character of individuals' existential resonances with God, and then respecting and promoting those that release radically creative activities. Recall that the "I" enables the self to gain the sort of critical purchase on its social inheritances, its various "me's," that enables it either to resist and transform those inheritances, or to shore up further their present forms in order to prevent resistance and transformation. In the theological terms of my argument, the "I" is either radically trustful or radically distrustful. Hence, communities that recognize the moral significance of individuality must take it upon themselves to discern the character of their members' individualities, and then figure out ways to respect and promote individuality that expresses radical faith and creativity.

My intent is to conclude my book by making these claims more material and less abstract. In the first section, I engage Niebuhr's discussion of symbols, in order to characterize existential resonance and to articulate one form of the radical creativity it funds, symbolic creativity, the perpetual reworking of our symbolic activity so that it properly expresses our existential resonance with God. The second section engages Niebuhr's discussion of virtue, in particular his re-working of the moral/theological distinction within virtue theory, in order to articulate another form of radical creativity, virtuous creativity. What should become clear is that symbolic and virtuous creativity work through the transformation of symbolic and virtuous activity, rendered possible by the transformation of our existential existence with God. That is, the transformation of communal activities like symbolization and virtue, so that they are radically creative, depends on the transformation of our social faiths into radical faith. The third and final section makes a christological connection in order to articulate how God can be understood to morally form us. If the first two sections discuss symbol and virtue in order to articulate how communities can morally form us to be radically trustful and creative, then the final section seeks to account for how communities that manage to do this are responding fittingly to God's action upon us. As the Son of God, Christ exemplifies how and enables us to engage in radical creativity, and crucially, this includes enabling us to reflect our radical creativity back upon his own example, which is to say, back on social inheritances focused on him. In other words, Christian moral formation submits the variety of traditions that constitute Christianity itself, to the critical transformation of radical faith and creativity.

SYMBOLIC CREATIVITY

The use of the term *direct* to describe an individual relation to God that funds communal transformation has two things to recommend it. First, Niebuhr uses it himself, rendering it at the very least exegetically appropriate. In a late essay in which he reflects back on his own career and looks forward to what he thinks the theological shape of the continuing reformation of "the church" should be, Niebuhr remarks that a proper "resymbolization of the message and the life of faith in the One God," a form of religious revival or renewal that encompasses both "pregnant words" and "symbolic deeds," demands "*direct* relations in the immediacy of personal life to the actualities to which people in another time referred with the aid of such symbols."[1] This remark reflects Niebuhr's deepening his prior turn to divine sovereignty, recognizing that God's objective reality escapes not only liberal value-terminology, but more significantly, any and all theological formulation. At the same time, this remark refers to a particular mode of access to God and reality, distinguishable from the mediation of social inheritances: "We *sense* reality in the powers and processes that we seek to apprehend and to communicate with the aid of these symbolic words or verbal symbols."[2] The symbols bequeathed to us by our social inheritances allow us to apprehend and communicate objective realities, but beyond this we sense or experience them. Such sense or experience is direct in the sense that it is not ultimately beholden to mediating symbols, and as such, allows us to critically reflect on the adequacy of those symbols.

This leads into the second recommendation for using the term *direct*: direct is distinct from *immediate*.[3] To say that our relation to God is immediate can suggest that it is entirely anterior to, or completely bypasses, all social mediation. This may lead us to focus our attention on our experience of God, rather than on God. Since immediate experience is purportedly exterior to social mediation, it would seem to take immense effort to grasp the character of this experience—as it would require abandoning language, symbols, etc.—and such effort tends to result in our focusing self-ward rather than God-ward.[4] Niebuhr's appreciation for the social thought of Royce and Mead, as well as his devotion to the symbol-saturated Christian tradition, hardly allows him to take this route. However, direct experience, on my account, can occur with social mediation. When we encounter another person for the first time, that encounter is often funded by our social inheritances, which organize the new experience so that we come to expect some things rather than others, and can prepare our responses accordingly. At the same time, if the encounter chafes against expectations, then our experience of that person, rather than just failing to compute, can motivate us to modify our social inheritances accordingly.

1. Niebuhr, "Reformation: Continuing Imperative," 144; emphasis mine.
2. Niebuhr, "Toward New Symbols," 28; emphasis mine.
3. Though Niebuhr uses the word "immediate," I believe the term "direct" makes better sense of his argument.
4. Early on, Niebuhr notes that such "subjectivistic inversion" is the temptation of all Protestant theology. See Niebuhr, *The Meaning of Revelation*, 14.

Here is a theological example of the coincidence of direct experience and social mediation that I will use throughout this chapter. The traditional and gendered Christian language of "God the Father" has arguably shaped the experience of individual Christians in a number of destructive ways. We come to understand God as male, which is to say, as exemplifying whatever characteristics our particular historical communities attribute to maleness, and this effectively makes an idol of God. Meanwhile, the collapse of divinity into maleness—which ramifies into andro-centric forms of theological anthropology, ecclesiology, redemption, etc. that understand females to be less than human, less than Christian, and so on—has contributed to historical expressions of chauvinism that have forced women to leave diminished, unhealthy, and un-flourishing lives, and continue to do so.[5] At the same time, "God the Father" language arguably funds an experience of God that is personal and interactive, rather than conceptual and detached. Many Christians may and do find such traditional language more fitting for a life that includes activities like worship and centers around the *person* of Jesus Christ, than language like ultimate concern, ground of being, Niebuhr's own one beyond the many, or even other traditional language, like "God our mighty fortress" or 'God our rock." It is possible that our experience of God can be shaped by the socially mediated language of "God the Father," such that we come to comport ourselves as persons toward God as person, while the directness of our experience of God allows us to critically reflect on the language that mediates it. For instance, for those who experience God more as a caring power devoted to the flourishing of creation, than as an authoritative power issuing commands and rules, "God the Father" might seem less adequate than "God the sustainer," if not "God the mother." Obviously, this example cannot, nor is it meant to, settle the larger issues of the power and authority dynamics that have complicated and corrupted the relation between gender and tradition. It is also not meant to endorse gendered God-talk. The point is to illustrate how social mediation and direct experience can operate together, with social mediation funding the direct experience that critically reflects back on it.

The question remains as to the character of our direct relation to, experience of, God. The answer is in the title, and elaborated in the content, of Niebuhr's third and final Cole lecture, "Toward the Recovery of Feeling." While the lecture is brief and programmatic, more of a recommendation than a theoretical reflection on its topic, it does provide an account of what characterizes our direct relation to God. Niebuhr's recovery of feeling or

---

5. See representatively, Daly, *Beyond God the Father*, and Reuther, *Sexism and God-Talk*.

THE TRANSFORMATION OF FAITH, TO TRANSFORM FAITH   153

emotion contends against two fronts, contemporary for him but still relevant today. First, the significance of emotion is denied by our predisposition for accepting "observing, spectator reason" and "technical intelligence" as the best ways to relate to reality. Analysis is preferred to valuation, on this view, because analysis puts us in touch with reality, while valuation distorts our view of reality by putting a miasma of personal attributions over it. Such a predisposition indicts the emotions on three counts: as subjective, they cannot provide objective knowledge; as private, they are not open to social verification; ultimately, the only practical objectives they can provide are false, in that they are necessarily unreliable and unverifiable.[6] Niebuhr does not directly defend the emotions against these indictments, though his rhetorical strategy provides an indirect defense. Since, as ineradicably faithful beings we are necessarily valuing beings, our preference and predisposition for spectatorial and technical analysis is rooted in an emotional attitude,[7] "our faith in the ability of our reasoning to outwit things."[8] Niebuhr's point is that the decrial of emotions is ultimately self-defeating since the decrial itself is emotionally and attitudinally funded. Moreover, if we can discern that objective analysis is emotionally funded, and also agree that such analysis still does provide objective knowledge (and so is not merely subjective), is still open to social verification (and so is not merely private), and so can provide reliable and verifiable practical ends, then it becomes possible to defend the emotions against the presupposition and indictments against them. Niebuhr neither notes nor pursues this, but it is a plausible extension of his rhetorical strategy.

The second front that Niebuhr's recovery contends against is "the continued and probably necessary tendency of institutional religion" to convert personal experiences "into something general, something that can be conceptually communicated." Specifically, emotional experiences like trust in God and the reception of forgiveness become "encapsuled in doctrinal forms," such that religious affiliation takes on the shape of minds sharing beliefs, rather than hearts participating in affections.[9] In his early work *The Meaning of Revelation*, Niebuhr discusses this as the conversion of internal into external history, or lived into observed history. His theological-methodological concern is to ensure that the lived experience of community members fund and control its conceptual articulations, but this includes a confidence that the external, observer perspective can be chastened and

---

6. Niebuhr, "Toward a Recovery of Feeling," 34–36.
7. Ibid., 36–37.
8. Ibid., 35.
9. Ibid., 37–38.

properly utilized for internal purposes, e.g., attempting to see oneself and one's community from God's perspective. In the later lectures, Niebuhr confronts the possibility that the necessary external formulations of the personal experiences that compose the history of the Christian community, can in fact work against attention to those experiences, especially when coupled with the influence of the contemporary predisposition for objective analysis.[10] As Niebuhr articulates the problem: "Symbols have lost vitality when they so merge with the realities to which they refer that communication between knower and known no longer takes place."[11] Two things should be noted about this claim. First, Niebuhr suggests that social mediation can so collapse into the reality it mediates, that a true relation to or experience of that reality is effectively prevented. This is idolatry; to understand God as male is to have turned "God the Father" into an idol. Second, by distorting our relation to God, such a collapse of symbol and reality also distorts the valid function of social mediation. Symbols are meant to put us in touch with objective realities, despite our propensity to take them as exhausting those realities. As if to underscore this point, Niebuhr argues that the recovery of the emotions is *fitting* to Christian faith, insofar as that faith is Scripturally based—which is to say *symbolically* based. The scriptures are "written largely in the language of the emotions." They present God as an emotional being, to whom we appropriately respond emotionally, and before whom our moral life is a matter of "rightly reorganized emotions." Rather than offering objective propositions, the scriptures "speak from feeling to feeling about the objects that elicit feeling and cannot be known without feeling." Niebuhr then outlines a theological strand, extending from Augustine through the early Reformers and (especially) Jonathan Edwards to Kierkegaard, whose work pioneers around this aspect of the scriptures.[12] His point is to show that Christianity includes a different strategy for dealing with the negative side of emotions (e.g., anarchic enthusiasm) than appealing to detached reason, namely, the reordering of our affections so that they are truly responsive to the character of God.

---

10. Our own version of this is the predisposition to trust historically particular conceptual schemes or rationalities instead of anything purporting to be universal. Theologians betray this predisposition insofar as they understand Christianity to interact with other historical forces by offering an alternative, competing language or rationality. I do not deny that Christianity has its own rationality—or better, that each of the many versions of Christianity is composed of a number of possible rationalities—which often conflicts with others, but that rationality shapes *something*, and my claim is that that something is direct experience of God and the world, which experience can then critically ramify its own shaping.

11. Niebuhr, "Toward New Symbols," 24.

12. Niebuhr, "Toward the Recovery of Feeling," 41–45.

Niebuhr's "hypothesis" is that the emotions "put us into touch with what is reliable, firm, real, enduring in ways that are inaccessible to the conceptual and spectator reason."[13] However, this is not to say that our emotions do not somehow fund the exercise of such reason, and reading Niebuhr in a Mead-oriented direction here will enable us to account for this and to save his work from a possible subjectivistic inversionist reading. When he claims that our knowledge of God and of ourselves before God is "an apprehension that involves the whole self, *including the emotions,*"[14] it sounds as though the emotions are a particular function or faculty of the self alongside others. On this account, the problem is not conceptual or doctrinal knowledge of God in and of itself, but the privileging of such knowledge over emotional knowledge. Unfortunately, Niebuhr does not discuss how emotions and reason relate to each other within a properly whole self. This is exacerbated by Niebuhr's endorsement of Jonathan Edward's notion of "true religion" as a matter of religious affections, which separates heart and head as modes of access to God without accounting for their connection.[15] This is problematic. On my theological interpretation of Mead's I/me distinction, the "I" occupies a direct relation to God, but understanding the "I" as simply the emotional aspect of the self would undermine Mead's attempt to overcome a faculty psychology that he saw as static. The "I" is a phase of the entire self, one's own holistic response not to some one part of one's self, but to one's whole self as socially formed, and so to one's social formation. Recall that Mead's example of Jesus exercising his "I" is Jesus' recognition of Samaritans as appropriate objects of God's care *according to his own religious tradition.* We can say that Jesus' emotional encounter with God and with Samaritans compelled him to recognize their moral worth, but according to Mead, Jesus was also carrying on what he took to be the *normative trajectory* of his tradition.[16] In other words, Jesus' "I" was simultaneously doing emotional and conceptual work. At the same time, what this multidimensional work responded to was not simply the conceptual scheme that socially formed Jesus, but also the emotional relations of trust and loyalty that undergirded personal devotion to that scheme. Mead himself discerns that the Pharisees'

13. Ibid., 48.

14. Ibid., 42.

15. The rhetorical explanation for this is that, as pointed out above, Niebuhr is explicitly confronting the negative ramifications of emphasizing the head over the heart. *The Meaning of Revelation,* which clears conceptual space for the heart rather than defends it against the head, has its own account of how heart and head can relate. My account will participate in its spirit, but not its letter.

16. I pick up the notion of normative trajectory from Hector, *Theology without Metaphysics.*

response to Jesus' work was the response of people feeling betrayed, not the response of a math teacher to a student who has miscalculated. If my theological reconstruction of Mead's I/me distinction is to avoid violating it, then the "I" cannot be identified with emotion to the exclusion of reason or of social inheritances.

Thankfully, Niebuhr makes some suggestive remarks that provide a way forward. He asserts, "[E]motional relations to otherness, to objective being, are prior *in meaningfulness* to intellectual relations." Trust or distrust in our parents "is prior in time and probably *personally prior*" to our conceptual identification of them as our parents, just as love or hate of God is prior to our conceptual formulations of who God is.[17] The suggestion is not that emotions are simply beside reason, but rather that emotions are primitive. Insofar as we are *persons*, we occupy *meaningful* relations to others and the world, and these relations—which are *felt* or *lived*—ground and fund our intellectual relations. Recall that, for Niebuhr, trust and distrust are hermeneutical, they *interpret* the character of others. The suggestion here is that these lived hermeneutical relations then give rise to images (God the friend) and concepts (God the good One beyond the many, working powerfully in and through the many) that can be intellectually considered apart from those relations. To the extent that our production and use of images and concepts remain tethered to the lived hermeneutical relations that fund them, those images and concepts remain existentially resonant, or in Niebuhr's own terms *vital*. In this way, doctrinal knowledge per se is not the problem, but rather doctrinal knowledge cut off from existential resonance. Existential resonance and doctrinal knowledge are meant to work together, in the sense that doctrinal knowledge is meant to be existentially resonant. Resonance and doctrine compete only when they are separated from each other.

I use the term "resonance" in order to suggest the simultaneous relation and difference that is meant to connect our lived hermeneutical relations to the world with the images and concepts we use to characterize those relations. Musical notes resonate with each other insofar they are not the same as each other, yet still create vibrations between them that give each a thickness or pregnant quality that they would not have if played alone. One might say, musical notes become more alive, more vital, as they resonant with others. If my experience of God is that of radical trust, then a theological image of God as the friend of creation and a theological concept of God as the One beyond yet working in and through the many, may well resonant with that experience. Such an image and concept gain existential

---

17. Niebuhr, "Toward the Recovery of Feeling," 48; emphasis mine.

validity because of this resonance, and in turn bolster my original experience by giving it a cultural form that enables me to share it with others and effects an evocation of the original experience in times of encroaching distrust. This regains existential validity for the image and concept, and so ideally the cycle continues. Crucially, such a cycle depends on a tensive gap between symbol (image, concept) and reality (God), which experience itself instantiates: in order for the self to experience another reality, neither can be absorbed into the other. Experience is resonance insofar as it is a vitalizing interaction between self and other. Hence, for a symbol to resonate with experience, it must respect the vitalizing difference between itself and the experience it mediates, which experience is itself a vitalizing difference between self and other.

However, once the image and concept become separated from the experience that gave rise to them—once doctrine becomes separated from existential resonance with God—symbols lose their function of putting us in touch with objective realities. Since symbols are the elements of our social inheritances, when they lose their proper function, they fall back on and become restricted to their only other function, which is to socialize us into the community that uses them. For Niebuhr, this means that the transmission of symbols for God that lack existential resonance forms us to put our trust and loyalty in our social inheritances, rather than in God—which is to say, it forms us into social rather than radical faith. The effects of this are noted in the last chapter: social faith forms communities whose mode of being is self-defense, thereby closing themselves off to criticism and transformation and abandoning them to competitive relations with other communities. Niebuhr's insistence is that the Christian community is vulnerable to this deformation insofar as it clings to dead symbols.

At the same time, given Niebuhr's claim that our fundamental relation to God is never neutral, but either trust interpreting God as friend or distrust interpreting God as enemy, the collapse of symbol into reality that de-vitalizes the symbol is the symptom rather than the disease. To say that humans are constituted by their faith in God is to say that we are constituted by our existential resonance with God. To the extent that we trust God, we are enabled to recognize the necessity of symbols for interpreting and relating to God, while appreciating the tensive gap between God and those symbols; to interpret God as our friend enables us to understand that, by the grace of God, our symbols can be existentially resonant, though not cognitively exhaustive, of the character of God. God accommodates Godself by vitalizing our symbols—that is, by relating to us in such a way that our language, images and concepts resonate with that God-initiated relation. What happens in situations of distrust is that our lived interpretation of

God as enemy chafes against a social inheritance that characterizes God as good, resonating with those aspects of the tradition that characterize God as judge. This lack of fit between our relation with God and our social inheritance prompts us to choose between them, and since we interpret God as hostile, we are likely to choose our social inheritance. The result is that we utter "God is good," but somehow mean "God is evil but our church community is good," and then endorse traditional depictions of God punishing or laying waste to other peoples as ideal images of our community's destiny over others. In a word, statements of radical faith come to embody social faith, so that symbols become de-vitalized, referring their users back to their communities rather than to God. The collapse of reality and symbol here is the collapse of God into community. The reason for this collapse is our warped existential resonance. This analysis is significant because it does not permit an appeal to existential resonance exclusive of symbol-use, which is to say, exclusive of social inheritances, *precisely because a form of such resonance is the problem*, exacerbated by but irreducible to the dynamics of finite communities. At the same time, existential resonance remains distinct enough from social inheritance to reflect critically on it. Those who trust God also discern a lack of ultimate fit between our relation to God and our social inheritances, but rather than respond to this as posing an exclusive option between mystical immediacy and social conformity, the faithful respond to it as an invitation to continue symbolization, though critically so.

I prefer the term "existential resonance" to emotion or feeling because it connotes a holistic response to realities that can lead to symbolic responses, and through reflection to conceptual responses, rather than a partial response from a particular faculty that is understood to be different in kind than more intellectual responses. This is where reconstructing Niebuhr is helpful, again with reference to Mead. Mead's account of human development is emergent: physical gestures become vocal gestures, which become language, which in turn becomes the condition for symbolic and conceptual thought. The intent is to demonstrate that even our private thinking is a function of social formation, but the implication is that our intellectual life is rooted in our bodily existence. Attention to the embodied character of human existence is what Mead contributes to Royce's notion of interpretation: before we interpret the symbolic signs of others, we interpret, with our bodies, others' bodily signs, as we participate in bodily endeavors. Recall that Mead's example of taking on the generalized other is participation on a baseball team, where each position player has to take on and organize the potential bodily actions of the other players. Significantly, such bodily interpretation persists in, and influences, occasions of more intellectual interpretation.[18] Niebuhr implicitly picks up on this bodily emphasis, in two ways. First, the affirmation of responsibility—"God is acting in all actions upon you. So respond so all actions upon you as to respond to his action."[19]—concerns divine *action*, and not simply divine manifestation or proclamation. The responsible life is a matter of interpreting what we *suffer*, not merely what we see and hear.[20] Obviously, an expansive sense of suffering includes the notion that we *undergo* others' self-presentations and words, but my point is precisely that this is an *inclusion*: we can be said to suffer manifestations and proclamations precisely because we are bodily beings. The responsible life is a matter of interpreting what happens to our bodies; another person's spoken claim is no more a sign to be interpreted as divine action than another person punching or feeding us. In this respect, it is appropriate that Niebuhr endorses Edwards as "a psychosomatic thinker" attuned to how the body is affected.[21]

Second, in Niebuhr's discussion of symbolism he includes deeds besides words, bodily actions besides images and concepts, as symbolic forms. Thus, attending to how we symbolize God requires attending not only to our God-talk but also to our "God-walk"—that is, our actions towards others. Again, it is true that our actions are exemplary, and so serve as signs of our character and of the characters of those we take to be normative. At the same time, insofar as our actions affect other persons, they are not only signs to be interpreted conceptually but also concrete bodily aids or inflictions. The divine significance of feeding the hungry, for instance, has less to do with how the action is available to interpretation outside the endeavor of feeding the hungry, and more to do with what the endeavor actually accomplishes, satisfying the hunger of the needy. More generously, what such feeding signifies outside of the endeavor itself will prove to have less vitality if the hungry are not actually fed. In short, existential resonance is holistic because it is grounded in bodily significance, and such resonance can only be perceived fully within bodily endeavors.

---

18. See the work of Erving Goffman and Randall Collins, two American sociologists who extend the work of Mead in ways that appreciate the significance of the human body, especially Goffman, *The Presentation of Self* and *Interaction Ritual,* and Collins, *Interaction Ritual Chains.*

19. Niebuhr, *The Responsible Self,* 126.

20. Proclamation and manifestation are two traditional ways of understanding how God reveals Godself in the world. I am suggesting that if God is understood to work in and through all actions upon us, then privileging these two senses may hinder us from discerning the full bodily influence of God's activity. Speech is action, but not all action is speech.

21. Niebuhr, "Toward the Recovery of Feeling," 44.

It is essential to see that existential resonance is amenable to conceptualization without necessarily endangering the vitality of the resonance. Recall my assertion that experience *is* resonance, the vitalizing interaction between self and other that presupposes their distinction from each other. Symbols and concepts, in turn, express this experience by resonating with it, which means respecting the vitalizing difference between themselves and experience. Niebuhr suggests something similar in his first Cole lecture. He advocates that we orient "ourselves by reference to our relations to some of the great polarities that characterize our human existence," such as past/future, subject/object, and contemplative/practical reasoning.[22] Niebuhr explicitly contrasts polarities with dualities: in the former, the terms cannot be defined without each other. God/Satan is a dualism because we can define God without reference to Satan, but subject/object is a polarity because the two mutually constitute each other. Niebuhr's concern in this lecture is theological method, but there is an implicit anthropology. To say that human existence is characterized by "great polarities" is to say that human life is lived in and through interactions, for example, between subjectivity and objectivity, a polarity that suggests experience understood as resonance. On this account, conceptualization, and thus doctrine, are ultimately rooted in our lived—and hence, bodily—relations with and within the world. Existential resonance connotes the primitive relations from (not against) which our reflective capacities emerge and regarding which these capacities consequently construct accounts, which then become social inheritances. Reason and tradition, whether in the form of natural science or theological doctrine, fulfill their function to the extent that they respect and attest the existential resonance that birthed them, and it is precisely the strength of this respect and attestation that serves as the criterion of evaluation. For Niebuhr, this might mean that the articulation of existentially resonant liturgical forms should be the final purpose of doctrinal theology, not its addendum.[23]

If we reconstruct Niebuhr along these lines, understanding existential resonance as a sort of primitive transaction that gives rise to our reflective capacities, then we can escape a possible subjectivistic introversionist reading of that resonance. On such a reading, emphasizing existential resonance with God as the criterion for the adequacy or value of doctrine entails making human life the measure of God, or at least individual experience the measure of tradition. The result is a humanistic individualism that ceases to count as theology because its object is humanity, and potentially

---

22. Niebuhr, "Position of Theology Today," 3–4.

23. See Niebuhr, "Toward the Recovery of Feeling," 46, for his gestures in this direction.

just individuals, rather than God. This reading includes all of the indictments against emotions that Niebuhr discerned: merely subjective, merely private, and so objectively misleading. However, existential resonance with God is not merely subjective because it refers to our relation to God; that is, existential resonance puts us in touch with God. Moreover, existential resonance with God is not merely private because it can emerge from reflective activities like symbolization and conceptualization that we pursue with others; that is, existential resonance submits itself to social verification. Finally, since existential resonance puts us in touch with God and is amenable to the critical reflection of others, a reflection that is itself rooted in such resonance, then we cannot categorically deny objectivity to existential resonance. Existential resonance, though self-constitutive as our life-orienting faith, is other-regarding, responsive to God as objectively real.

As noted above, our existential resonance with God can be warped, insofar as it is distrust that interprets God as enemy, and if such distrust becomes socially endorsed, the result is a finite community turning in on itself through social faith, even as it utters radically faithful statements and appears to perform radically faithful deeds. Again, the appeal to existential resonance exclusive of social inheritance cannot resolve this, but neither can an appeal to social inheritance exclusive of existential resonance. In other words, the appeal to some particularly Christian language, narrative, or rationality, without attention to the lived experience that funds them, can only play into the hands of social faith, insofar as it convinces us to fit ourselves into the workings of a particular community while neglecting the character of the faith that animates it.

To say that the self is composed of an "I" and "me" is to say that the self is constituted by the relations between its existential resonance with surrounding objective realities and the social inheritances which enable it to express that resonance because these inheritances are, among other things, repositories of such expressions. Theologically construed, the "I" is the self's existential resonance with God, and the "me" is the self as formed by the forms and examples of God-talk and God-walk provided in its finite communities. Following this, to say that the "I" constitutes the self's creative response to the "me," is to say that the self's existential resonance with God bears down on the self with such power that it throbs through the self's socially mediated religious traditions, enabling it to discern where those traditions have in the past released or muffled its resonance with God, as well as how presently it does and in the future might release or muffle its resonance. When I say that existential resonance *throbs through* social mediation, I mean this in two senses, positive and negative. Positively, it means that social mediation may serve as an appropriate vehicle of existential resonance. In other words, symbols can and often do disclose (something of) the character of objective reality, insofar as they express the character of our relation with that reality, thus enabling us to reflect on it. Despite the ill consequences of its history and uses, "God the Father" discloses that the character of our relation to God is personal, like that of our relation to a parent. Negatively, the throbbing of existential resonance through social mediation means that such resonance must often work against that mediation. Symbols can and often do distort the character of objective reality, insofar as they distort the character of our relation to that reality, most usually by coming to stand in for, replace, or otherwise (claim to) cognitively exhaust, that relation. Thus, if "God the Father" is taken to mean that our relation to God is like that of our relation to parents with male genitalia, so that we come to think that the only appropriate social mediation of God must pass through male humans; or, similarly, that our relation to God is like that of our relation to humans with qualities that are deemed conventionally to be particularly male or fatherly, e.g., distantly authoritative, punitive, etc.; then it distorts the character of our relation to God. In this case, the throb of our existential resonance with God through "God the Father," if responded to in faith rather than in distrust, should motivate us to explore and expand upon the *personalist* ramifications of this symbolic affirmation, rather than to defend its paternalist, masculine heritage.

Recall that for Mead, the "me" forms or structures the "I," and yet the "I" is able to creatively respond to this form or structure, especially by expanding its area of concern, and more specifically by demonstrating how certain of its concepts or categories apply beyond their finite, social provenance. Those whose "I's" are particularly strong, who Mead calls social geniuses, speak against the present shape of their social inheritances, but from the resources of those inheritances, and for the sake of their future shape. So, the self formed by a social inheritance that affirms "God the Father," may end up affirming "God the mother," insofar as the traditional affirmation attunes the self to the personal character of its relation to God, even as the self's existential resonance with God communicates divine qualities that are better comprehended by the (admittedly conventional) language of motherhood, e.g. qualities of care for the sake of flourishing, rather than of authority and rule. In this way, the creative activity of the "I," the work that flows from the radical faith that is nothing other than the self's existential resonance with God, can be understood as symbolic novelty. This is a form of contingent creativity, and in two senses. First, symbolic novelty depends upon a socially mediated tradition of symbolization and its effects; "God the mother" remains for many Christians a radical and challenging response to the traditional "God the Father," but its challenging character is funded by that traditional symbol, particularly as it attests to the unfortunate history of male-female relations. That is, "God the mother" is a fitting and existentially resonant challenge to "God the Father" due to the contingencies of human history. Second, symbolic novelty depends upon the character of our existential resonance with God; the deadening effect of "God the Father" would only motivate us to find a new symbol to the extent that that existential resonance throbbed heretofore under-appreciated and under-recognized qualities of personal caring against the traditional symbol. Such throbbing is contingent on God, which is to say that radical faith in the form of trust is a divine gift.

Above I spoke of divine accommodation as God vitalizing our symbols by relating to us in such a way that our symbols resonate with that relation. This means that "God the Father" remains legitimate, insofar as it resonates with a *personal* relation to God. At the same time, it means that "God the mother," spoken as a human judgment on the ill historical effects and uses of "God the Father," may incarnate the divine judgment on those very effects and uses. In this way, divine accommodation to our symbolic activity means that God legitimates the human activity of carrying on a social inheritance through tradition *and* underwrites the criticism of particular accomplishments of traditions. In Mead's language, this means that God relates to both the self's "me" and "I." The difference between these relations is that, God relates to the "me" by resonating with symbols and other aspects of social inheritances, but relates to the "I" by resonating with individual existences. We can still understand social inheritances as repositories of symbols that resonate with God (precisely *because* they initially emerge from the existential resonances of their individual participants) while affirming that God will judge and disrupt particular symbols by relating to individuals through direct existential resonance, and not only through available resonant symbols. Since such direct existential resonance will result in the production of new symbols that will inevitably become conventional—that is, become more resonant with finite communal life than with God—God will continually renew direct existential resonance and so continually fund symbolic novelty. God's freedom over human activity, symbolic and otherwise, works simultaneously against and through that activity.

Niebuhr notes that repentance over the loss of symbolic vitality that happens when symbol collapses into reality, and so when our relation to God collapses into our relation to community, involves the recognition that symbols are necessary but insufficient for discerning our relation to God.[24] Stated otherwise, repentance entails the recognition that social faith, which

---

24. Niebuhr, "Toward New Symbols," 30.

includes symbolization, is a necessary but insufficient vehicle for radical trust and loyalty. In other words, radical faith must be communicated if it is to have its transformative effects on human life, but no particular communication of it should be reified as an absolute portrait of that faith. In light of this, Niebuhr rejects an apophatic response as divinely and humanly unfitting: the Trinitarian character of God is meant to enable our "communication with God through Christ in the Holy Spirit," and the responsible character of human life entails the necessity of communicating with finite others. Perhaps paradoxically, the proper repentant response to our warped symbolic activity is the multiplication of symbols, "so that not one of them will ever be accepted by ourselves or those with whom we communicate as adequate or as identical with the reality interpreted with its aid." We might consider this the democratizing of symbolic authority: the more symbols we use that put us in touch with God, the less authority any particular symbol or symbol-set will wield. Niebuhr insists that such symbolic multiplication is the "way of Scripture" and of religious history more generally.[25] Thus, the way of symbolic multiplication is fitting to the reality of God in relation to us *and* to the Christian tradition.

Two specifications should be made about the creativity of symbolic multiplication. First, the contingency of symbolic creativity consists in the fact that it does not produce entirely new words, but rather uses available words to refer to our relation to God. For instance, God is spoken of as occupying available social positions in finite communities: King, Judge, Captain, Father, etc. The danger of using only one is that collapse whereby symbol becomes reality and God becomes a community-functionary. The advantage of multiplying these symbols is that God will not be understood to occupy such roles towards us in any straightforward fashion. More methodologically, this creativity means that our relation to God is spoken of in the language (e.g., alienation, encounter, anxiety) of multiple human disciplines (e.g., philosophy, sociology, psychology). Thus, traditional religious and theological language should not be understood as "a language that ought to be kept pure at all costs," but rather as a language striving to resonate with the many dimensions of human life that our disciplines explore, because it is precisely these many dimensions to which God relates. Second, the symbolic creativity works by *renewal*, not replacement. New symbols do not simply take over for old symbols, but rather refresh the old symbols. So, "God the Creator" may challenge any tribalism perceived in the "God of Abraham, Isaac, and Jacob," but in doing so should give us a renewed understanding of the earlier symbol, i.e., that the "God of the fathers"

25. Ibid., 31–32.

expresses less a divine desire for tribal politics, and more the divine strategy of carrying out divine purposes in and through finite particulars.[26] More controversially, "God the mother" challenges the attendant andro-centrism of "God the Father," but in doing so should enable us to recognize that the old symbol can express relations of personal care, insofar as it connotes parenthood rather than maleness, and so is not necessarily destined to reproduce and continue violence towards women. Such renewal is possible only to the extent that the old and new symbols are used together, so that the old symbols are *reinterpreted* in light of the new symbols. Symbolic multiplication democratizes authority, not only through the dispersal of authority, but more importantly, through the renewal of the authority of past symbols, by re-authorizing them through new symbols.

This last point is significant once we integrate into this discussion the distinction between social and radical creativity that I noted in chapter 4. Social creativity is that form of creativity funded by the social faith that is our trust in and loyalty to our finite communities, motivated by the radical distrust that interprets God as enemy and the world as hostile; such creativity operates within a social inheritance, for the purpose of defending it against others. Radical creativity is that form of creativity funded by the radical trust that interprets God as friend and the world as ultimately beneficent and that grounds loyalty to God's cause, the universal community of being; radical creativity operates not only within, but also upon social inheritances, and so entails the exposure of those inheritances and their communities to the judgment of others, which judgment is ultimately understood to be God's. What distinguishes these forms of creativity is the character of the faith that animates them, and not necessarily the character of the creative activities themselves. This means that we cannot simply align radical creativity with the production of new symbols. Niebuhr is clear: "Each new symbol doubtless brings with it the danger of a new dogmatism and a new idolatry in which the category takes the place of the reality it was meant to interpret."[27] In this way, the use of a new symbol to completely replace an old symbol is likely to be an expression of social faith to the extent that particular groups or communities, present *and* historical, are understood to align with each symbol. For instance, the use of "God the Creator" to replace the "God of Abraham, Isaac, and Jacob" may be a self-defensive expression of Christian social faith *against* its Jewish heritage. Again, and more controversially, the use of "God the mother" to replace "God the Father" may be similarly self-defensive if it *merely* functions as an expression of identity politics within

26. Ibid., 32.
27. Ibid.

a Christian community.[28] The upshot of this is that symbolic creativity can only be understood as radical to the extent that it is (potentially) *reconstructive of* an *entire* tradition, neither simply rejecting parts of it nor co-opting others for some finite, social cause. Just as the radicality of faith concerns its extent and character, as trust in and loyalty to the *universal* community of being which is ultimately *good*, so the radicality of symbolic creativity concerns the extent and character of its ramifications, as the reconstruction of the social inheritance itself that is simultaneously its revaluation. "God the mother" will be radically creative, not simply as that particular provocative symbol that is meant to indicates its users' anti-sexism, but rather as an expression of our existential resonance with God which has transformative effects on our particular community's theology, Christology, pneumatology, anthropology, soteriology, ecclesiology, biblical exegesis, homiletics, liturgics, pastoral care, daily church life and so on. Radical faith affirms that God, though beyond all finite agencies, nevertheless works in and through them, and a ramification of this affirmation is that radical faith itself emerges as the transformation of social faith, opening it up to and for the universal goodness of all being. Similarly, radical symbolic creativity emerges as the transformation of social creativity, opening up the symbolic production within a social inheritance to the influence of an existential resonance with God that has been heretofore under-appreciated and under-recognized, an influence that, precisely because it is the communication of the divine Spirit, can and (by the grace of God) will "spirate" throughout the tradition.

Insofar as radical symbolic creativity is so extensively reconstructive, it is better understood as a process than a single act, and so as ultimately communal rather than individual. At the same time, insofar as radical symbolic creativity is a process, it unfolds over time, so that the communal form it will take is not necessarily some sort of consensus involving a final commitment to a reached decision, but rather and more likely an emerging conversation whose members are bound to each other by the resonance between the individual existential resonance of each with God. In other words, radical creativity entails a communal form that preserves the individuality of its participants. Recall that in my interpretation of Mead's notion of the social genius I asserted that the social genius's creativity is worked out

28. Obviously, I am wading into dangerous waters here. After all, the suggestion that any later Christian symbol should reinterpret rather than replace "the God of Abraham, Isaac, and Jacob" could simply be a form of benevolent supercessionism. Moreover, the fear that an historically concrete symbol that's contemporarily salient—such as "God is black" or "Jesus was an immigrant"—will end up as exclusive as what it replaces, is just as likely an expression of the fear of the loss of the status quo and my privileged place within it. My full answer to these possible objections will develop, in stages, throughout the rest of the chapter.

through followers; that is, if the work of the particularly strong "I" of the social genius is actually to transform the community, to eventually take on the form of the "me," it must be met and realized by the similarly strong "I's" of others in the community who recognize what the social genius first articulates, if not first discerns. In this way, the radical creativity of "God the mother" concerns not its original utterance and use, but the eventual outcomes that it funds. The author of "God the mother" expresses her own existential resonance with God, her own "I," by articulating that symbol. Others, who share that author's "me," find that this symbol expressively resonates with their own existential resonance with God, their own "I's," in such a strong way that they realize the limitations of the available symbols (e.g., paradigmatically, 'God the father), and yet also discern their possibilities if reconstructed by the new symbol. Still others, also co-participants in the author's "me," discern the challenge that the new symbol poses to the old symbols and exercise their "I's" in the defense of those symbols, which may take the form of social creativity—say, producing other symbols that express maleness or authoritarianism, or attempting to include feminine elements. In this way, the social genius is one who precipitates a crisis within her community, provoking a conflict between those who willing to transform the shared social inheritance in light of the articulation of an under-recognized existential resonance with God, and those defending the current form of the social inheritance precisely from such transformation. The social genius's creativity is worked out through this struggle and is validated insofar as her followers win out, that is, insofar as radical creativity trumps social creativity.

It is at this point that the issue of time becomes significant, for the triumph of radical creativity can only be seen in retrospect, once the activity of the "I's" of the social genius and her followers has settled into a new "me." Recall that on Mead's conception of time, the "I" emerges in the present as the passage from the past to the future, and can only be discerned once the future that its activity precipitated has become the past. Radical faith and creativity should be understood similarly: they emerge in the present to transform a social inheritance that has turned in on itself into one that is open to otherness, but can only be discerned once the new form of the social inheritance has settled. This has two ramifications for confronting radical symbolic creativity. First, judgments as to whether or not the new symbol "God the mother" has or will win out must remain provisional since the taking up of the symbol by others is a personal rather than mechanical process. Potential followers must discern and judge for themselves whether or not the new symbol resonates with their resonance with God, and though the judgment must be made singly, self by self, the process of discernment is communal. Such discernment would require a series of conversations with the social genius herself and/or her current followers about their existential resonances and the symbols that resonate with them, as well as the impact these have on traditional symbols. If one finds oneself resonating with them, that is, if one discerns a resonance between one's own resonance with God and their resonances with God, than it would be incumbent on one to become a follower. The point is that this is a process that takes time, which means that one's initial No may become an ultimate Yes. Second, once the new symbol has won out in a particular community, and so once the resonance of the new symbol has become taken for granted—to the extent that it resonates enough with member's lives and with the traditional symbols that vital for them—the radicality of the symbol has diminished, and its creativity is in danger of becoming merely social, and so of becoming an instrument of defense. For those committed to radical faith, this means that the moment of recognizing a new symbol's triumph coincides with the moment of recognizing that it needs to be engaged critically. Perhaps this is an instance of affirming that we are simultaneously justified and sinner—"justified" in the sense that we can affirm that God has accommodated Godself to us by vitalizing our new symbol, by resonating first with individual and then with communal uses of the symbol; "sinner" in the sense that we can admit that we may take up the new symbol as a tool for justifying our particular community, rather than as an articulation of resonance with God.

However, it is important not to split these two ramifications into stages, whereby discernment is undertaken as a self-contained process that prepares for, but is not vulnerable to, criticism. The process of discerning the resonant scope of a new symbol must be critical itself, especially because the conflict between radical creativity and social creativity necessarily manifests as a social conflict between developing groups within a community, and so as a conflict between two forms of social creativity, one open to divine transformation through an emergent radical faith and one closed in on itself and guarded by social faith. In short, judging whether or not one is engaging in a merely social conflict between factions for supremacy within the community, or in a conflict between radical and social faith where what is at stake is the status of the community before God, itself requires a process of discernment! The downside of recognizing this is the temptation to crippling self-reflection, a form of self-involvement that could easily become defensive because it instantiates an (impossible) effort to insure that we are participating in the right conflict. Instead, we should commit ourselves more deeply to the social aspect of discernment, and this requires attending to another layer of the notion of social verification. On the one hand, social verification just means that individual personal experience is to be verified according to the personal experience of others. I find J on initial contact to be blunt and aloof, but others who know him better assure me that he is actually straightforward and shy. On the other hand, social verification also means that the 'sociableness'—by which I mean, the *faithfulness*—of those involved in the verification process must be personally verified. If I am to come around to the view that J is in fact straightforward and shy rather than blunt and aloof, I must personally experience the faithfulness of those correcting me about J *and* I must personally experience J's behavior as straightforward and shy. If on continuing contact J proves to be loquacious and generous with everyone but me, or with people who are of a different race, gender, or class than me, than some form of deception is occurring. Either there is a conspiracy against me to enable J's treatment of me, or there is some form of self-deception among those who corrected my initial assessment.[29] This is precisely when the discernment of J's true behavior becomes critical, requiring us to challenge our fellows' self-understandings and understandings of others.

This means that when discerning the resonant scope of a new symbol, part of what needs to be discerned is the behavior of those articulating and endorsing the new symbol. This is not an invitation to moralism, e.g., "The person who first proposed 'God the mother' cheated on her spouse, so we can't possibly take her proposal seriously." Rather, the point is a pragmatist one. As Sidney Hook asserts, "More important than any belief a man holds is the way he holds it."[30] This is a brief against dogmatism, and it holds true for symbols as well as beliefs: since no human symbol can ever fully capture God, the value of symbolic production and communication has to do with its contribution to a faithful, loving, and hopeful life before God, not with the particular symbols articulated and used. This is not to say that a symbol correctly captures God only to the extent that its articulation and use result in some specific and manifest social behavior in a religious community. Rather, it is to say that symbolic production and communication are parts of a larger form of life, and so nested within and connected to a number of other practices. The idea is that the existential resonance of any symbol will become compromised if it is articulated and used dogmatically to defend some current form of one's particular community. Hence, the justification of a linguistic utterance like "God the mother" takes place practically, that is, its justification occurs not only through its coherent connection to other symbolic utterances, but more significantly through the manner of life in

---

29. The form of this example, as well as the point about defensive (and thus vicious) self-involvement, are inspired by Murdoch, *The Sovereignty of Good*.

30. The epigraph to Hook, *Sidney Hook*.

which it is employed.[31] A particular religious community that is proud of its history of the public use and affirmation of the validity of "God the mother" might be expected to have a better history of female leadership than its peer communities who cling to "God the Father." If our community consistently articulates "God the mother" while consistently opting to install males in leadership positions, then we should critically examine its commitment to the new symbol, the fit between its linguistic and practical behaviors. The point of such criticism is not—and in fact cannot be—to insure the presence of radical faith in those who appear to resist some aspect of social faith (e.g., by using 'God the mother'), but rather to denounce those forms of social faith that persist in resisting transformation, and so implicitly to announce the possibility of transformation. The only justification of such criticism is that it be willing to turn back on itself.

The pedagogical upshot of this long discussion is that mastery of a particular community's inheritance of symbols turns out to be a necessary but insufficient approach to the moral formation of persons. Necessary because mastery of the traditional and historical symbols enables us to converse with each other about the reality those symbols put us in touch with, which in turn enables us to criticize those symbols insofar as we discern the adequacy of the symbols to that reality. Insufficient because, as my reading of Niebuhr insists, religious symbols fundamentally express an existential resonance with God that is irreducibly individual, a resonance that can be neglected, denied, or attacked by our community's articulation and use of religious symbols. Niebuhr's insight regards not only the positive contribution of mediating social forms to the very possibility of human communal life, but also the sinful character such forms can take on. I have suggested that God accommodates Godself to our symbolic activity by vivifying symbols such that they come to resonate with God, but that those symbols originally emerge as expressive of individual existential resonances with God. This might suggest that the difference between the merely socially faithful and the radically faithful is that the former subordinate their direct existential resonance with God to the resonance of their community's symbols with God, while the latter allow their community's symbolic resonance with God to be beholden to their own individual existential resonance with God. However, it is important to remember that the option of the merely socially faithful to live by symbolic resonance is oriented by the negative character of their direct and individual existential resonance with God. "God the Father" is an expression of social faith insofar as it expresses an ascription of

---

31. While Hans Urs von Balthasar has his problems with liberation theology, the agreement uniting them is that the justification of theology is anchored in the conduct of life. See Balthasar, "Theology and Sanctity."

ultimacy to the male gender or certain qualities taken to be male, *as part of a more general endeavor to defend the status of males, which endeavor is itself a response to God interpreted in radical distrust as enemy.* In short, not only may devotion to the social inheritance of a religious community be used as a tool of social faith, but ultimately such use may be grounded in each individual community member's direct relation with God in the form of hostile resonance. The solution to this problem cannot simply be alternative socialization, since many efforts at socialization are themselves symptoms of radical distrust. Instead, the solution must consist in some development of our individuality before God, from radical distrust to radical trust. Admittedly, such development cannot be a solitary task. At the same time, the community's contribution to this is more likely to involve absorbing the novelty of its individual members, rather than absorbing the individual members into its social inheritance,[32] and this involves an openness to criticism that runs parallel to an openness toward God. That is, one significant way that a community is open towards God is to be open towards its individual members' existential resonances with God.

Before developing this last point to its fullest, I need to move on from issues of symbolization to issues of virtue, for two reasons. First, as noted above, symbolic activity is one practice amidst a variety of practices within any community, such that the moral validity of symbolic activity is intrinsically tied to the moral validity of the total conduct that transpires within that community. As recent philosophical and theological ethics have affirmed, the language of the virtues, understood as those capacities and dispositions to certain acts that a community habituates its members to exercise, is a fruitful way to approach the total moral conduct that occurs within communities—communities can be examined morally as to the virtues (or vices!) of their individual members resulting from their communal formation. In other words, habituation into virtues is the larger context of socialization within which the socializing force of symbolic activity operates. In order for a community to form its members in its particular way of life, those individuals who undertake the formative task must already have been formed in that particular way.

Second, Niebuhr's discussion of symbolic activity notes that it includes symbolic deeds, but he does not develop the point. The point is suggestive, though. Just as the utterance "God the mother" symbolizes some characteristic of the divine-human relation, so do our particular actions; if uttering "God the mother" expresses that God's relation to humans is one of care, so does raising money for a family whose provider has lost her job. Meanwhile,

---

32. I am deliberately skewing George Lindbeck's language of absorption here.

our particular actions also symbolize our relation to God. This is the implication of Jesus' statement in Gospel, "Whatever you do to the least of these you do for me"—how we treat human others renders legible our comportment toward God. To care for those in need may express a recognition and endorsement of the divine care. In this sense, actions are subject to the same vicissitude as linguistic symbols. The utterance "God the Father" can express the personal character of the divine sovereignty over all of creation *and* the privileging of the male gender within its community of utterance; similarly, raising money for a family within one's own finite community can express one's radical loyalty to the divine cause of caring for the universal community of being, a loyalty which would manifest in raising money for families outside of one's finite communities, *and* the radically distrustful defense of one's finite community against others, and ultimately against God understood as enemy, in which case one's active care would be exclusive. Insofar as our particular actions proceed from more settled dispositions, the virtues and vices, then there may in fact be layers of symbolization: actions symbolize our relation to God, but through the mediation of the virtues, which enables us to turn the other way and say that the virtues express our relation to God, but only as they are expressed in actions. Just as the character of our faith determines the character of our symbolic activity, so the character of our faith orients the exercise of our virtues. The Christian tradition has discussed this dynamic by distinguishing between non-theological and theological virtues: faith, love, and hope do not manifest directly in particular actions, but rather form or infuse those intellectual and moral virtues that dispose us to particular actions. Niebuhr himself contributed to this historical discussion in an essay made available only posthumously, and so we turn to this.

RESPONSIBLE VIRTUOUS CREATIVITY

Before turning to this essay, a note is in order. The turn to virtue would seem to be a turn to the symbol of purposiveness, which Niebuhr rejects for the symbol of responsibility. According to Niebuhr, purposiveness affirms, "we act toward an end or are purposive; and, we act upon ourselves, we fashion ourselves, we give ourselves a form."[33] Virtue discourse, especially in its recent form, is precisely about how moral agents form themselves, in order to pursue certain ends—responsibility discourse purports to push our thinking in another direction. The discussion of virtue that follows is intended neither to characterize Niebuhr as primarily a virtue theorist

33. Niebuhr, *The Responsible Self*, 49.

(though Hauerwas, perhaps Christian ethics's best-known recent virtue theorist, was influenced by Niebuhr),[34] nor to shift my argument into a different moral-theoretical register. Rather, as the concluding paragraphs of the prior section express, I believe a discussion of virtue is implied by Niebuhr's discussion of symbolization and fitting in an argument about moral formation. What should become clear in this section is that Niebuhr understood virtue along the lines of responsibility, not purposiveness; the thinker he distinguishes himself from, Thomas Aquinas, is Christianity's magisterial purposive thinker. Meanwhile, it is worth remembering that Niebuhr's endorsement of responsibility is not a categorical rejection of other symbols of the moral life, like purposiveness and citizenship, but rather their inclusion within a more encompassing symbol. Responsibility discourse would reject a reduction of the moral life to the life of virtue, but the responsible moral life does include virtuous activity. My turn to virtue also has a rhetorical point. Virtue ethics is often appealed to regarding the maintenance of the lives of particular communities. If I can show how radical creativity operates in virtuous activity, then I can disrupt conventional connections between the virtues and particular historical communities. In this sense, I am (humbly) enacting creativity upon moral discourse.

In his posthumous essay "Reflections on Faith, Hope and Love," Niebuhr claims that "the idea of virtue itself has no real place in Christian ethics," at least "insofar as virtue means good conduct in the power of the agent and insofar as it means habit." For the Christian who discerns good conduct "in the perspective of faith," virtue should be understood as "neither achievement nor habit, but gift and response," and more specifically, as *given relation*. He describes the virtues as "relations which depend for their continuance on the constancy with which the objective good, to which the self is related in these ways, is given."[35] Christian virtues are responses to God, which are understood to be gifts because we are only able to respond to God insofar as God gives Godself to us in personal actions that call for personal response. Radical faith is a given relation: our trust in God's ultimate friendliness and our loyalty to God's universal cause are possible only because God continually gives Godself to us through actions that demonstrate divine trustworthiness and loyalty. Niebuhr does not note this explicitly, but it cannot be the mere presence of an objective other and her personal actions that enables us to exercise virtues as given responses; the other's personal actions upon us must include some vivification of our capacities to respond appropriately. Thus, an essential aspect of what is given

---

34. See Werpehowski, *American Protestant Ethics*, chapter 5.
35. Niebuhr, "Reflections on Faith, Hope and Love," 152.

with radical faith is the renewal of our capacity to trust in and be loyal to God, which Niebuhr describes as a conversion of our hermeneutical capacity to discern events in the world as disclosing divine friendliness rather than divine hostility. The point is that what is given in virtue is simultaneously external (manifest personal actions that evoke response) and internal (renewal of our capacities to so respond). Consider the theological virtue that Niebuhr tends to neglect, love. We are enabled to love God because God first loved us (cf. 1 John 4:10), but such divine love is not primarily a matter of God conferring external benefits (e.g., what Job lost and then had restored), nor simply a matter of God giving Godself as the proper end of our actions and desires (e.g., the *sunnum bonum* as union with God); rather, divine love must crucially include God's renewal of our capacity to love God and neighbor properly (e.g., the gift of the Holy Spirit). Of course, what is interiorly given in a virtue is intrinsically connected to what is exteriorly given—the renewal of our capacity to trust in and be loyal to God and God's cause makes little sense without some manifest divine action that evokes trust and loyalty—but the interior gift is essential, and Niebuhr neglects it.

I emphasize this last point because Niebuhr is up to something in this essay on which he does not follow through, but which is connected to his rejection of the Thomistic account of virtue. On that account, there is a distinction between moral and theological virtues; the former are acquired by habit, the latter are infused by grace. This distinction is grounded in the larger Thomistic distinction between nature and grace. While formation in the moral virtues is a matter of humans enabling humans to achieve our natural end of happiness, the theological virtues of faith, hope, and love are "supernatural additions" to our moral achievements that enable us to attain our supernatural end, blessed union with God. Niebuhr's response to this account is to deny the exclusivity of faith, hope, and love as theological virtues: these three "are not *the* theological virtues which may be added as gifts to achieved moral virtues—courage, temperance, justice and prudence—but the chief or most inclusive theological virtues," a group that includes endurance, patience, self-control, righteousness, humility, and "other kinds of gracious behavior." The only legitimate distinction between moral and theological virtues is that "between the habits which put one in the way of receiving the gifts and the gifts themselves."[36] On Niebuhr's account, all virtues ultimately concern gift. This is indebted to an alternate construal of the relation between nature and grace. Niebuhr asserts, "The love of God and of neighbor in God are not foreign to man's nature or, better, to man in his natural situation; but in our fallen situation they are present as love

---

36. Ibid.

of idol and love of neighbor in relation to idols."[37] There appears to be an elision here between nature and sin, similar to the way that, in *Faith on Earth*, Niebuhr characterizes natural religion as negative, or sinful, faith.[38] The problem is that such a construal suggests that grace must replace rather than perfect nature. However, as I mentioned in chapter 4, Niebuhr rejects construing the relation between natural religion and revealed religion/historical faith as one of mutual exclusion (as well as of developmental continuity); rather, the latter transforms or converts the former.[39] Insofar as this relation is an instance of that between nature and grace, then it becomes clear that Niebuhr would not understand grace to replace nature. He affirms, "The love of God is the *restoration and perfection* of a response which has always been present in misdirected or inverted form."[40] While Niebuhr uses the Thomistic language here, putting it in the context of his larger work enables us to discern that he means something different. While Thomas understands the theological virtues to be additive gifts, enabling us to move on from our natural to our supernatural end, Niebuhr understands them to be gifts of conversion, enabling us to turn from the idolatry ensuing from radical distrust and disloyalty to the true interpretation of God achieved in radical trust and loyalty. The point of aligning our natural and fallen situation is not to disparage creation, but to insist that what is ultimately redeemed *is* creation. The dignity of pagan virtue is that, because it is an aspect of created (if fallen) nature, it is redeemable, transformable into an expression of positive radical faith.[41]

What Niebuhr implies in this discussion is that there is no compelling *structural* distinction between moral and theological virtues. According to his example, the theological virtue of love is the transformation of a human form of love. Moreover, it should be clear from chapter 4 that the bulk of Niebuhr's most significant work characterizes radical faith as a theological virtue that transforms distorted human forms of faith. Thus, the theological virtues are human virtues transformed: as "the restoration and perfection to its true activity of a personal capacity for response which has been perverted," theological virtues are simply "virtues insofar as they are theological."[42] We can say that *any* virtue may become theological, insofar as it becomes a

37. Ibid., 153.
38. Niebuhr, *Faith on Earth*, 67–68.
39. Niebuhr, *The Meaning of Revelation*, xxxiii.
40. Niebuhr, "Reflections on Faith, Hope and Love," 153; emphasis mine.
41. I recognize that Niebuhr's account of the Thomistic account of virtue may be controversial; I neither defend nor endorse it. My reason for discussing it is the integral part in plays in Niebuhr's own account of virtue.
42. Niebuhr, "Reflections on Faith, Hope and Love," 153.

disposition leading to acts that are responsive to the true character of God, to God understood as ultimately beneficent. Meanwhile, any virtue remains merely moral insofar as it remains a disposition leading to acts that are responses to God interpreted as enemy. On this account, we can characterize the virtues in general as *hermeneutical responsive dispositions*: virtues are "dispositions" because they dispose us to act in certain ways; virtues are "responsive" because the acts they dispose us to are responses to acts we suffer; and virtues are "hermeneutical" because the acts we suffer and respond to are comprehended within a larger pattern of interpretation.[43] What distinguishes the moral and theological virtues is not the nature of the end they enable us to attain, nor (as I will show shortly) the manner of their acquisition, but rather the character of the larger pattern of interpretation that orients the responsive acts they issue forth. Courage as a merely moral virtue is the disposition to respond to fearsome acts upon us as the acts of a hostile God, disposing us to defend ourselves and our proximate finite communities against all aggression. Courage as a theological virtue is the disposition to respond to fearsome acts upon us as the acts of an ultimately friendly God, disposing us to treat aggression as an opportunity to respond to such a God. While moral courage enables us to defend ourselves and our finite communities against external criticisms, theological courage enables us to respond to such criticism as though to divine judgment, discerned as ultimately pedagogical more than punitive. I think it can be a genuine instance of moral courage to defend the traditional, patriarchal language of "God the Father" within a prevailing climate of theological reconstruction that pressures us to reform. At the same time, as the first section of this chapter should suggest, I think such an instance is a failure of theological courage, a failure to respond to new symbols like "God the mother" as an opportunity to rethink the character of our symbolic activity, and thus, of our existential resonance with God.[44] Theological courage transforms moral courage by reframing our personal capacities for endurance within a wider, more life-affirming context, and affirming this entails recognizing the value of such capacities and what they can accomplish.

43. The phrase "responsive disposition" is taken from Robert Brandom's notion of "reliable differential responsive disposition," but for purposes alien to his work. See Brandom, "The Centrality of Sellars's Two-Ply Account."

44. Obviously, this account becomes much more complicated in situations of physical endangerment, whether more local (spousal abuse) or global (war, terrorism, etc.); I don't think the difference between moral and theological courage simply reduces to that between resistance and non-resistance, or violent and non-violent resistance. Still, militarily defending ourselves against threats to our life can be more or less sensitive to the long-term consequences of the *manner* of that defense. Our conduct during and after a war will affect the likelihood of future belligerence.

To understand virtues as hermeneutical responsive dispositions is to understand all virtues, even the merely moral, as gifts. When Niebuhr describes the moral virtues as habits *as opposed to* given relations, he seems to be suggesting that they are solely "achievements or products of training," and so necessarily non-gifted. While the theological virtues are "relations which depend for their continuance on the constancy with which the objective good . . . is given," the continuance of moral virtues apparently depends solely on subjective, human capacities that are not given. Again, Niebuhr fails to learn from Mead, which would enable him to complicate this distinction. Recall that, according to Mead, the self learns the various social roles of its community by taking them on, internalizing them one by one until able to take on and so participate in larger cooperative endeavors involving multiple roles and multiple interactions between them. One point of Mead's account is to contest a mimetic account of human development, whereby we are understood to take on the social roles of others simply through imitation. For Mead, the problem with the mimetic account is that it presumes that the self is substantively complete from the start, that all of the social activities to be imitated are already within us, waiting to be evoked by exterior examples. To take the social aspect of human development seriously is to appreciate that these social activities must be written into us. On Mead's account, this occurs through the various conversations of gestures that are part of our upbringing, which eventually develop into actual linguistic conversations that sustain cooperative endeavors. The significance of participating in a conversation of gestures is that we play *different* roles that evoke *different* actions from each other; whether boxing or child-care, the action proceeds by the mutual responsiveness of *different* gestures. On this account, a child does not learn to parent by simply witnessing her parents and doing likewise. Rather, the child is able to do likewise in this case because what the child is doing is what was done *to* her. The suggestion is that we can only come to imitate well what we have *suffered*, or at least what we can imagine suffering *based on what we have in fact suffered*,[45] where suffer is understood in the neutral sense of undergo. Successful social cooperation based on mutual, alternating role-taking requires participants to anticipate each other's action, and such anticipation involves imagining how another will respond to our actions, and to imagine this is to imagine them suffering our actions, and such imagination relies on our having suffered identical or similar actions. In short, our capacities for social interaction and participation are

---

45. If mindedness is ultimately rooted in gesture, as it is for Mead, than our imaginative capacities, which enable us to fore-discern alternatives, are ultimately rooted in what has happened to and with our bodies.

given to us insofar as others enact upon us, such that we suffer, the activities that sustain our communities.

Mead's account of human development in this regard has ramifications for understanding the virtues. Insofar as our responses to others are given to us in and through those relations responsible for our development, and insofar as all virtues can be understood as responsive dispositions, all virtues can be understood as gifts. Consider moral courage as the disposition to respond to fearsome and possibly painful acts so as to confront rather than flee from them. On Mead's account, we *fully* learn the virtue of courage, not merely by witnessing and imitating it, but more significantly by suffering or undergoing courageous acts. In what would such moral suffering consist? I can think of two options. First, we may experience someone courageously confronting us when we act fearsomely towards her. This is perhaps the most direct way to suffer courage, but as a moral-pedagogical avenue it is limited because it relies on our being able to discern such a confrontation as an exemplification of a virtue rather than as simply a counter-attack—that is, as an overcoming of fear rather than as an aggressive act. In other words, learning from this relies on our recognizing virtue *despite* our self-interest, and such recognition seems to presume rather than ground virtue. The second option does not have this limitation: it is the experience of someone performing a courageous act on our behalf. Recall that, for Mead, the mutual play of responses in conversations of gestures is practical, because its function is to keep the social endeavor going. The function of virtues as responsive dispositions is similar: their enactment serves the social participation of their agent. Thus, courageous acts include those that defend a social endeavor from threats. In this case, to suffer a courageous act is to suffer the defense of the community in which one participates. For instance, a child suffers his mother's courage when she confronts a threat to their familial unit. Such suffering involves more than gaining epistemic access to some external exemplar, because the child in this case shares both the fear that the mother's courage overcomes and the benefit resulting from the courageous act. All of this is to say that the situation in which the mother exercises her courage *existentially resonates* with the child, who comes to grasp the meaning of courage through its place in that situation. Courage is the disposition to so respond to fear as to confront it for the sake of the community from which we derive value. The mother's courage is a gift to the child because it is by undergoing situations in which courageous acts are experienced as responsible for resolving fearsome threats that the child is enabled to take on his mother's courage in future situations.

If the dichotomy between moral and theological virtues can be dissolved insofar as both can be understood structurally as gifts, then we can deepen this dissolution by seeing that the gifted-character of virtues does not compete with their habit-character. Again, in order to see this we need to take Niebuhr beyond himself. His allergy to understanding virtues as habits seems to stem from the typically Protestant anxiety about works-righteousness. As I noted above, the distinction between gifts and habits appears to be that between depending on an objective good and being subjectively self-sufficient; while habits may prepare us to receive gifts, they cannot achieve what the gifts do. Niebuhr seems to be worried that understanding virtues as habits will lead people to persist in their idolatry, rather than to be open to God. This might dovetail with the more general worry that habits are necessarily routine, in the sense of deadeningly repetitive, tools of a social faith seeking to absorb our agency into its self-defensive protocols. In both cases, Niebuhr is neglecting his own resources. First, both Luther and Calvin recognized a difference between works before and after justification; while the former are efforts at self-justification, the latter are expressions of divine justification, through acts of neighbor-love and aspirations to Christian progress. Following this tradition and Niebuhr's own logic in the article under discussion, a similar distinction could be made between courage as a merely moral and as a theological virtue. As merely moral, courage is the habit of self-defense in the face of fear; as theological, courage is the habit, in the face of fear, of opening one's self and finite communities to others as fallible exemplars, that is, as exemplifying a way of life that is life-giving rather than death-dealing, but fallibly so, such that an aspect of its life-giving character is its openness to external criticisms. Both versions of courage entail human activity, and so can be understood as human achievements. Moreover, both versions can be understood as habits *enabled* by their gifted character; whether merely moral or robustly theological, courage can only be taken on insofar as it is suffered as an aspect of what is given in the transmission of a social inheritance. As we will see soon, part of what distinguishes the character of courage is the character of the community, loyalty to which the Christian inheritance demands. Still, even if we admit that theological virtues can include properly human achievement, the worry about routine remains. Could not theological courage devolve or ossify into merely moral courage, if our acts of openness become acts intended to shame others by the fact of our openness?

On the one hand, we must affirm this possibility, for it is a possibility opened by the fact of sin. Insofar as we remain sinful, we may re-pervert the personal capacity for response that God restores and perfects. This is why Niebuhr characterizes the Christian life as one of 'permanent revolution.'[46]

---

46. See Niebuhr, *The Meaning of Revelation*.

Humans do achieve something through the theological virtues, but such achievements are never final. If we neglect this second part, we can all too easily turn some past achievement into a rigid blueprint for response, which can be ironically unresponsive to changing circumstances.[47] On the other hand, that the possibility of such devolution into deadening routine is endemic to virtue does not mean that virtue is fated to it. By conceiving of virtues as *responsive* dispositions, I mean to affirm that virtues at their best are open and flexible, in the sense that they are responsive to novel circumstances. What courage entails in particular situations is as various as the sorts of fearsomeness that arise to evoke courage. Recall that Mead's example of taking on a communal endeavor, which involves the ability, at least imaginatively, to take on all of the roles that compose that endeavor, is playing baseball. Any particular position player is able to field successively because they can take on all of the roles, and the potential actions proceeding from them, which are involved in any particular play. The upshot of this example is to show that coming to take one's place within a community involves the capacity to interact with others in changing circumstances, not to occupy a station whose role exhaustively determines in advance the range of one's actions. Similarly, learning to be courageous involves not only learning *that* we should confront rather than flee from fearsome danger, but more importantly, learning *how* to confront the various forms of danger that we encounter in various situations. Suffering courage provides personal resources for such learning, and the more variously we have suffered courage the richer those resources are. Still, more is required, such as learning the place of courage within communal life more generally, including its place among the other virtues, as well as learning its place within the tendencies of our own capacities, all of which comes with the continuing experience of communal participation and our reflection on it. In short, there is an intrinsic creativity to virtue understood as responsive disposition, but only and precisely insofar as our responses are not pre-determined. Creativity, *not* routine, is an essential aspect of the habit of virtue.

To summarize briefly, before pressing on: moral virtues are, structurally speaking, gifts as much as theological virtues. In both cases, virtues are given exteriorly, in manifest exemplars, and interiorly, in the renewal of our responsive capacities. Meanwhile, my detour through Mead enables us to see that the exterior and interior aspects of gifted virtues are inextricable, because our responsive capacities are enabled by the manifest actions we suffer. We do not have to posit something magical or mysterious to account

---

47. For an example of this, see Eddie Glaude's discussion of the contemporary relevance for black politics of the civil rights movement, in Glaude, *In a Shade of Blue*, chapter 6.

for interior renewal. On this account, development occurs from the outside in; the exercise of our responsive capacities in a new situation partly results from situations we have undergone in a participatory manner in the past. Thus, virtuous agents can be understood to give virtues insofar as they provide external examples that, within the context of a situation, renew our internal capacities themselves. Moreover, virtues are as much habits as they are gifts. What is given in the renewal of internal capacities is precisely the capacity to enact a habit. Significantly, part of that habit is creativity.

Now I need to press my point about the gifted character of virtue one more step, which should clarify how virtues can be understood as creative habits. I have conceived the virtues as "*hermeneutic* responsive dispositions" because, on Niebuhr's account of responsibility, the exercise of our responsive capacities is oriented by interpretive frameworks that are responsible for characterizing the actions that evoke our responsive capacities. These interpretive frameworks are part of what is given by the virtuous to the members of their communities through their virtuous acts. Admittedly, the transmission of such a framework can be disarticulated from explicit moral activity—e.g., by isolating it as a specific, scholastic function of communal formation—but each performance of a virtue transmits that framework insofar as each performance instantiates the framework. Moreover, the virtuous transmission of interpretive frameworks is likely to be more significant than the scholastic transmission, for at least two reasons. First, since the virtues are responsive dispositions exercised in everyday, existentially resonant situations, their lessons are likely to stick. Second, insofar as we are at root practical creatures, whatever interpretive framework becomes manifest in our virtuous acts is the one we truly live by, regardless of the one we claim to live by. Exploring the hermeneutic character of virtue requires turning to the classic theological virtues.

As my discussion in chapter 4 bore out, Niebuhr's theo-ethical position is funded by an understanding of the character and significance of faith, which makes no appeal to love and hope. This is to say, Niebuhr's account and use of faith is disengaged from a larger account of the classic theological virtues. Because of this fact about his larger corpus, it is surprising that his essay on virtue does *not* privilege faith, insisting that each of the classic theological virtues "has its distinctive character, but none of them can be in action without the others." Love regards our "existence in devotion to the good" and is characterized by the double response "to God as the self's good, fulfilling all its need, and to all creaturely beings which are good for God, whether or not their goodness for the self has become evident." Faith regards our "existence in covenant relations" and is characterized by the double response "to God as the faithful One who keeps his promises, and to his creatures to whom he has made his promises and to whom the self is united in covenant." Niebuhr is clear that there is no hierarchy between these two. It is a matter of personal contingency whether one's first existentially significant response is love or faith, though the Christian life demands that whichever comes first be perfected by the other. While love and faith are ascribed to God in scripture, hope is not so ascribed, and so is itself "the particularly human theological virtue." Hope regards our "existence in time" and has two sides. First, hope is a three-fold expectation: of the manifestation of God's love and faith; of the self's perfection in love and faith; and of the kingdom of God, which consists of relations of perfected love and faith between finite beings, and between finite beings and God. Second, hope is "the exercise of faith and love in the temporal dimension," or the form of faith and love in regard to the future, and then from there, to the present and past.[48] Niebuhr is suggesting that faith and love complete each other, while hope humanizes them eschatologically, putting them to work in human life by orienting that life before the horizon of God's promised goodness.

In light of his larger corpus, this scant account of the unity of the classic theological virtues is peculiar. Each virtue is aligned with a typical human response: love, to the good; faith, to the reliability (understood as both trustworthiness and loyalty) of relations; hope, to our timefullness. By insisting that each virtue is distinctive, HRN is implying that faith does *not* regard the good, *nor* time. However, this is in tension with his account of faith in *The Responsible Self*, where radical trust is understood to interpret God as good rather than evil, and so to interpret the world as governed by a teleology of resurrection rather than of entombment. On this account, faith enables us to love rather than hate God and to confront time as pregnant with possibility rather than determined to death. Even structurally, regardless of its character as radical or social, faith as trust and loyalty is intrinsically oriented to time and the good. To trust someone is to expect that in the *future* she will act in a particular way, and such trust is often based on *past* experience. To be loyal to some cause entails *valuing* that cause, recognizing it as *good*. When loyalty to some cause is based on trust in the person endorsing the cause, then the value of the cause is inferred from the value of that person. Meanwhile, enduring loyalty to a cause would seem to involve the expectation that the cause remain good across time, again, an expectation often based on past loyal experience. Now, the point of this quibbling is not to demonstrate that Niebuhr is inconsistent, nor to claim that love and hope are reducible to faith. Rather, it reflects how rich his conception of faith is. At the same time, I mean to mark that my reconstruction of

---

48. Niebuhr, "Reflections on Faith, Hope and Love," 154–56.

Niebuhr's account of virtue departs from Niebuhr's own explicit discussion of virtue, similar to the way my reconstruction of Niebuhr's account of faith in light of Mead's I/me distinction departs from Niebuhr's own discussion of Mead. Granted, Niebuhr's explicit account of the classic theological virtues in the posthumous essay is more traditional, but building off of the richness of his privileging of faith is more fitting to the trajectory of his entire work.

I will take up Niebuhr's suggestion that the theological virtues are best understood as reconstructed moral virtues, which expands the number of properly theological virtues, so that what distinguishes the classic theological virtues is chief-ness or inclusivity. Virtues in general can be understood as hermeneutic responsive dispositions. As the restoration and perfection of such dispositions, the specifically theological virtues can be understood as transformed moral virtues, and perhaps more specifically as the moral virtues made theo-centric. So, we might say that courage has a theological form as the confrontation of fearsome danger before God, as well as a merely moral form as the confrontation of fearsome danger vis-à-vis our finite communities. However, the distinction between moral and theological is more complicated, and this will become clear once I give an account of faith as a theological virtue.

I have already noted that the hermeneutic aspect of virtue is responsible for the difference between the merely moral and the theological: merely moral virtues are exercised in a narrow context, surrounded by what the self discerns to be hostile forces, while theological virtues are exercised in a cosmic context and responsive to perceived threats as opportunities to contribute to the life of permanent revolution. This is to say that the difference between merely moral and theological virtues regards whether they are oriented by radical faith as radically distrusting and disloyal or as radically trusting and loyal. The transformation of moral virtues into theological virtues is thus a function of the transformation of our faith. In this way, radical faith can be understood as the most chief and inclusive of the theological virtues, for it is responsible for the transformation of the interpretive framework which is itself responsible for the character of all other virtues. While it is intuitive to affirm that the theological virtues are the moral virtues made theo-centric, Niebuhr's account of faith complicates this. The merely moral virtues are not less oriented in their exercise by a relation to God than the theological virtues, but rather oriented by a relation to God that is misinterpreted. Because radical distrust construes God as enemy and God's world as a web of hostile forces, it restricts the exercise of our virtues so that they become the tools of finite communal self-defense. We can say that, in terms of their exercise the merely moral virtues are community-centric, but in terms of their animating hermeneutic they are distrustfully theo-centric.

So, while the exercise of courage as merely moral reduces to communal self-defense, the virtue itself is animated by a theological form of faith that is radically distrustful. The way to transform courage, or any other moral virtue, so that its exercise becomes properly theological is to transform the character of the theological faith that animates it.

What is peculiar about this account is that faith—as radical, which is to say, as a theological virtue—can no longer be understood as necessarily good. The account would be simpler if we could understand the merely moral virtues to be animated by social (and so a merely moral form of) faith, and the theological virtues to be animated by radical faith. Instead, Niebuhr implies a more dynamic model. Just as the merely moral virtues cannot be understood as constitutively non-theological or a-theological, so the properly theological virtues cannot be understood as disconnected from the social faiths with which we conduct our life with finite others in finite communities. Recall that radical faith emerges as the transformation of social faith; just so, the theological virtues emerge as the transformations of moral virtues. In fact, the former transformation can now be understood as the privileged instance of the latter transformation. This means that the theological/moral distinction in virtue aligns with the theologically reconstructed I/me distinction in the self, though the distinction between exercising merely moral and properly theological virtues regards the character of the "I," which in light of last section we can understand as the character of our existential resonance with God. In other words, the moral virtues are aspects of our social inheritances, and so aspects of our various "me's," while the theological virtues, those virtues animated by radical faith, emerge as their modifications through our "I." What is responsible for the transformation of our moral virtues into theological virtues is the transformation of our social faith into radical faith, and what is responsible for the transformation of our exercise of the moral virtues, so that they are exercised as properly theological rather than merely moral, is the transformation of our radical faith from distrust to trust. Just as radical faith manifests as a way or manner of living out social faith, so the theological virtues manifest as a way or manner of exercising the moral virtues. Insofar as our "I" is attuned distrustfully to God as enemy, we exercise the moral virtues dogmatically, as static dispositions of communal self-defense in a world construed as fundamentally hostile. Insofar as our "I" is attuned trustfully to God as friend, we exercise the moral virtues as flexible dispositions, open to transformation because their sphere of concern is understood to be that sphere about which God is concerned, the universal community of being. I have affirmed that virtues are dispositions, but it is essential to see that this does not mean that virtues are, or even ever become, fixed states. The Christian life of "permanent revolution" means, for our moral life, that our exercise of moral virtues be ceaselessly renovated.

The place of the *exercise* of the virtues in our theo-ethical life is structurally similar to that of symbols, in the sense that both are aspects of the social life of finite communities by which we orient our lives to God. With the use of linguistic symbols, we characterize the divine-human relation, and with symbolic deeds, we characterize human life, both individually and collectively, in hermeneutically responsive relation to God. Now, insofar as our deeds spring from our virtues, the character of our deeds, by which they characterize human life, is a function of the character of our virtues, which is itself a function of the character of our theological faith, that is, of our "I," our existential resonance with God. Of course, the use of linguistic symbols is itself a deed, and as we saw in the prior section, the manner in which we carry this out is also a function of the character of our existential resonance. Given the orienting connection between radical faith and the moral virtues, we can now understand our linguistic symbolic activity to be performed according to the character of our moral virtues. It is one thing to existentially resonate with God in such a way that "God the mother" strikes us as a fitting symbol, but it takes some degree of courage to utter it and propose it to others in a context in which the male gender is still taken to be normative. This point about context is especially crucial when considering the virtues, since I have also suggested that defending traditional symbols like "God the Father" can also be courageous in particular circumstances, i.e., those of overwhelming reform. What distinguishes merely moral from theological courage is the *ultimate* context in which the self construes its exercise of courage to occur. It is courageous to swim against the grain of social convention or prevailing trends, but such courage fails to be radical if its impetus is merely the grain of another convention or trend. Courageously defending traditional symbols is merely moral to the extent that its point is to defend the privileged place that males are perceived to have lost. On the other hand, courageously using and endorsing new symbols is properly theological only to the extent that its purpose is to confess a God who is ultimately beneficent and calls us to devote ourselves to God's own cause, the universal community of being. Meanwhile, our use of new symbols will become restricted to conflicts between social faiths insofar as the theological courage motivating it becomes merely moral, which will happen insofar as our theological faith fails to be radically trustful. The emergence of radical trust in one instance does not guarantee its enduring presence, though it enables us to await its coming.

So, the character of our symbolic activity is a function of, and thus expresses, our moral character, which in turn is a function of, and thus expresses, the character of our faith. If radically distrustful, we will regard the current status of the moral virtues in our communities as a static blueprint to guide future conduct, and we will regard the currently accepted symbols as final characterizations of our relation to God. If radically trustful, we will regard our moral virtues as flexible dispositions able to be shaped and reshaped in light of novel circumstances, and we will regard our current stock of symbols as susceptible to renewal with the influx of new symbols. Thus, radical creativity is a matter of novel symbolization *and* novel practical action. As with the renewal of symbols, so with the reshaping of the virtues: it is a process that takes time, so that judging whether or not particular exercises of a virtue are violating or reshaping the virtue requires continuous critical discernment. Using and endorsing "God the mother," and (more politically) appointing a female bishop, can be easily understood to express cowardice rather than courage, and so betray rather than fidelity, because they seem to be the capitulation of traditional Christian language and social structure to impinging political forces, rather than a robust defense of the church against her critics. To recognize the emergent character of radical trust is to recognize, first, that endorsing "God the mother" and appointing a female bishop may in fact initially be capitulation to external pressures, but second, that they could become a new manner of confessing the one good God, a manner of confession that expresses a new form of courage because it involves confronting *internal*, rather than external, pressures. Again, critical discernment cannot involve insuring that it is positive radical faith rather than social faith that animates such actions, since only God is privy to that, and since the point of this example is to suggest that the dynamism of emergence means attending to what virtues can become, not what they were at some point. Still, critical discernment can identify and resist forms of social faith that resist transformation, not only the faith of the old guard, but also that of any new guard that ends up triumphing.

I have argued that the justification of critical discernment is its willingness to turn back on itself. In fact, such willingness can be understood as the distinguishing quality of radical creativity, a sign of the intended permanently revolutionary character of Christian life. Symbolic creativity issues in new symbols, but such creativity is radical only to the extent that it is willing to renew older symbols *and* make its own symbols vulnerable to renewal through whatever newer symbols may emerge. Virtuous creativity issues in novel actions, in new ways of expressing our responsive dispositions that reshape them, but this is radical only to the extent that it is willing to make its reshaped virtues vulnerable to even further reshaping. I think the paradigmatic instance of this is when the exercise of moral virtues is turned back against their communal home. Let me explain. I take it that one important function of the moral virtues, as responsive dispositions that are exercised in social interaction, is to maintain that form of social life through which a particular community persists over time. To use my privileged example, a function of courage is to dispose the members of a community to confront rather than flee dangerous threats so that the community does not disintegrate whenever it is met with fearsome challenges. Given our sinful tendency to self-defense, courage easily becomes routinized as the disposition to defend our community from any and all external criticism. One obvious example of *radical* virtuous creativity, which I have been noting throughout this section, is when the exercise of courage involves confronting fearsome threats to the universal community of being that come from *within* one's own finite community. In this instance, courage transforms from being an exercise of self-defense against external criticism to becoming an exercise of internal criticism. In this regard, I have been discussing the status of women in Christian communities throughout this chapter, but a discussion of Bartelomo de las Casas's defense of the American Indians would be fitting as well.

The radicality of virtuous creativity does not necessitate this measure of communal self-criticism, nor does it necessarily preclude the criticism of other communities. For example, the transformation of the exercise of justice may involve revising the scope of its exercise, though not in response to any injustice being exercised within the community. A community may come to realize, as their social faith is being renovated into positive radical faith, that justice demands attending not only to the equality of present access to goods and opportunities, but also to the equality of capacities that are historically conditioned, and this may involve instituting inequalities at the level of present access in order to redress inequalities at the level of capacities. Such virtuous creativity would involve re-contextualizing justice, widening its scope to include what Niebuhr would call the timefulness of selves, but it would depend on the perceived failure of justice in its present form, rather than on the perpetration of injustice within the community. Meanwhile, radical virtuous creativity may also involve critically retrieving a seemingly outdated virtue like modesty insofar as it now strikes us as a fitting response to the dangers of overconsumption, overdevelopment, and an oversexualized media.[49] Such retrieval might be motivated by the discernment of these vices in surrounding communities and the fear that they are invading one's own communities. Still, insofar as this retrieval is meant to resist these vices everywhere, and not only within our own communities, and insofar as it involves the recognition that we are just as likely

---

49. See Hartman, "A Proposal for Modesty."

as anyone to participate in such vices, then our resistance to external vice is less likely to get caught up in a conflict of merely social faiths. In short, the radicality of virtuous creativity neither demands resistance to internal vice, nor excludes resistance to external vice. It only requires the willingness of communities to reshape their virtues, again and again, allowing them to solidify but never freeze, even and especially when this involves internal criticism of our own virtuous achievements.

Just as symbolic creativity is a contingent form of creativity, so is virtuous creativity. First, it depends upon a socially mediated tradition of the virtues and their characteristic exercises. To use the example of courage, it can be challenging to discern that resistance to one's own community—from within it and possibly funded by external criticisms—is an exercise of courage, precisely because courage is a virtue often understood to be properly in service to some form of self-defense. Such an exercise of courage is a fitting challenge to past exercises of courage only because of the contingencies of courage's own history. Second, virtuous creativity depends upon the character of our existential resonance with God, which is to say, on the character of our most chief virtue, faith. Courage as merely moral and routinized could only become properly theological to the extent that our necessarily social faith is becoming properly theological. This transformation is contingent on God. In this second respect, we can discern the duplex character of virtuous creativity. God transforms our negative radical faith into positive radical faith, which renders to us a transformed relation to our social faith, so that we occupy it as open and flexible rather than closed and fixed. This in turn renders the transformation of our moral virtues, from being merely moral to becoming properly theological. This double dynamic captures the double sense of this book's title: "transforming faith" means, first, the faith that is transformed by God, and second, the faith that transforms our virtuous life from being conducted merely intra-communally, to becoming a way of responsible engagement with God's universe. The transformation of our radical faith entails that our naturally political virtuous life become cosmic, the feedback effect of which is the transformation of the political character of that life. To use a popular term in Christian ethics, the relevant *polis* for the Christian virtuous life is the good cosmos God creates and redeems, not the Christian community. What should distinguish the Christian community, as a finite *polis* among others, is its willingness to having its social faith transformed so that it may be open to the cosmos. The potential signs of this distinction are forms of creativity: virtuous creativity, which may involve the exercise of moral virtues against the Christian community itself, as well as symbolic creativity, which often involves the criticism of that community's own traditional language.

Linguistic symbolic creativity is an instance of virtuous creativity. I have been suggesting that properly theological courage is the transformed disposition that enables us to engage in and endorse novel symbolization, but it would be possible to show that other virtues are involved, such as justice (e.g., using "God the mother" exemplifies the recognition of the equal status of women before God) or temperance (e.g., for males, using "God the mother" might exemplify restraining the impulse to overidentify with God). If we expand the sense of symbolic however, then virtuous creativity simply is a form of symbolic creativity. Recall again that Niebuhr refers to deeds as symbolic; part of my intention in this section has been to follow up on the implications of this. Deeds are symbolic of the virtues that dispose them, of the hermeneutical responsive dispositions from which our deeds spring. Since, as hermeneutical, all virtues are shaped by a radical interpretation of the divine agency, and since faith is responsible for that interpretation, then all deeds are also symbolic, through the virtues that dispose them, of the character of our faith. So, deeds symbolize virtues, which in turn symbolize the chief virtue, faith. Linguistic symbolic creativity is such a deed, and insofar as such creativity is motivated by the existential resonance with God that *is* our faith, then linguistic symbolic creativity can be understood as reflexive creativity, that is, the form of creativity that allows us to reflect on our virtuous creativity. One function of using and endorsing "God the mother," besides trying to understand our relation with God appropriately, is to provoke reflection on the character of that relation, and so to provoke reflection on what the character of our actions in the world, which are responses to that relation, should be. We might say that (linguistic) symbolic creativity is the theoretical counterpart to the practical activity of virtuous creativity. Using and endorsing "God the mother" should provoke reflection on what properly characterizes theological courage, justice, temperance, etc., and the deeds they motivate. In this way, affirming "God the mother" involves more than uttering words about our relation to God; it also involves the transformation of our virtues so that they responsively dispose deeds that symbolize that very relation. Thus, acts of justice may become more characterized by personal and involved care, than by detached calculations whose primary purpose is to thwart self-interest. Understood so expansively, symbolic creativity is at the heart of the Christian life: it is the permanent revolution of symbolic creativity, both practically, as the ceaseless transformation of our virtuous life before God in the world, and theoretically, as the ceaseless transformation of the language we use to reflect on that life.

My description of the responsible Christian life as the permanent revolution of symbolic creativity might seem to privilege human achievement. But as with all Christian anthropologies, grace must play a role. The theological virtues are not the result of humans reconstructing their moral virtues on their own, but rather of God's reconstruction of our radical faith from its natural negative form to its emergent positive form, which both enables and helps us to reconstruct our moral virtues. I claimed in the first section that our linguistic symbols of God are existentially resonant because God accommodates Godself to our symbolic activity. Understanding symbolism expansively, we can say something similar about our deeds and virtues: though particular to the individual exercising them, they come to symbolize positive radical faith more generally insofar as they resonant with others' individual existential resonances with God. In this way, to speak of theological virtues and deeds as symbols is to speak of them as exemplifications of the radically faithful responsible life before God in the world. The exemplary resonance of such virtues and deeds is a function of divine accommodation, but in this case that accommodation takes a particular historical form. Recall from chapter 4 that Niebuhr spoke of Jesus Christ as both historical figure and symbolic form. The divine grace that reconstructs our faith, thereby enabling the reconstruction of our moral virtues, is communicated to us through Jesus Christ insofar as he is symbolic.

I will conclude this chapter with a discussion about how God can be understood to morally form us through Jesus Christ. If God is to be understood as our moral former, then God must be understood to (re)create the proper faith relations between Godself and humans as well as between humans, and God must be understood to enable us to participate in the permanent revolution of symbolic creativity. God accomplishes this through Jesus Christ. As risen, Jesus Christ transforms our radical distrust into radical trust in God; as symbolic, Christ functions as enabling exemplar for the radically faithful responsible life, the shape of whose loyalty is symbolic creativity. Moreover, insofar as Christ is not only the other of radically faithful selves, but also the object of self-other interactions—that is, insofar as Christ is not only the other in the theo-centric triad of self-other-God, but also the common third in the subordinate triad of self-other-Jesus Christ— he mediates the responsible life between humans, such that his own work becomes material to be transformed rather than mechanically followed. Christ's pedagogical function is not to provide information, but to show us *how* and enable us to live a radically faithful responsible life before God, even to the point of transforming Christ's own historical example.

CONCLUDING CHRISTOLOGICAL REFLECTIONS

The point of this section is not to offer a full Christology, but rather to specify how God morally forms us through Jesus Christ as an enabling exemplar of positive radical faith and creativity. I am picking up on some more of Niebuhr's explicit christological discussions, but again the aim is reconstructive. I hope to show how Niebuhr's Christology enables us to characterize God as a moral former of humans. Though the argument here is focused on Jesus Christ, it should become clear that the position is centered on God, or better, centered on the irreducibly individual relation between Christ and God, which is an index of the individuality I have been promoting throughout this book.

Niebuhr does not distinguish between the Jesus of history and the Christ of faith, but between "Jesus Christ in history, and the symbolic Christ within."[50] While the former formulation can suggest that faith operates above or outside of history, such that the personal significance of Jesus Christ can be unmoored from his historical appearance, Niebuhr's explicit formulation suggests that the personal significance of Jesus Christ regards the internalization of his historical appearance. This enables Niebuhr to affirm historical similarities between the responsibility ethics of Jesus Christ and the ethics of "Stoic and Spinozistic universalism," while simultaneously affirming the uniqueness of Jesus Christ's ethics—not merely because Jesus Christ is the Son of God and Epictetus and Spinoza are not, but because, as Son of God, Jesus Christ is able to *accomplish* responsibility within us, beyond simply instructing us about it.[51] As I suggested in chapter 4, the key to Jesus Christ's uniqueness in this regard, and what binds his historical and symbolic aspects, is the resurrection. As an event *within* Jesus Christ's historical appearance, the resurrection is God's endorsement of his radical trust-grounded ethics, and so their establishment as divine Father and Son. As an event of "his continuing Lordship—his session at the right hand of power,"[52] the resurrection is Jesus Christ's symbolic power to reconstruct our faith *through his historical appearance*. A similar dynamic is implied but not specified in Niebuhr's early classic *The Meaning of Revelation*. Here, the concern is to find the proper historical locus for the revelation of Jesus Christ. Niebuhr distinguishes between external and internal history, which are two perspectives on the same historical events, detached observation, and practical participation. From the former perspective, Jesus is under-

---

50. Niebuhr, *The Responsible Self*, 176.
51. Ibid., 170–77.
52. Ibid., 177.

stood as "a complex of ideas about ethics and eschatology, of psychological biological elements," comparable to other such complexes.[53] As revealed of God, Jesus Christ must be discerned from the latter perspective, as the event in our lived history "in whom we see the righteousness of God, his power and wisdom," and from whom we "derive the concepts which make possible the elucidation of all the events in our history."[54] What Niebuhr's later works specify is that the resurrection is both the validation of Jesus Christ's historical existence as the revelation of God's righteousness, power and wisdom, *and* the power of that historical appearance to orient human life.

As risen, Jesus Christ is the symbol of God for us. More specifically, Jesus Christ's historical life symbolizes God's relation to the world and exemplifies the proper response to that relation, and insofar as he is risen, that life enables us to live likewise. In the first section, I drew a connection between symbols and existential resonance. Human life consists in existentially resonant—lived, experienced, personally significant—interaction with others and the world. From Mead's developmental perspective, this interaction is initially bodily, occurring through conversations of gestures, which then become linguistic and conceptual. The symbols we use expressively articulate our existential resonance, which is not to say that they are merely subjective; "existential resonance" refers to our lived interaction with objective realities, so symbols that successfully articulate that resonance can put us in touch with those realities. Thus, symbols themselves can become existentially resonant, and end up being used and endorsed by those whose lived experience with others in the world they articulate. Social inheritances, in turn, can be understood as depositories of precisely such symbols. Now, to speak of Jesus Christ as *symbol of God* is to say that Jesus Christ puts us in touch with the reality of God, through his existential resonance with God. This is one aspect of Niebuhr's insistence, "Not eschatology but sonship to God is the key to Jesus' ethics," that is, not "extreme hopefulness, with the repentance it entails," but instead the "realization of the present rule of God in the course of daily and natural events."[55] Jesus Christ symbolizes God because through him God, the One who is beyond the many, becomes present to the many. Importantly, the mechanism of such making-present can only be the communication of existential resonance, and such communication can only occur appropriately through Jesus Christ's historical existence, the teaching and conduct characterized by that very "unique devotion to" and "single-hearted trust in" God which constitute his sonship.

---

53. Niebuhr, *The Meaning of Revelation*, 34.
54. Ibid., 50.
55. Niebuhr, *Christ and Culture*, 22.

Niebuhr explains, "He does not direct attention away from this world to another; but from all worlds, present and future, material and spiritual, to the One who creates all worlds, who is the Other of all worlds."[56] In other words, Jesus Christ refers us away from our particular human values, powers, and histories, but only to put us in touch with a God who works in and through all values, power, and histories.[57] The point is that Jesus Christ does not represent God as some being separated or absent from the world, who could be satisfactorily captured in some impersonal media, but rather is himself God's reverberation throughout the world. The only way to participate in this divine reverberation, so as to be in touch with God, is to be in community with Jesus Christ, so as to become resonant with his existential resonance with God.

Moreover, Jesus Christ is the symbol of God *for us*. Niebuhr characterizes the divine sonship as an "ambivalent process" with a "double movement": "he is a single person wholly directed as man toward God and wholly directed in his unity with the Father toward men."[58] Insofar as Jesus Christ symbolizes God's relation to the world in and through his historical existence, he is human moving toward God; insofar as his historical existence is a resonant force in our lives that enables us to live a similarly devoted and single-heartedly trustful existence, he is God (now as Son of the Father) moving toward humanity. This resonant enabling is the work of the Spirit. Recall from chapter 4 that, as the "principle of communion" that is an attribute of the Father and the Son, the Spirit "makes it possible for us to be selves with them," which is to say that the Spirit enables us to participate in the same faith relation that unites Jesus Christ and God as Son and Father, to be positively radically trustful in God and loyal to God's cause.[59] Of course, it is precisely this participation that, in turn, enables us to engage in our own symbolic and virtuous creativity. Following this, the duplex character of virtuous creativity can be construed along the traditional lines of justification and sanctification. The Spirit's work is justification, the transformation of our natural negative radical faith into positive radical faith, of our radical distrust into radical trust.[60] Our "Spirited" work, our own

---

56. Ibid., 27–28.

57. Despite connotations of distance, to call God the "Other" of all human worlds is to identify God as the One able to relate to all human worlds.

58. Niebuhr, *Christ and Culture*, 28–29.

59. Niebuhr, *Faith on Earth*, 105.

60. Recall that Niebuhr interprets redemption as "the liberty to interpret in trust all that happens as contained within an intention and a total activity that includes death within the domain of life, that destroys only to re-establish and renew." See Niebuhr, *The Responsible Self*, 142.

work oriented and animated by the emergence of radical trust, is sanctification, the transformation of human life, both individual and social, from a rebellious, hostile existence into one of service to the divine cause, precisely through radical symbolic and virtuous creativity.

In this sense, radical creativity is sanctified creativity. Pressing our social faiths and the moral virtues they orient and animate into service to the divine cause of loyalty to the universal community of being requires divine aid. Whether or not a particular example of creativity is in fact sanctified is not something that is presently evident, but only discerned in retrospect. Hence, using and endorsing "God the mother" as an act of courageous resistance against the self-defensive tendencies of a merely social faith within one's own Christian community, may in the long run come to be seen as an example of sanctification, so long as such use and endorsement does not become expressive of self-defensive tendencies of another merely social faith within one's Christian community. This particular example seems to emphasize self-expression over self-denial, and so perhaps pride over humility, insofar it emphasizes the self's creativity. However, it is important to recall that a properly theological use of "God the mother" expresses not the self isolated from all lateral and transcendent relations, but the existential resonance between self and God. At the same time, such self-expression involves a form of self-denial, that is, the denial of those selves ceaselessly given to us through those social relations that constitute our finite communities and demand social faith, as ultimate.

It is essential to appreciate that the self-denial constitutive of sanctified creativity is not the categorical denial of our social selves, our selves insofar as they are conditioned by social inheritances, but rather the denial of those selves as our true selves. A major aspect of Jesus Christ's symbolic function is to exemplify and enable the re-interpretation of social inheritances, pressing them into service to the divine cause despite their resistance to it. In this respect, in order to occupy any social inheritance as Jesus Christ would, we must be willing to continually re-interpret it anew, to keep it open and flexible so that it is less likely to curve in on itself and can more easily be pressed into divine service. Paradoxically, this willingness must extend to those social inheritances that center on Jesus Christ. Consider Calvin's account of the Decalogue; for each negative injunction, he delineates a positive injunction, so that obedience to the divine command requires, beyond withholding maleficent actions, the performance of beneficent actions.[61] On my account, to follow Jesus Christ requires something similar, in the sense that it involves re-working traditions centered on Jesus Christ. What Calvin did

---

61. Calvin, *Institutes*, 367–415.

to the Decalogue, we must do to Jesus Christ's parables and sermons. Of course, New Testament scholarship affirms that the gospels, both canonical and non-canonical, are the result of precisely such re-working. The Markan Jesus offers no great sermon, and while both the Matthean and Lukan Jesus do, only the latter adds curses to its benedictions; meanwhile, the Johannine Jesus seems to occupy a very different narrative and symbolic universe. To the extent that Christians affirm this sort of variety, there would seem to be no Christian presumption against the creative use of Christian traditions. My point is that Jesus Christ is the enabling exemplar of such use, and as such, can be turned back against social inheritances that center on him. Jesus Christ invoked God as Father, but as I have been arguing throughout this chapter, following Jesus Christ today may mean creatively using that invocation, by invoking God as Mother.

In order to understand how this might work, we must renew the discussion of the triads of faith from chapter 4. Recall that Niebuhr understood the triad of Christian faith to be composed of the human self, Jesus Christ as our other, and God as the common third, with the Spirit binding all three together. Through interaction with Jesus Christ, empowered by the Spirit, the human self is put in touch with God; from another perspective, God encounters the human self decisively through divine interaction with Jesus Christ. Recall also that this triad includes a subordinate triad, composed of the human self, human and companionate others, and Jesus Christ as the common third. To recognize this subordinate triad means to recognize that Jesus Christ is historically and socially mediated. Meanwhile, to recognize this triad as subordinate means to recognize that the historically and socially mediated Jesus Christ, the one who emerges from responsible relations between human selves, is not the full Jesus Christ. Because we are human, historical-social mediation will necessarily condition our encounter with Jesus Christ; because Jesus Christ is divine, such mediation should not determine that encounter. The subordinate triad is meant to open onto the theo-centric triad, and this is possible because the resurrection has decisively installed Jesus Christ as the Son of the God who can now be understood as Father. I have said that the resurrection renders Jesus Christ an existentially resonant force in our lives; because he is risen, his historical example is no longer a curiosity shut up in the past, but a present event that evokes response. In this sense, the resurrection renders Jesus Christ that responsible other for us who can put us in touch with God.

This has ramifications for the way we occupy the subordinate triad. The point of constructing and participating in communities and traditions that center on Jesus Christ is to bring people together so that they can be led by Jesus Christ to God. Properly speaking, Christian traditions should not be about Jesus Christ, but about God through Jesus Christ. The faith that Christian communities propagate should not be a trust in and loyalty to Jesus Christ, isolated from trust in and loyalty to God; as Niebuhr notes, this all too easily becomes faith in Christian communities themselves. Rather, Christian communities should help us to become participants in Jesus Christ's own faith: trust in God as the good Father of all, and loyalty to that Father's cause of ultimate benevolence toward the universal community of being. Since his faith involved creatively using his own religious tradition, in order to render it appropriate for serving God—the parable of the Good Samaritan, etc.—participating in his faith requires a similar creative use of our own religious traditions. The peculiarity of our Christian faith is that it involves creatively using those very religious traditions that focus on the exemplar of such symbolic and virtuous creativity. Participating in Jesus Christ's own faith involves the reworking of those very social inheritances that are the first and most enduring sources of our access to Jesus Christ and his faith. Jesus Christ's *own* faith demands the radical transformation of any and all finite faiths, especially faiths that are *about* Jesus Christ.

The work of Jesus Christ, accomplished through the Spirit, is to pull us from the subordinate triad that focuses on him, into the theo-centric triad of Christian faith proper, which centers on God. Our work as participants in Jesus Christ's own faith, also accomplished through the Spirit, is to occupy the subordinate triad non-dogmatically, which means to be willing to engage in and endorse symbolic and virtuous creativity that re-works social inheritances that center on Jesus Christ, so that they ultimately center on God. These are more complete understandings of justification and sanctification, respectively. Because such creativity is irreducibly individual, insofar as it is funded by an irreducibly individual radical faith, by forming us to engage in this creativity, Jesus Christ is contributing to the form of moral formation I have been endorsing throughout this book, one in which individual development inclusive of yet beyond socialization is the goal. Jesus Christ's moral formation turns on transforming faith, in the two senses that this chapter has articulated it. First, the risen Jesus Christ, through the Spirit and in God, transforms our natural negative radical faith into positive radical faith. This transformation is not reducible to socialization; after all, justification is not reducible to becoming a participant in some Christian community. Rather, the transformation of our radical faith is something that can and should occur within Christian communities, insofar as negative radical faith can manifest as social faith in these communities. Such transformation does not categorically cut against the grain of socialization, as though all social inheritances were inescapably on the road to perdition. Rather, it results in a renewed reflexive posture towards our social inheritances, a posture that understands them to be flexible and vulnerable to change rather than static blueprints and tools for reproduction—redeemable rather than fated. This posture is necessarily individual, in the sense that it resists becoming reduced to a communal function, but it is hardly isolated. It is the posture of a self that is caught up in the faith relations that bind Father and Son, and that seeks companions in a human form of community that has yet to emerge.

Second, the risen Jesus Christ, again through the Spirit and in God, serves as an enabling exemplar for the transformative work that follows from positive radical faith. I take it as axiomatic that a substantial aspect of Jesus Christ's mission was the broadening of his followers' moral imaginations so that they might come to recognize those excluded by the boundaries of their finite communities as proper objects of their active moral concern, exemplified in Paul's own mission as the broadening of Jesus Christ's mission so that it included Gentiles. My point is that this broadening will often require a transformation of our social inheritances, those various "me's" that socially form us, since these are responsible for defining the borders of our moral imaginations. Such transformative work is irreducibly individual, the work of social geniuses funded by their "I's," that is, funded by their irreducibly individual positive radical faith. Jesus Christ exemplifies how and enables us to transform the various socials faiths that constitute our finite communities from the posture of a transformed radical faith. This is the second sense of 'transforming faith': transformed (radical) faith transforms (social) faith. On this account, the transformation of human life through Christian faith cannot be a matter of a social Christian faith, the social faith of a particular Christian community, forming other social faiths. Instead, the transformation of human life through Christian faith works through the ceaseless, internal transformation of Christian faith itself, from being a merely social Christian faith to being positively radical. In this way, creatively reworking one's Christian social inheritance becomes the paradigm for creatively reworking the other social inheritances we occupy. To put it in pedagogical terms, Jesus Christ's moral formation is a matter of know-how rather than know-that. To receive transformed radical faith is not to receive a body of knowledge regarding the transformation of social faiths—e.g., economic forms should be socialist, political forms should be democratic, etc.—but rather to be enabled to occupy our various social inheritances as so many venues for serving the divine cause. This account can affirm that Jesus Christ has his own politics without demanding that that politics appear as a form of social faith. Instead, such politics would be the creative integration of all social faiths, including those that constitute Christian communities, into God's cosmos, thereby transforming them into forms of life whose ultimate purpose is divine service.

Above I argued that the resurrection—understood as God's endorsement of Jesus Christ's historical existence of radical faith, which institutes God as Father and Jesus Christ as Son—renders Jesus Christ that other for us who can put us in touch with God. I also argued that this "putting in touch" is a matter of existential resonance. By existentially resonating with Jesus Christ through community with him, we participate in his existential resonance with God. I want to conclude by tracing the pedagogical ramifications of these claims. The resurrection establishes God as a moral former of humans through Jesus Christ; insofar as the raising of the historical Jesus Christ renders him symbolic, the resurrection turns Jesus Christ into God's moral curriculum for human life. This is significant: God's moral curriculum is nothing but the radically faithful historical existence of an individual human, Jesus Christ. That God elects a human individual to be the divine moral curriculum would seem to be an endorsement of existential resonance as a criterion for proper moral formation. God did not become incarnate in abstract humanity, but in a particular human individual raised in a particular cultural world and occupying a particular social location, which is to say, in a person who would existentially resonate in particular ways but not in others. Indeed, existential resonance is a matter of particularity: certain symbols of God resonant with us, but not others. Thus, the human particularity of God's moral curriculum is an index of its existential resonance.

Now, that the particular historical existence of Jesus Christ is God's chosen moral curriculum means either that God intends us to be morally formed simply *by and into* Jesus' particular existential resonance, or that God intends us to be morally formed *through* his particular existential resonance in order to resonant with God in a participative manner and so become loyal to God's cause, the universal community of particular beings. It is hopefully clear at this point that the first option stops short at a social faith in Jesus Christ, while the second option is an attempt to incarnate radical faith through a social faith in Jesus Christ. In other words, the second option makes clear that just as Jesus Christ functions as God's moral curriculum to mediate between God and humans, so he functions to mediate the radically faithful responsible life between humans trying to discern the radicality of their faith and creativity. From birth to crucifixion, Jesus Christ mediates directly between God and humans through the shape of his historical existence. The resurrection is then the provision of this individual historical existence as a moral curriculum to be utilized between humans—*not* in order to be learned as end in itself, but as a means to be put in touch with God. Post-resurrection, the historical existence of Jesus Christ is a curriculum that humans must discern together, in order to discern God.

This means that God's moral formation of humanity through Jesus Christ is not a matter of know-that—of revealing information about Godself heretofore unknown—but rather of know-how—of exemplifying a manner of human life, in all of its social complexity, that is in proper relation to God. What God teaches through Jesus Christ's own faith, is the radical faith that interprets Godself properly.

The two kinds of creativity I have discussed in this chapter, symbolic and virtuous, are the paradigmatic transformative practices that express radical faith. Hence, what God teaches through Jesus Christ's radical faith is less the deliverances of these particular practices—e.g., particular symbols and particular virtues—than the practices themselves. The point of symbolic creativity is to ensure that our symbolic activity remains truly transformative, truly open to the positive radical faith that presses it into divine service. To say "God the mother" is to denounce the ill patriarchal effects of the traditional "God the Father," but also to announce, say, an understanding of social relations that can be occupied both within and without the Christian community, which turn less on authoritarian structure of command and obedience and more on responsively sensitive structures of care and empowerment. It is precisely such social reconstruction within the Christian community that enables individual Christians to engage in social reconstruction beyond church walls. Moreover, the practice of symbolic creativity involves being critically reflexive upon its own resulting symbols. In the first instance, this means that Christians, both socially and individually, must critically reflect on the symbols provided by their moral curriculum, that is, the symbols used by Jesus Christ. That he used "God the Father" in his attempt to put us in touch in God does not entail that we simply repeat it, especially since that now-traditional symbol can be understood as a product of Jesus Christ's own symbolic creativity. In the second instance, Christians must critically reflect on the products of their own symbolic creativity. Despite any good transformative effects, "God the mother" should not be held immune from criticism. To so immunize it would be to de-radicalize the very symbolic creativity that rendered it, and so to close that creativity off from radical faith, making it expressive of a merely social faith.

Meanwhile, the point of virtuous creativity is to ensure that the exercise and development of our hermeneutic responsive dispositions also remain truly transformative, truly open to becoming properly theological rather than merely moral, such that they become expressive of positive radical faith transforming our social faiths. To exercise the virtues in a merely moral way is to exercise them merely for the purpose of maintaining the social life of the community from which they have arisen; merely moral courage is exercised paradigmatically as self-defense. To exercise virtuous creativity is to allow our merely moral virtuous activity to become theological, expressive of loyalty to God's cause, even and especially if that means that such virtuous activity must turn back critically against its home community. In this case, we become able to exercise courage as self-criticism and as openness to external criticism, even and especially if that criticism is directed toward our exercise of courage. Thus, virtuous creativity is critically reflexive virtuous activity. Again, the point is not to slavishly imitate Jesus Christ's particular expressions of radical faith through his virtuous activity and deeds, nor to rest content with our own discerned-to-be successful expressions of radical faith. Instead of drawing up tables of virtues and their exemplary deeds that distinguish the Christian community from others, because we can identify them either as those that Jesus Christ practiced or as those that are promoted by or necessary to some specific form of Christian life, individual Christians should take stock of all dispositions exercised in their various communities that are considered to be virtues, no matter how obnoxious on face value, and then continually practice transforming them so as to be expressive of radical rather than social faith. To immunize any particular virtue-become-theological from transformation, whether by resting content with it or characterizing it as irredeemable, is but another way to de-radicalize that very creativity that rendered the virtue theological in the first place, which is simply to slide back into social faith.

I have argued throughout that socialization is a necessary but insufficient moral-pedagogical task. The aim of moral formation is individual development, which is intended to fund communal development. What is at stake theologically is radical faith, our irreducibly individual and direct relation to God. So long as socialization remains the *de facto* end of moral formation, not only will the moral life of the community remain dumb to the transformative possibilities of radical trust in God and loyalty to the divine cause, but it will also remain unable to confront the radical distrust that keeps it closed to transformation. The moral point of the individual is to keep the community open, primarily to divine transformation, and so thereby to human criticism and resistance. Such transformation is the free gift of the One beyond the many, but it comes through the finite agencies that compose the many. The proper response to this transformation is radical faith, which ensures that moral communities remain open to transformation from the individuals within them, precisely by ensuring that those individuals remain open to transformation. Radical faith keeps individuals responsibly attuned to the agency of God, who in turn often works divine transformation through individuals. The expression of this theo-centric relation is the radical creativity whose exercise is ineradicably individual.

— 6 —

Conclusion

My intention throughout this book has been to argue that moral formation must ultimately be oriented toward individual development. Socialization into particular communities' traditions is essential to that task, but finally insufficient. The proclivity of moral communities to turn in on themselves—such that the scope of their moral concern contracts to the scope of their membership, while the scope of membership contracts to include primarily those attributes and performances that can be closely monitored by communal leaders and that sharply distinguish one's own community from others—demands an approach to moral formation that can form individuals to resist such contraction. Importantly, such individual resistance does not need to be a categorical opposition to community, but rather, may be the agent of communal transformation, funded by the social inheritance of the very community being transformed. In this respect, my account of individuality is confident that moral communities do in fact have the resources to contribute to their own transformation, even if their first response to such transformation is to contest it as treason. At the same time, given the fact that most people live in multiple moral communities—families, neighborhoods, occupational affiliations, churches, nations, etc.—it is probable that individual resistance to one community will also be funded by the social inheritances of other communities. For instance, feminist reformulation of traditional Christian God-talk is often taken as a violation of Christian tradition, partly because it is seen as collusion with, e.g., liberal America. What is at stake in the possibility of something like feminist Christian God-talk is the recognition of internal diversity within the Christian community, abetted by the recognition of external diversity alongside the Christian community. The figures of such diversity are individuals irreducible to their various communal relations, and it behooves moral communities in an increasingly globalized world to develop individual members who can transact with other communities in such a way that these communities can contribute to each other's moral lives. The alternatives to such transaction seem to be, at worst, hostility, and at best, indifference. Given the increasing global character of our world through technology and media, which decrease distance between geographically separated communities, indifference is an unlikely option. Humans tend to judge each other. Meanwhile, given the complexities of current life and the burden of equally complex histories, restricting one's moral purview to one's own communities seems to offer safety and security. What is needed is a non-defensive, creative transaction between communities. Because individuals are the agents of such transaction, I have been arguing, moral formation must aim for communally funded individual development.

I have articulated my argument both theologically and pedagogically. My argument required an account of individuality that could critically and creatively reflect on its social inheritances, in order to serve communal relations. To accomplish this, I appealed to the thought of H. Richard Niebuhr, read through his American intellectual heritage exemplified in Josiah Royce and George Herbert Mead. Niebuhr's notions of radical faith and social faith enabled me to articulate individuality as the self's direct relation to God (radical faith), irreducible to socially mediated relations to God and to relations with human others within communities (social faith). This direct relation to God secures the unity of the individual amidst her various communal attachments, and so is responsible for the character of her communal conduct. What is particularly useful about Niebuhr's account of faith is that it does not oppose individual and community, but rather good and bad forms of both. Radical faith takes the form of either radical distrust in God as our enemy or radical trust in God as our friend. If the former, the individual self must live in its communities self-defensively, protecting itself against divine threats by contracting the scope of its communal life. If the latter, the individual self lives in its communities in a critically creative manner, bending the social inheritances of her various communities to serve not only their own causes, but through them the divine and ultimately benevolent cause of the universal community of being. Building off of Niebuhr's account of faith, I formulated two forms of creativity, social and radical. Social creativity is the transformation of social inheritances that enables communities to better secure themselves against internal and external criticism. Radical creativity is the transformation of social inheritances that opens communities to the recognition of and service to the universal community of being in which they participate. Just as radical faith consists in the continual transformation of social faiths, so radical creativity consists in the continual transformation of social creativity; this is my articulation of what Niebuhr calls the Christian life of permanent revolution. Given communities' proclivity to moral contraction, radical creativity is more disruptive than reparative, more likely to disrupt than bolster present forms of communal life. In this respect, I have argued that Niebuhr is ultimately more devoted to Mead than to Royce.

With this formal account of faith creativity in hand, I exploited some of Niebuhr's later work in order to provide a fuller account of the character of our direct relation to God, as well as to illustrate how social and radical creativity might appear in Christian communities. I articulated our direct, irreducibly individual relation to God as existential resonance, which can take a radically trustful or distrustful form. I then articulated two forms of radical creativity, symbolic and virtuous creativity, rooted in our positive individual existential resonance with God and enabling the transformation of the symbolic and moral resources of the social inheritances of Christian communities. To flesh this out theologically, I offered a brief pedagogical Christology, in which God is understood to morally form us through Jesus Christ. God accomplishes this by offering Jesus Christ as our enabling exemplar of radical creativity whereby our social faith is transformed into radical faith and we transform our social inheritances through symbolic and virtuous creativity. That God accomplishes this through an individual, to whom we are meant to have a direct relation, irreducible to though funded by our socially mediated relations, only bolsters my portrait of individuality as an agent of communal transformation in and through its very irreducibility to social relations, as secured by its theo-centric reference.

In the end, I hope to have cleared the ground conceptually for exploring moral formation as ultimately oriented toward individual development, understood as a theologically and morally paradigmatic agency for communal development. On the one hand, the concern for individual development has a negative valence: the point is to protect individuals from tyrannical communal relations. On the other hand, the concern has a positive valence: the point is to recognize and enable the creativity of individuals that follows from a properly individual, if communally funded, relation to God. I have endeavored to show that if we balance these valences, then to protect individuality is not necessarily to protect some creation of Western liberal modernity, but rather to hallow those relations to God that each of us can only know by analogy to our own. Meanwhile, if we recognize proper individual creativity to be in service to communal development, then the hallowing of such individual relations to God does not and cannot mean the privatization of religious life. What need to be investigated further are the various shapes that individuality and radical individual creativity may take. I have discussed two examples, symbolization and virtue, and I have tried to emphasize that radical creativity is exercised as much in recognizing and endorsing novelty as in producing novelty, and that such recognition has an ineradicable temporal dimension. Further work ought to attend to these less apparent, receptive exercises of radical creativity, because they probably compose the majority of such exercises. Specifying these would ideally accomplish two things. First, it would make the life of radical faith and creativity more accessible, not in the sense of easier to live out, but in the sense of easier to begin. Since the life of radical faith and creativity is one of transforming social faith and creativity, it ought to be emphasized that initiating such a life does not mean the replacement of our social life with some heroic career, but rather the transformative renewal of our social life, down to its humblest aspects. Second, specification of more ordinary exercises of radical creativity would enable more concrete pedagogical proposals. As stated, I stuck to conceptual ground clearing rather than programmatic retooling, mostly because such retooling needs to be articulated conceptually. Still, the ground clearing is for naught if the pedagogical vision has no concrete traction.

More conceptual work needs to be done with *individuality* as well, for there is another side of the story regarding the destiny of individual lives in contemporary life. The rhetoric of this book has been to valorize the community-resistant aspects of individuality, but social theorists have recently begun discussing a dynamic referred to as 'institutional individualization'[1] or the 'new individualism.'[2] These terms describe the plight of individuals unmoored from traditional communities that provided value and meaning, but embedded in a dizzying array of globalized institutions that promise value and meaning, but only insofar as individuals figure out how to negotiate the institutional terrain. The idea is that today individuals are forced to make their own individuality significant, but the only available resources for doing so are often existentially "irresonant": plastic surgery, social media presence, consumerism, and so on. This dynamic is not an index of moral communities insulating themselves against internal and external criticism and transformation, but rather of those communities failing to gain a significant foothold in individual lives at all, much less a tyrannical foothold. In order to be morally plausible and efficacious, my theological account of individuality needs to engage these global forces and articulate how radical

---

1. Beck, *Risk Society*, chapter 5.
2. Elliot and Lemert, *The New Individualism*.

creativity relates to but differs from these rather impersonal possibilities of self-reinvention. Given the transformative vision of my argument, it is important not to be pejorative about these trends, while remaining attuned to their moral ramifications. If in fact the task of individuality is being increasingly forced upon us, then attending to the moral shape of individuality becomes that much more important.

Bibliography

Aboulafia, Mitchell. *The Cosmopolitan Self: George Herbert Mead and Continental Philosophy*. Urbana: University of Illinois Press, 2001.

———. "Introduction." In *Philosophy, Social Theory, and the Thought of George Herbert Mead*, edited by Mitchell Aboulafia, 3–17. Albany: State University of New York Press, 1991.

———. *The Mediating Self: Mead, Sartre, and Self-Determination*. New Haven: Yale University Press, 1986.

Aulen, Gustaf. *Christus Victor: An Historical Study of the Three Main Types of the Idea of Atonement*. Translated by A. G. Herbert. New York: Macmillan, 1969.

Baier, Annette. "Demoralization, Trust, and the Virtues." In *Reflections on How We Live*, 173–88. Oxford: Oxford University Press, 2010.

———. *Moral Prejudices: Essays on Ethics*. Cambridge, MA: Harvard University Press, 1995.

Balthasar, Hans Urs von. "Theology and Sanctity." In *Explorations in Theology I: The Word Made Flesh*, 181–209. San Francisco: Ignatius, 1989.

Barth, Karl. "Evangelical Theology in the Nineteenth Century." Translated by Thomas Wieser. In *The Humanity of God*, 11–33. Louisville: Westminster John Knox, 1960.

Beach-Verhey, Timothy A. *Robust Liberalism: H. Richard Niebuhr and the Ethics of American Public Life*. Waco, TX: Baylor University Press, 2011.

Beck, Ulrich. *Risk Society: Towards a New Modernity*. Translated by Mark Ritter. London: Sage, 1992.

Biggar, Nigel. *Behaving in Public: How to Do Christian Ethics*. Grand Rapids: Eerdmans, 2011.

Blumer, Herbert. *Symbolic Interactionism: Perspective and Method*. Berkeley: University of California Press, 1986.

Brandom, Robert. "The Centrality of Sellars's Two-Ply Account of Observation to the Arguments of 'Empiricism and the Philosophy of Mind.'" In *Tales of the Mighty Dead: Historical Essays in the Metaphysics of Intentionality*, 348–67. Cambridge, MA: Harvard University Press, 2002.

Byrnes, Thomas A. "H. Richard Niebuhr's Reconstruction of Jonathan Edward's Moral Theology." *The Annual of the Society of Christian Ethics* (1985) 33–55.

Calvin, John. *Institutes of the Christian Religion*. Edited by John T. McNeill. Translated by Ford Lewis Battle. Louisville: Westminster John Knox, 1960.

Clebsch, William. *American Religious Thought*. Chicago: University of Chicago Press, 1973.

Collins, Randall. *Interaction Ritual Chains*. Princeton: Princeton University Press, 2004.
Cook, Gary A. *George Herbert Mead: The Making of a Social Pragmatist*. Urbana: University of Illinois Press, 1993.
Cook, Martin L. *The Open Circle: Confessional Method in Theology*. Minneapolis: Fortress, 1991.
Daly, Mary. *Beyond God the Father: Towards a Philosophy of Women's Liberation*. Boston: Beacon, 1973.
Daniel, Joshua. "Cultivating Trust: Vulnerability and Creativity in Moral Education." Religion and Culture Web Forum, Martin Marty Center, June 2011. http://divinity.uchicago.edu/martycenter/publications/webforum/archive.shtml
Davidson, Donald. "On the Very Idea of a Conceptual Scheme." In *The Essential Davidson*, 196–208. Oxford: Oxford University Press, 2006.
Elliot, Anthony, and Charles Lemert. *The New Individualism: The Emotional Costs of Globalization*. Rev. ed. London: Routledge, 2009.
Fowler, James W. *To See the Kingdom: The Theological Vision of H. Richard Niebuhr*. Lanham, MD: University Press of America, 1974.
Frei, Hans. "Niebuhr's Theological Background." In *Faith and Ethics: The Theology of H. Richard Niebuhr*, edited by Paul Ramsey, 9–64. New York: Harper & Row, 1957.
———. "The Theology of H. Richard Niebuhr." In *Faith and Ethics: The Theology of H. Richard Niebuhr*, edited by Paul Ramsey, 65–116. New York: Harper & Row, 1957.
Fuss, Peter. *The Moral Philosophy of Josiah Royce*. Cambridge, MA: Harvard University Press, 1965.
Glaude, Eddie S., Jr. *In a Shade of Blue: Pragmatism and the Politics of Black America*. Chicago: University of Chicago Press, 2007.
Godsey, John D. *The Promise of H. Richard Niebuhr*. Philadelphia: J. B. Lippincott, 1970.
Goffman, Erving. *Interaction Ritual: Essays on Face-to-Face Behavior*. Garden City, NY: Anchor, 1967.
———. *The Presentation of Self in Everyday Life*. New York: Anchor, 1959.
Grant, C. David. *God the Center of Value: Value Theory in the Theology of H. Richard Niebuhr*. Fort Worth: Texas Christian University Press, 1984.
Gregory of Nyssa. "An Address on Religious Instruction." Translated by Cyril C. Richardson. In *Christology of the Later Fathers*, edited by Edward R. Hardy and Cyril C. Richardson, 268–323. Louisville: Westminster John Knox, 1953.
Gunton, Colin. *The Promise of Trinitarian Theology*. Edinburgh: T. & T. Clark, 1997.
Gustafson, James. "Preface." In *Christ and Culture*, by H. Richard Niebuhr, xxi–xxxv. Exp. ed. New York: HarperSanFrancisco, 2001.
Hartman, Laura M. *The Christian Consumer: Living Faithfully in a Fragile World*. Oxford: Oxford University Press, 2011.
———. "A Proposal for Modesty." Paper delivered at the Annual Meeting of the Society of Christian Ethics, Washington, DC, January 7th, 2012.
Hauerwas, Stanley. *The Peaceable Kingdom: A Primer in Christian Ethics*. Notre Dame: University of Notre Dame Press, 1983.
Hauerwas, Stanley, and Charles Pinches. *Christians Among the Virtues: Theological Conversations with Ancient and Modern Ethics*. Notre Dame: University of Notre Dame Press, 1997.
Hector, Kevin W. *Theology without Metaphysics: God, Language, and the Spirit of Recognition*. Cambridge: Cambridge University Press, 2011.

Hoedemaker, Libertus A. *The Theology of H. Richard Niebuhr*. Philadelphia: Pilgrim, 1970.
Hook, Sidney. *Sidney Hook on Pragmatism, Democracy, and Freedom*. Edited by Robert B. Talisse and Robert Tempio. Amherst, NY: Prometheus, 2002.
Hunsinger, George. *The Eucharist and Ecumenism*. Cambridge: Cambridge University Press, 2008.
Jenson, Robert W. *Systematic Theology*. 2 vols. New York: Oxford University Press, 1997–99.
Joas, Hans. *G. H. Mead: A Contemporary Re-examination of His Thought*. Translated by Raymond Meyer. Cambridge, MA: MIT Press, 1997.
———. *Pragmatism and Social Theory*. Chicago: University of Chicago Press, 1993.
Kegley, Jacquelyn. *Genuine Individuals and Genuine Communities: A Roycean Public Philosophy*. Nashville: Vanderbilt University Press, 1997.
Keiser, R. Melvin. *Roots of Relational Ethics: Responsibility in Origin and Maturity in H. Richard Niebuhr*. Atlanta: Scholars Press, 1996.
Kliever, Lonnie. "The Christology of H. Richard Niebuhr." *Journal of Religion* 50 (1970) 33–57.
LaCugna, Catherine Mowry. *God for Us: The Trinity and the Christian Life*. New York: HarperOne, 1991.
Lewis, J. David. "A Social Behaviorist Interpretation of the Meadian 'I.'" In *Philosophy, Social Theory, and the Thought of George Herbert Mead*, edited by Mitchell Aboulafia, 110–33. Albany: State University of New York Press, 1991.
Lindbeck, George. "The Gospel's Uniqueness: Election and Untranslatability." In *The Church in a Postliberal Age*, edited by James Buckley, 223–52. Grand Rapids: Eerdmans, 2002.
———. *The Nature of Doctrine: Religion and Theology in a Postliberal Age*. Louisville: Westminster John Knox, 1984.
———. "Scripture, Consensus and Community." In *The Church in a Postliberal Age*, edited by James Buckley, 201–22. Grand Rapids: Eerdmans, 2002.
Luther, Martin. "The Large Catechism." In *The Book of Concord*, edited by Robert Kolb and Timothy J. Wengert, 377–480. Minneapolis: Fortress, 2000.
Markell, Patchen. "The Potential and the Actual: Mead, Haunch, and the 'I.'" In *Recognition and Power: Axel Honneth and the Tradition of Critical Social Theory*, edited by Bert Van Den Brink and David Owen, 101–29. New York: Cambridge University Press, 2007.
Mathews, Donald G. *Religion in the Old South*. Chicago: University of Chicago Press, 1977.
Mead, George Herbert. "The Mechanism of Social Consciousness." In *Selected Writings*, edited by Andrew J. Reck, 134–41. Chicago: University of Chicago Press, 1964.
———. *Mind, Self, and Society: From the Standpoint of a Social Behaviorist*. Edited by Charles W. Morris. Chicago: University of Chicago Press, 1962.
———. "Philanthropy from the Point of View of Ethics." In *Selected Writings*, edited by Andrew J. Reck, 392–407. Chicago: University of Chicago Press, 1964.
———. "The Philosophies of Royce, James, and Dewey in Their American Setting." In *Selected Writings*, edited by Andrew J. Reck, 371–91. Chicago: University of Chicago Press, 1964.
———. *The Philosophy of the Present*. Amherst, NY: Prometheus, 2002.

———. "Social Psychology as Counterpart to Physiological Psychology." In *Selected Writings*, edited by Andrew J. Reck, 94–104. Chicago: University of Chicago Press, 1964.

———. "The Social Self." In *Selected Writings*, edited by Andrew J. Reck, 142–49. Chicago: University of Chicago Press, 1964.

Meilander, Gilbert. *The Theory and Practice of Virtue*. Notre Dame: University of Notre Dame Press, 1984.

Miller, David L. "Josiah Royce and George H. Mead on the Nature of the Self." *Transactions of the Charles S. Peirce Society* 11 (1975) 67–89.

Moltmann, Jürgen. *The Trinity and the Kingdom*. Minneapolis: Fortress, 1993.

Murdoch, Iris. *The Sovereignty of Good*. London: Routledge, 1970.

Niebuhr, H. Richard. *Christ and Culture*. Exp. ed. New York: HarperSanFrancisco, 2001.

———. "The Doctrine of the Trinity and the Unity of the Church." In *H. Richard Niebuhr: Theology, History, and Culture: Major Unpublished Writings*, edited by William Stacy Johnson, 50–62. New Haven: Yale University Press, 1996.

———. "The Ego-Alter Dialectic and the Conscience." *Journal of Philosophy* 42 (1945) 352–59.

———. *Faith on Earth: An Inquiry into the Structure of Human Faith*. New Haven: Yale University Press, 1989.

———. *The Meaning of Revelation*. Louisville: Westminster John Knox, 2006.

———. "The Position of Theology Today (Cole Lectures)." In *H. Richard Niebuhr: Theology, History and, Culture: Major Unpublished Writings*, edited by William Stacy Johnson, 3–18. New Haven: Yale University Press, 1996.

———. *Radical Monotheism and Western Culture, With Supplementary Essays*. Louisville: Westminster John Knox, 1970.

———. "Reflections on Faith, Hope, and Love." *Journal of Religious Ethics* 2 (1974) 151–56.

———. "Reformation: Continuing Imperative." In *"The Responsibility of the Church for Society" and Other Essays by H. Richard Niebuhr*, edited by Kristine Culp, 138–44. Louisville: Westminster John Knox, 2008.

———. *The Responsible Self: An Essay in Christian Moral Philosophy*. Louisville: Westminster John Knox, 1999.

———. "Toward a Recovery of Feeling (The Cole Lectures)." In *H. Richard Niebuhr: Theology, History, and Culture: Major Unpublished Writings*, edited by William Stacy Johnson, 34–49. New Haven: Yale University Press, 1996.

———. "Toward New Symbols (The Cole Lectures)." In *H. Richard Niebuhr: Theology, History, and Culture: Major Unpublished Writings*, edited by William Stacy Johnson, 19–33. New Haven: Yale University Press, 1996.

Oppenheim, Frank. *Reverence for the Relations of Life: Re-imagining Pragmatism via Josiah Royce's Interactions with Peirce, James, and Dewey*. Notre Dame: University of Notre Dame Press, 2005.

———. *Royce's Mature Ethics*. Notre Dame: University of Notre Dame Press, 1993.

———. *Royce's Mature Philosophy of Religion*. Notre Dame: University of Notre Dame Press, 1987.

Ottati, Douglas F. "Meaning and Method in H. Richard Niebuhr's Thought." PhD diss., University of Chicago Divinity School, 1980.

Pagano, Joseph S. *The Origins and Development of the Triadic Structure of Faith in H. Richard Niebuhr: A Study of the Kantian and Pragmatic Background of Niebhur's Thought*. Lanham, MD: University Press of America, 2005.
Ray, Darby Kathleen. *Deceiving the Devil: Atonement, Abuse, and Ransom*. Cleveland: Pilgrim, 1998.
Reuther, Rosemary Radford. *Sexism and God-Talk: Towards a Feminist Theology*. Boston: Beacon, 1983.
Rivera, Mayra. *The Touch of Transcendence: A Postcolonial Theology of God*. Louisville: Westminster John Knox, 2007.
Royce, Josiah. "The Philosophy of Loyalty." In *The Basic Writings of Josiah Royce, Volume 2: Logic, Loyalty, and Community*, edited by John J. McDermott, 855–1013. New York: Fordham University Press, 2005.
———. *The Problem of Christianity*. Washington, DC: Catholic University of America Press, 2001.
———. "What Is Vital in Christianity?" In *William James and Other Essays in the Philosophy of Life*, 99–183. New York: Macmillan, 1911.
Shriver, Donald W., Jr. *H. Richard Niebuhr*. Nashville: Abingdon, 2009.
Silva, Filipe Carreira da. *G. H. Mead: A Critical Introduction*. Malden, MA: Polity, 2007.
Smith, John E. *America's Philosophical Vision*. Chicago: University of Chicago Press, 1992.
———. *Royce's Social Infinite: The Community of Interpretation*. Hamden, CT: Archon, 1969.
———. *The Spirit of American Philosophy*. Albany: State University of New York Press, 1983.
Sobrino, Jon. *Witness to the Kingdom: The Martyrs of El Salvador and the Crucified Peoples*. Maryknoll, NY: Orbis, 2003.
Stassen, Glen H. "Concrete Christological Norms for Transformation." In *Authentic Transformation: A New Vision of Christ and Culture*, 127–89. Nashville: Abingdon, 1996.
———. "A New Vision. " In *Authentic Transformation: A New Vision of Christ and Culture*, 191–268 Nashville: Abingdon, 1996.
Stassen, Glen H., et al. *Authentic Transformation: A New Vision of Christ and Culture*. Nashville: Abingdon, 1996.
Tunstall, Dwayne. *Yes, But Not Quite: Encountering Josiah Royce's Ethico-Religious Insight*. New York: Fordham University Press, 2009.
Weaver, J. Denny. *The Nonviolent Atonement*. Grand Rapids: Eerdmans, 2001.
Werpehowski, William. *American Protestant Ethics and Legacy of H. Richard Niebuhr*. Washington, DC: Georgetown University Press, 2002.
Yoder, John Howard. "How H. Richard Niebuhr Reasoned: A Critique of Christ and Culture." In *Authentic Transformation: A New Vision of Christ and Culture*, 31–89. Nashville: Abingdon, 1996.
———. *The Politics of Jesus: Vicit Agnus Noster*. Grand Rapids: Eerdmans, 1994.

Index

absolute, 25–26, 109–11
acknowledgment, 105, 109–10
association, 107
Atonement, 24, 27, 45–54, 57–58, 127, 139–41
attitude, 62–63, 69–72, 74–75
   economic/religious, 82–83
attunement (to God), 129, 133–36, 184

Barth, Karl, 8–9, 12, 19, 94–95, 206
Beloved Community, 27–29, 32–33, 37–38, 41–43, 53–55, 58, 98–99, 114
bodily existence, 158–60

Calvin, John, 194–95, 206
cause, 33–37, 41, 44–45, 98–100, 102, 107–9, 117–18, 120–22, 127–30, 148–49, 165–66, 172–73, 182, 193–94, 196–98, 200, 202
   moral, 6–8
Christianity, 26–27, 28, 110, 114–15, 139, 154
church, 8, 10–12, 14–17, 37–38, 41–42, 114, 119–20
citizenship, as symbol of the moral life, 122–23, 173
collectivism, 31, 38, 39, 43–45, 53
Collins, Randall, 4–6, 169n18, 207
common social endeavor, 61, 63–64, 66–71, 75–77, 81, 83, 126
   and faith, 104, 106
communal development, 18–19, 22, 57, 76–77, 90–91, 200, 202–3

communal norms, 2–3, 5, 7–8
community, 2–6, 8, 9–10, 12–13, 37–45, 47–55, 56–59, 70–71, 73–86, 89–92, 100, 107–9, 119–20, 127–28, 140–42
   Christian, 9–11, 41–42, 119–20, 157, 188
   democratic, 78, 84–87
   Royce's metaphysics of, 26, 48–49
   universal, 37, 41, 82, 84, 130
   of being, 132, 142, 145, 165–66, 172, 184–85, 187, 194, 196; of faith, 119–20

consciousness, 29–31, 61, 64–65
concept, 155–61
conceptual reconstruction, method of, 20
cooperation, 39–40, 67
courage, 176, 178–80, 183
covenant, 10–11, 105–7, 181–82
creativity, 51, 87–88, 143–44, 146, 166–67, 180–81
   as social reconstruction, 90–91
   contingent, 51, 89, 98, 118–19, 162–63, 188
   disruptive model of, 67, 77, 86, 90
   radical/social, 144–46, 165–68
   sanctified, 194
   symbolic, 164, 166–67, 186, 188–90, 196, 199
   virtuous, 186–89, 193–94, 196, 199–200
critical discernment, 168–69, 186

Decalogue, 194–95
democracy, 79, 81–84
direct experience, 127–28, 131–33, 151–52, 154n10
direct relations, 11–12, 18–19, 20–21, 94, 103, 116, 121, 126, 128–30, 147–52, 200, 202–3
distrust, 105–7, 109–14, 117–21, 132–37, 144–46, 156–58
   natural, 110–13, 118–19, 133–37
   radical, 121, 145, 148–50, 171–72, 183–84, 190, 193, 200
divine accommodation, 22, 157, 163, 168, 170, 190
doctrine, 15, 17, 156–57, 160
doctrine of signs, 48–49

ethics, 122–23, 135
   Christian, 14–15, 95–96
   Jesus', 191–92
   responsibility, 123, 139
   theological, 22
   virtue, 173
existential resonance, 21, 149–50, 156–63, 166–71, 185, 188–90, 192–93, 198
expectation, 63, 111, 137
experience, 4–8, 12, 16–17, 26–27, 35, 39, 122–23, 131, 151–54, 156–57, 160

faith, 97–99, 100, 103–13, 120, 132, 139–40, 142–44, 181–84, 188–89
   broken, 113, 115–16
   Christian, 115–20, 138, 196–97
   human, 99–100, 109, 117–18
   of Jesus Christ, 113–18, 138–39, 193–200
   natural or negative, 110–11, 118–19
   pluralistic (polytheism), 100–101, 112–13, 135
   radical, 113–15, 118–21, 141–42, 144–45, 166–68, 173–74, 183–84, 188, 190, 196–200
   social (henotheism), 99–101, 108–9, 112–13, 144–45, 165–66, 170–71, 184, 188, 194, 197–200
Father, 99, 116, 118, 191, 193, 195–98

feeling/emotion, 153–54, 156, 158
fitting/fittingness, 51–52, 61–62, 123, 127
freedom, 6–7, 14, 106–7, 136, 146

generalized other, 68–72, 125–26
gesture(s), 60–64, 158, 177–78
   conversation of, 62, 67, 177–78, 192
God, 7–12, 99, 101–2, 115–19, 131–33, 139, 146, 151, 157, 170, 188, 190–93, 198–99
   interpreted as enemy or friend, 130, 132, 134–37, 141, 157, 176, 184
"God the Father," 152, 154, 162–63, 165, 170, 172, 176, 185, 199
"God the Mother," 152, 162–63, 165–67, 169–70, 171, 176, 185–86, 189, 194–95, 199
grace, 42–43, 146, 174–75, 189–90
grammar, 17–18
grief, 35, 52, 145

Hauerwas, Stanley, 13–15, 17, 207

"I". See I/me distinction
ideal extension, 40
idealization, 35, 39, 52
idolatry, 8–9, 154
image(s), 137, 156–57, 159
imagination, 35, 52–53
   moral, 197
I/me distinction, 67–68, 71–80, 84, 89–90, 121, 128–29, 132–33, 134, 135, 143, 148–50, 155–56, 162–63, 167, 194
imitation, 61–62
incarnation, 114–15
individual(s), 2–8, 10–12, 26–29, 35–36, 37, 42, 57–58, 67, 70, 77–78, 84
individual development, 53, 75–76, 81, 94, 96, 147, 171, 200, 202–3
individual self. See individual(s)
individualism, 1, 9–10, 16–17, 31–32, 38, 39, 43–45, 53
individuality, 2–5, 11–13, 31–32, 48, 53, 94–95, 149–50

interpretation, 28, 38, 40, 45–49,
    51–52, 57, 64, 76–77, 124–25,
    126–28, 132–33, 158–59
  reinterpretation, 136–38
  Will to Interpret, 47–49, 51, 56
interpretive frameworks, 181

James, William, 26, 68n39
Jesus Christ, 76–77, 110, 113–18,
    138–39, 155–56, 190–200
  as risen, 98–99, 103, 114–16, 138,
    190, 192, 195–97
  as symbolic, 138, 190–91, 194, 198
justice, 187, 189

knowledge, 104–5, 155–56

language, 5, 63–67, 104–5, 152
Lindbeck, George, 13, 15–17, 171n32,
    208
Lost Individual (Moral Burden of the
    Individual), 27–29, 31, 53
love, 40–45, 98–99, 174–75, 181–82
loyalty, 32–37, 41–45, 52–53, 98–102,
    103–12, 114–18, 120, 127–28,
    140, 182, 196
  Royce's metaphysics of, 35–36,
    48–49

"me". *See* I/me distinction
Mead, George Herbert, 23–25, 54–55,
    56–92, 93–97, 94–95, 115,
    118–19, 124–34, 136, 140–41,
    143, 145–47, 148–49, 155–56,
    158, 162–63, 177–78, 208–9,
meaning, 25, 54, 63–66, 124, 126,
metanoia, 110, 118, 141, 144–46. *See
    also* permanent revolution
Miller, David L., 24–26, 54, 56, 58,
    209
mind(s), 37–38, 46–49, 60–61, 64,
    65n29, 66–67, 70, 78, 87–88, 124
  social, 37–38, 53, 142
modernity, 1–2, 16–18, 32
moral formation, 12, 18, 23–24, 35,
    38, 47, 53, 96, 106, 147, 170,
    196–200
moral self-consciousness, 29–31

narrative, 15–16
neighbor, 40–41, 174–75
Niebuhr, H. Richard, 23–24, 82,
    93–147, 148–65, 170–75, 177,
    179, 181–84, 191–93, 209
novelty 74–77, 86–87
  symbolic, 162–63

particularity, 14–17, 26, 34, 122
Paul, 28, 32, 40–41, 43, 197
permanent revolution, 91, 110, 115,
    119, 179, 183, 185, 189, 203
post-liberalism(ism), 9, 11–13, 15
principle of being, 101–2, 111
promise(s), 105–7, 181–82
prophecy, 10–11
purposiveness, as symbol of moral
    life, 122–23, 172–73

radical action, 130–33
radical monotheism, 100–102, 108,
    110–11, 113–15, 118. *See also*
    faith, radical
realm of being, 102, 108, 112, 114.
    See also universal community of
    being
reconstruction, 88–92, 115
  of faith, 117–21, 190
  social, 91, 199
repentance, 134–35, 163–64
response(s), 61–66, 71–73, 76, 98,
    102, 104–6, 120, 123–30, 132–33,
    135–37, 158, 173–74, 175–76,
    178–82
responsive(ness), 120, 122–23, 129,
    176–78, 180–81,
responsibility, 121–27, 159, 172–73
  as symbol of the moral life, 122–23,
    172–73
  universal, 130, 139
  See also ethics, responsibility
resurrection, 115, 117–18, 138–39,
    191–92, 195, 198
revelation, 110
role(s), 62–63, 65, 68–70, 81, 90,
    104–6, 126, 143, 177, 180

Royce, Josiah, 23–55, 56–60, 64, 91–92, 96–97, 98–104, 106–9, 113–14, 116, 120, 127, 140–42

self, 57–58, 61–63, 68–74, 78–79, 89–90, 97–102, 110–11, 122–36, 141–44, 155, 161–62, 177, 195
  moral, 30–31, 38, 105
  responsible, 130–31, 133, 139–40
self-defense, 96n9, 144–47, 149, 157
self-development, 31, 34, 36, 42, 48–49, 71–72, 75–76
self-expression, 31, 34, 36, 39, 42, 45, 48–49
sign(s), 46–48, 54, 57. See also doctrine of signs
sin, 29, 32–33, 44–45, 113, 141, 145
social act, 61, 64, 113, 124
  of faith, 104–6, 115–16, 120, 140
social behaviorism, 57–58
social contrasts, 30
social genius, 74–77, 79–81, 166–68
social inheritance, 58, 77, 90, 126, 128, 158, 161–63, 165–67, 171, 194, 197
social interaction, 58, 61–62
social training, 29–34, 44, 101, 113
social will, 29–32, 38
sociality, 86–87, 89, 119
socialization, 23–24, 53, 67, 77–78, 143, 147, 171, 196, 200
society, 31, 37–38, 70, 74–75, 78. 99–100, 141
Son, 116–18, 191, 193, 195, 197–98
spirit, 42–43, 50, 98–99, 116
Spirit, 116, 166, 193, 195–97
symbol, 122–23, 150–51, 154, 157–58, 162, 170, 172–73, 185–86, 190, 192–93
  significant symbol, 62, 65–68

symbolic activity, 163–64, 170–72, 185–86

time/temporality, 38–40, 47, 51–52, 86–91, 119, 130–31, 136, 166–68, 182, 186–87
tradition, 160–64, 166, 195–96
transformation, 110, 118–21, 141, 144–46, 149–50, 166–67, 170, 183–84, 187–89, 196–97, 200
treason, 33, 36–37, 44–45, 49–53, 91–92, 101, 107, 113, 140–42
triad/triadic structure
  of Christian faith, 116–17, 195–96
  of faith, 107–8, 113
  of human experience, 5–6
  of knowledge, 104
  of meaning, 64
  of responsibility, 126–27
trust, 63, 65, 69, 81–82, 86, 98–107, 110–12, 117–18, 120, 139–42, 144, 156, 182
  radical, 121, 182, 185–86
Tunstall, Dwayne, 26, 36, 55n100, 210

universal community, 37, 41, 82, 84, 130
  of being, 132, 142, 145, 165–66, 172, 184–85, 187, 194, 196
  of faith, 119–20

virtue(s), 14–15, 99n12, 171–90, 199–200
  as hermeneutical responsive disposition, 176–77, 189
  moral/theological, 174–80, 183–88, 190, 199–200
  Thomistic account, 174–75

Yoder, John Howard, 9, 210

www.ingramcontent.com/pod-product-compliance
Lightning Source LLC
Chambersburg PA
CBHW070254230426
43664CB00014B/2528